MILITARY BOUNTY LAND
1776-1855

MILITARY BOUNTY LAND 1776-1855

by

Christine Rose

SAN JOSE, CALIFORNIA

2011

ISBN 978-0-929626-20-8

First printing 2011

10 9 8 7 6 5 4 3 2 1

Published by CR Publications
1474 Montelegre Dr., San Jose, CA 95120-4831
www.CRPublications.net

Printed by Thomson Shore, Inc., Dexter, MI

Author:
email: christine@christine4rose.com
www.Christine4Rose.com

Cover design: Ann Silberlicht

Dedicated to Lloyd deWitt Bockstruck in appreciation of his many contributions
in books, articles, and lectures about military and bounty land records.
Thank you, my friend.

About the Author

Christine Rose, CG, CGL, FASG, is a Certified Genealogist and a Certified Genealogical Lecturer. She was elected a Fellow, American Society of Genealogists, an honor bestowed by peers based on quantity and quality of publications, and limited to only fifty at any time. She was the recipient of the prestigious Donald Lines Jacobus award in 1987 for two genealogy books; the recipient of the Association of Professional Genealogist's Professional Achievement Award in 2010, and the recipient of the Lloyd deWitt Bockstruck Distinquished Service Award by the Dallas Genealogical Society in the same year. She is the compiler of numerous genealogies and articles; is a Trustee of the Board for Certification of Genealogists, a former Vice President of the Association of Professional Genealogists and of the Federation of Genealogical Societies, and long-time columnist for the latter's *Forum*. Christine has lectured at national conferences, at the National Institute of Historical Research in Washington, D.C., and has been on the faculty and a course coordinator of the Samford University Institute of Genealogy and Historical Research for many years. She is the founder and editor of the *Rose Family Association*. Her published titles include *Genealogical Proof Standard, Courthouse Research for Family Historians, Courthouse Indexes Illustrated, Nicknames: Past & Present, Military Pension Acts 1776-1858,* and *Family Associations: Organization and Management.* She also authored two full-size genealogies and several genealogical booklets, and co-authored the highly acclaimed *The Complete Idiot's Guide to Genealogy*.

Christine's specialities include onsite research in courthouses and repositories across America; also military research and federal land records.

Table of Contents

SOME ABBREVIATIONS

ASP   American State Papers
ARC   Archival Research Catalog
BLM   Bureau of Land Management
BLM-ES   Bureau of Land Management-Eastern States
CMSR   Compiled Military Service Record
DP   Descriptive Pamphlet
GLO   General Land Office
NARA   National Archives and Records Administration
NUCMC   National Union Catalog of Manuscript Collections
PI   Preliminary Inventory
PM   Principal Meridian
RG   Record Group
Stat.   Statute
Twp.   Township
USMD   United States Military District
VMD   Virginia Military District
WT   Warrant

List of Figures

Acknowledgements

So many deserve thanks for their able and valuable help.

First, to Sandra Hargreaves Luebking, FUGA, who read the whole manuscript and wrote the Foreword: deepest thanks. You shared your expertise on land records and on editing, and you never flagged in your enthusiasm for the project. Your input was invaluable.

To James L. Hansen, FASG, Reference Librarian at the Wisconsin Historical Society Library: your detailed suggestions were of tremendous assistance, and your insight from your own expertise on federal land records enhanced the project.

To Lloyd deWitt Bockstruck, FNGS, retired librarian of the Dallas Public Library, Rick Sayre, CG, and Claire Mire Bettag, CG, CGL—what gems you all are for taking the time to examine the draft and offering important comments and advice.

Others read selected chapters in the area of their own expertise. Kandie Adkinson, Administrative Supervisor, Land Office Division, Office of Kentucky's Secretary of State read Chapter Two and answered many questions; Jonathan R. Stayer, Head, Reference Section, Pennsylvania State Archives, offered excellent suggestions to enhance that section so readers would get a good sense of the records available in Pennsylvania; Tom Rieder, Archivist of the Ohio State Historical Society Library answered questions about the remarkable Ohio records; Russell P. Baker, retired Archivist of the Arkansas History Commission provided his knowledge on that state's records; J. Mark Lowe, CG, FUGA, made important additions on the North Carolina/Tennessee section, and Barbara Vines Little, CG, CGL, whose expert observations assisted with the Virginia section. My thanks to each one of you.

To Patricia M. Tyler, Branch Chief, GLO Automation, Bureau of Land Management, my thanks for answering questions and demonstrating the new BLM website and also for arranging a tour of their facility in Springfield, Virginia. We are fortunate to have her and her team at the BLM.

To Pamela Boyer Sayre, CG, CGL, my thanks for a variety of editing suggestions. She added commas, corrected dashes, and assisted in making the text flow smoothly.

Others who helped by supplying documents, articles, or answering questions were Brent Holcomb, professional genealogist of Columbia, South Carolina, Thomas Rose, Executive Staff Assistant at Trulaske College of Business at the University of Missouri, Pamela S. Eagleson, CG, of Kennebunk, Maine, the Research Services Department at the Virginia State Library, and George R. Shaner and George T. Briscoe, consultants of Record Group 49 at the National Archives. And, thanks to my husband Seymour T. Rose who read, and read, and read, always with enthusiasm and offering good suggestions and encouragement.

It seems so little to say "thank you." But I do so with deepest gratitude, for each helped make this a better book.

Foreword

It was a turbulent era, 1783-1855. Surging forth from the heart of England into the realities of economic shifts, court supremacy debates, slave revolts and class restructuring, this country seemed liquid when one viewed its unremitting flow west. All of this, set against the backdrop of more war against Great Britain, then against the Mexicans, was interspersed with military encounters and forced migrations of Native Americans.

As the acquisition of public lands by the federal government increased the westward flow to a flood, advantages were seen in compensating veterans with land while moving the battle-seasoned fighters to vulnerable border areas. This decision served to create a compelling inducement to enlist or to remain in service. Although a constant topic of congressional debate, the distribution of military bounty lands in lieu of cash incentives, grew to incredible proportions. By 1855 the government had shifted more than 60 million acres of land to the private sector. Thus was created the vast collection of records known as military bounty land warrants.

One great value of the records of military bounty lands is the broad range of opportunity to find a subject of research interest. At least four factors are inherent in creating this expanse of prospects: the number of participants, the lack of gender limitation, the time span, and the geographical coverage these records represent.

The number who participated is great. More than 550,000 veterans, widows, and minor heirs received land, including some who may have applied more than once as qualifications were reduced or additional land offered under later acts. Gender was not exclusively male as the laws allowed widows or, when legal heirs, mothers or daughters to apply. The range of time these records cover, eight decades from 1776 to 1855, makes a three generation search possible. Consider, too, the breadth of geographic coverage: military bounty land could bring a veteran and his family from the east coast to areas west of the Mississippi River.

"It was a turbulent era ..."

"More than 550,000 veterans, widows, and minor heirs received land ..."

The warrants are an important part of the bounty land story. Yet other records are involved in a comprehensive search, such as the federal patent, exchanged for the warrant, that authenticated ownership. The new General Land Office website of the Bureau of Land Management provides an index to help locate both the patentee and the warrantee. This is important as many veterans chose not to use but to sell the warrant.

Prior to the publication of this book, the value of military bounty land warrants as a research source was underestimated. The lack of a cohesive and explicit guide to understanding and locating these records made them difficult to use. No longer is this a problem. This scholarly yet concise work offers a digest of the laws that governed the awarding and distribution of public land to military veterans or their heirs. The explanation of the contents of these records, the listing of specific finding aids and indexes, and the relationship between warrants and federal patents bring together the processes needed to explore the richness of information that these records can provide.

Christine Rose's knowledge of and familiarity with military bounty land law and its implementation is readily apparent and the contents of these pages will greatly assist a wide audience. Family historians and professional genealogists will find this work indispensible. Economists studying the national network that formed to redistribute warrants purchased from veterans, geographers examining migration patterns, and historians contemplating mining the rich lode of original warrant materials will find this book valuable as well. Whether focused on a specific individual or a broad subject, such as political and society attitudes towards land distribution, there is a need to have factual and useful information for easy consultation. This book provides that.

Sandra Hargreaves Luebking
Co-editor, *The Source: A Guide to American Genealogy*
Author, Chapter 8, "Research in Land and Tax Records."

"Prior to the publication of this book, the value of military bounty land warrants as a research source was underestimated."

Preface

Documents produced by the process initiated by federal bounty land legislation can be impressive. Evidence of marriages, deaths, Bible records, letters written by family members, physical description, names of heirs, and much more might be found in the document packets. The key to navigating the maze is to understand the laws which distributed bounty land and the process applicants followed from the initial application of the claim to the final disposition.

Federal bounty land was granted as an inducement to enlist or an inducement to remain in military service for a longer period, or, after service was completed, as a reward for service rendered. If a claim was accepted, a bounty land warrant was issued for a specific number of acres. This warrant represented the right of the veteran to settle on free land in the public domain, that is, on land owned by the government. It also evidenced the gratitude of a nation for the hardships endured by these veterans, and, not as obvious, the warrant represented the hope of a country that these experienced men would settle on and help protect the frontier.

This book covers bounty land from the Revolution to the mid-nineteenth century when the last bounty act rewarding service was passed. During these eighty years an astounding number of records flowed through the system.

For land claims based on Revolutionary War service there are two classes—rewards by the federal government, and the bounty offered by some states fortunate to own ample land. This book covers both classes. After the Revolution only the federal government used the inducement of land during subsequent wars.

Diligent searchers may find up to a dozen or more items emanating from one bounty land application. Even though some records may be lost through fires, carelessness or other misfortunes, at least one or two involving the warrant are likely to have survived.

Searching bounty land records based on Revolutionary War service? Check for both federal and state bounty awards.

This book is intended as a guide to the voluminous records accumulated from 1776 onward. The book is arranged starting with the earliest bounty warrants issued for the Revolution, and continuing to the last act awarding land for service performed in 1855 or earlier. Applications continued for a number of years, though later awards were based on pre-1855 service.

ARRANGEMENT OF CHAPTERS. Each chapter starts with information on the background of the pertinent related acts for that segment. This is followed in most instances by a discussion of the *application* files, followed by information on the *warrant* files. The applications are what initiated the claim for bounty land. Once the application was approved the warrant was used to claim the allotted acreage.

In Appendix A are reproduced the major acts defining the land and requirements to be used to fulfill the government's obligations and regulating the distribution. Marginal notes from the original text have been eliminated because most are far outdated. Any existing marginal notes were added by the present author. It is crucial to a clear understanding of bounty land that the statutes be examined for it is in their wording that clarification will result.

All successful claims for land based on federal military service, whether the land was actually settled by the soldier or an assignee, led to issuance of a patent by the federal government. Chapter Six covers the patent search. (Claims for Revolutionary War bounty land under state laws resulted in either a patent or grant from the pertinent state and is covered in Chapters Two and Three.)

This book offers researchers the tools to pursue these priceless documents, leading, it is hoped, to nuggets of family data. Often neglected and greatly underused, bounty land documents can help illuminate the lives of our ancestors.

"... bounty land documents can help illuminate the lives of our ancestors."

Introduction

Bounty land is a story of the hope of the men who enlisted for military service, convinced that they would be justly rewarded after discharge with a few acres of land. It is also the story of the obstacles that often prevented the fulfillment of that hope.

The Continental Congress, in an effort to provide an incentive to colonists to join the ranks of the American army, passed a resolution offering land, in differing quantities depending upon rank, for enlistment during the Revolution. No matter that the fledgling Congress didn't own any land; they were confident they would win the fight and, thus, the land. Their initial promise in 1776 gave every man the hope that after the war he would have a piece of land of his own, a place on which to settle and perhaps raise crops, livestock, and his family.

Congress had more than one reason for promising the land. Foremost was the need to fill the ranks with men and officers who would serve beyond a short enlistment. But Congress also presumed that when these men were discharged and initiated their claim, they would migrate to the unsettled western lands and provide a buffer to help protect the frontier.

When the war ended in 1783 all eyes turned to the Ohio country in the Northwest Territory as the logical location of wartime promises. But an immediate obstacle loomed — several states claimed interests in that area from previous charters by the King. For Congress to utilize this land required cessions from those states, and it would not be easy. But finally, starting with New York in 1780, followed by Virginia and others, it was accomplished. Virginia's cession was contingent upon reserving a tract in what became Ohio so that bounty promises to that colony's Revolutionary War veterans could be fulfilled. After much debate the condition was accepted by the fledgling United States Congress.

Library of Congress
Formerly a chicken coop, this housed one of the large families who settled in the west.

The government's hoped-for result of frontier settlement by former soldiers in the western lands was disappointing. Ohio, still troubled by Indian problems, was not attracting families. Though veterans were allowed to locate in the first of the federal lands to be surveyed in eastern Ohio, few did so. When General "Mad Anthony" Wayne and his Legion of the Army won a decisive victory at the Battle of Fallen Timbers in 1794, the outlook dramatically changed and settlers poured into Ohio. But it was too late for many soldiers who had already sold or assigned their warrants, usually to speculators.

Soon another war loomed and was fought, again with Great Britain, this time from 1812–1815. And again bounty was used as an inducement to enlist and to serve until the end of the war. This time the veterans would be restricted by the provision that the warrants were not assignable. But the military tracts the government set aside did not entice most veterans to uproot their homes and move west. Additionally, unscrupulous agents and speculators took advantage of the innocence of many of the soldiers and obtained the soldiers' warrants through fraudulent means.

Twenty-five years passed before a series of additional acts, generous in nature, benefitted men for their service in sundry disturbances, some with as little as fourteen days. This series to 1855 (with an additional act in 1856 for revolutionary service) produced more surrendered warrants than any of the previous acts.

Did Congress achieve its goal in awarding bounty land? Not really. Those men who had served in the Revolution did not settle the frontier because until the mid-1790s there was no place set aside for them to take up the warrants. War of 1812 veterans were restricted for many years to tracts in three territories that were largely unsettled and sparsely populated—not an attractive incentive to uproot their eastern homes. In a large sense, the bounty land experience was a failure, as only a small percentage of veterans did actually locate their own warrants and settle on western lands.

No new acts awarding land for service later than 1855 were enacted, though the possibility was hotly debated when the Civil War was imminent. However, another form of public domain land disbursement had been introduced as a viable alternative and was enacted in 1862, the first Homestead Act. Those who had not borne arms against the United States were eligible. The land, up to 160 acres, was free if certain requirements were fulfilled. The era of a bounty-land system passed but the legacy of the records it produced still assists us, descendants of its intended beneficiaries, in our studies today.

C.R.

1 THE REVOLUTION: Federal Bounty

AN INCENTIVE TO JOIN

The Revolutionary War period was not the first time bounty land was awarded to those serving in the military. Lloyd deWitt Bockstruck in his comprehensive *Bounty and Donation Land Grants in British Colonial America*[1] discusses pre-revolutionary bounty, particularly the land granted by King George III by the proclamation of October 7, 1763, for French and Indian War service. From the text of this proclamation:

> ... And whereas we are desirous, upon all occasions, to testify our royal sense and approbation of the conduct and bravery of the officers and soldiers of our armies, and to reward the same, we do hereby command and empower our governors of the said three new colonies, and all other governors of our said provinces on the continent of North America, to grant without fee or reward, to such reduced officers as have served in North America during the late war, and to such private soldiers as have been, or shall be disbanded in America; and are actually residing there, and shall personally apply for the same, the following quantities of lands, subject at the expiration of ten years, to the same quitrents as other lands are subject to in the province within which they are granted, as also subject to the same conditions of cultivation and improvement, viz.
>
> To every person having the rank of a field officer, five thousand acres; to every captain, three thousand acres; to every subaltern or staff officer, two thousand acres; to every non-commissioned officer, two hundred acres; to every private man fifty acres.
>
> We do likewise authorize and require the governors and commanders in chief of all our said colonies upon the continent of North America, to grant the like quantities of land, and upon the same conditions, to such reduced officers of our navy, of like rank as served on board our ships of war in North America at the times of the reduction

Precedents for rewarding service with bounty land preceded the Revolutionary War.

---

1   Lloyd deWitt Bockstruck, *Bounty and Donation Land Grants in British Colonial America* (Baltimore, Md.: Genealogical Publishing Company, 2007), i.–xvi.

of Louisbourg and Quebec in the late war, and who shall personally apply to our respective governors for such grants.[2]

Following the precedent set in earlier wars the Continental Congress passed a resolution on September 16, 1776, which promised free government land to officers and soldiers who continued to serve during the Revolutionary War or, if they were killed, to their representatives or heirs.[3] The resolution provided that a private or noncommissioned officer would be entitled to 100 acres of bounty land, an ensign 150 acres, a lieutenant 200 acres, a captain 300 acres, a major 400 acres, a lieutenant colonel 450 acres and a colonel 500 acres. This resolution, the first general act promising bounty land for Revolutionary War service, set in motion a flow of documents that would continue for decades. A few days after the 1776 act, Congress additionally resolved that the warrants were not to be assignable, that is, the warrants could not be transferred by any means (including sale or gift) to another person. This restriction on assignments did not change for a dozen years.[4]

DEFINITION
A warrant that was assignable could be alienated or transferred by any means to another person or persons.

Shortly before the initial resolution, Congress attempted to encourage desertion from British service by promising those who did so and who subsequently joined the American colonies a bounty of fifty acres of unappropriated land. This was intended to provoke the defection particularly of Hessians and German mercenaries into American service.[5] Few took up the offer.

As the war progressed, more bounty inducements were offered. Officers belonging to the medical department in the hospitals or army, that is, physicians general, surgeons general, the physician and surgeon general of the army, and a number of other named medical personnel who would continue during the war, were included for benefits. After the conclusion of the war they would be entitled to receive bounty land the same as did the officers by the 1776 resolve.[6]

Soon the provisions of 1776 were again extended to include a major general's award of 1,100 acres and a brigadier general's award of 850 acres.[7] A few months later provisions were added for the director (no

---

2   For the full proclamation see <www.sos.ky.gov/land/reference/legislation /vakypatents/kingproclamation1763.htm>.

3   Worthington C. Ford et al, editors, *Journals of the Continental Congress, 1774–1789* (Washington, D.C., 1904–37), 5:762–63, September 16, 1776, hereafter *JCC*. These journals *are* available online at the Library of Congress website located at <http://memory .loc.gov>.

4   *JCC* 5:787–88, September 20, 1776 and *JCC* 34:307–09, July 9, 1788.

5   *JCC* 5:654–655, August 14, 1776.

6   *JCC* 16:10–11, January 3, 1780.

7   *JCC* 17:726–27, August 12, 1780.

further identification of this director was given in the act) to have the same quantity as a brigadier general; chief physicians and purveyors the same as a colonel; physicians and surgeons and apothecary the same as lieutenant colonel; regimental surgeons and assistants to the purveyor and apothecary the same as a major; and hospital and regimental surgeons mates the same as a captain.[8]

The government intended to be generous to encourage enlistments and extensions of the time of service. It was, however, to be many years before any of these veterans could redeem their awards.

RESPONSIBILITY FOR ISSUING WARRANTS

After the war, the government was faced with the task of determining the process by which the promised land could be claimed, and delegating the departments to handle those claims. When the federal government was formed in 1789, the secretary of war retained the responsibility for processing applications and issuing bounty land warrants. The Treasury Department was in charge of the public domain and supervised the selection and location of land. The Treasury Department also issued the patents that gave actual title to the claim. In 1812 the General Land Office (GLO) was established in the Treasury Department to administer the public lands.[9] Ultimately

---

Federal Offices Handling Claims

By 1810 the Office of Military Bounty Lands and Pensions had been formed within the Office of the Secretary of War to examine claims and to issue warrants. In 1815 the pension and bounty land duties of the War Department were assigned to separate bureaus, and bounty land matters were handled thereafter by an administrative unit known successively as the Land Warrant Bureau, the Section of Bounty Lands, and the Bounty Land Office. On November 1, 1841, the Secretary of War placed the bounty land functions under the direction of the Commissioner of Pensions. This arrangement was formally authorized by an act of Congress approved January 20, 1843 (5 *U.S. Stat.* 597).

The laws relating to the granting of bounty land warrants were administered by the Department of the Interior after the Pension Office was transferred to that Department in 1849.

---

8   *JCC* 18:847, September 22, 1780.

9   Much later the GLO was placed into the Department of the Interior when that department was formed in 1849. Almost one hundred years later, on July 16, 1946, the GLO merged with the United States Grazing Service to become the Bureau of Land Management (BLM).

WARRANTS
After an application was filed and approved, the federal government issued a warrant designating the acreage due. Later when the land was claimed the holder of the warrant surrendered it in exchange for the acreage. (For surrendered warrants see Chapter Five.)

The process for Virginia was different than the federal government. (See Chapter Two.)

portions of these records were transferred to the National Archives Records and Administration (NARA) in Washington, D.C., and are part of Record Group 49 of the Archives. Other portions (as later will be seen) are held by the Bureau of Land Management, Eastern States (BLM-ES).[10]

THE PROCESS FOR OBTAINING THE LAND

A procedure was established in 1788 by which eligible veterans could finally apply for and obtain a warrant.[11] If a veteran's application was successful in fulfilling the requirements, the warrant was issued. The federal process for the various wars ultimately included the following, which will be discussed in this book.

- Applications
- Surrendered warrant files
- Patents

If the Revolutionary War veteran chose to dispose of his warrant, the same documents were generated except that the warrant would include one or more assignments, usually written on the reverse. The patent transferring ownership from the government was issued to the last person to whom the warrant was assigned.

Other assorted documents also were generated by the distribution of federal land—tract book entries, registers, correspondence, and others. This accumulation is a valuable source for genealogists.

LOCATION OF FEDERAL LANDS

The geographic area where the land warrants could be located had to be established. Several colonies held what were considered to be valid claims to the area in the Old Northwest Territory—that area which is now Ohio, Indiana, Illinois, Michigan, Wisconsin, and a portion of Minnesota. By a series of cessions starting in 1780, the states with claims relinquished those claims to the federal government.[12] It was now up to the United States to formulate a method by which to survey the lands, and then to dispense those lands to veterans.

Figure 1–1. States created from the Northwest Territory.

---

10   The National Archives and Records Administration (NARA) is located at 700 Pennsylvania Avenue, NW, Washington, DC 20408–0001. The Bureau of Land Management, Eastern States, (BLM-ES) is located at 7450 Boston Boulevard, Springfield, VA 22153–3121.

11   *JCC* 34:307–09, July 9, 1788.

12   These states ceded their interests in the Northwest Territory at various times: New York in 1780, Virginia 1781–1784 (reserving a tract for the Virginia Military District, see later), Massachusetts in 1785, Connecticut in 1786 and 1800 (reserving the Firelands and the Western Reserve in what became Ohio). North Carolina, South Carolina and Georgia also ceded minor interests.

1785 LAND ORDINANCE

The 1785 Land Ordinance passed by Congress was primarily responsible for setting the method by which the western lands would be surveyed; a tract was not to be sold or settled until a government survey was completed. A six-mile square rectangular system was chosen, each township to contain thirty six one-mile square sections.[13] The first surveys, which bordered the western line of Pennsylvania, were known as the Seven Ranges.[14]

1787 NORTHWEST ORDINANCE

Two years after the 1785 ordinance the 1787 Northwest Ordinance was also passed. This later ordinance directed how the area was to be governed and how states were to be admitted to the union.[15] The following year an additional ordinance concerning the surveying of the federal land was put into effect.[16]

> 375
>
> **FRIDAY, MAY 20, 1785.**
>
> Congress assembled.   Present as yesterday.
>
> Congress proceeded in the third reading of the Ordinance for ascertaining the mode of disposing of lands in the western territory, and the same being gone through, was passed as follows:
>
> An Ordinance for ascertaining the mode of disposing of Lands in the Western Territory.
>
> Be it ordained by the United States in Congress assembled, that the territory ceded by individual States to the United States, which has been purchased of the Indian inhabitants, shall be disposed of in the following manner:

Figure 1–2. From the 1785 Land Ordinance.

TWO PLANNED MILITARY TRACTS ABANDONED

In 1787 Congress set aside two tracts in the Northwest Territory for the use of veterans, one in Ohio and the other in Illinois.[17] Trouble with the Indians forced the abandonment of these plans and slowed the choice of a replacement. Finally, after the defeat of Brigadier General Josiah Harmer (1790–91) and the disastrous campaign of Major General Arthur St. Clair (1791) against the Ohio Indians, General "Mad Anthony" Wayne and his Legion of the United States Army achieved a victory at the Battle of Fallen Timbers in northwest Ohio. The resulting Treaty of Greenville in 1795 stabilized the Ohio country and enabled the government the following year to designate the United States Military Tract (later known as USMD) in Ohio.

Monument at Fallen Timbers near Toledo, Ohio. The resulting Treaty of Greenville in 1795 made Ohio more attractive to settlers. This had some influence on the opening of the United States Military District the following year. Those who had ancestors at Fallen Timbers should particularly check the Unindexed Bounty Land applications (Chapter Five).

---

13   *JCC* 28:375–386, May 20, 1785. Go to <http://memory.loc.gov/ammem/amlaw/lwjc.html> for online viewing of this 1785 Land Ordinance.

14   Paul W. Gates, *History of Public Land Law Development, with Chapter by Robert W. Swenson* (Washington, D.C.: Public Land Law Review Commission, 1968), hereafter Gates, *Public Land Law*. This is an excellent reference for federal land history including the various surveys and acquisitions.

15   See a copy of the Northwest Ordinance of 1787 at <http://avalon.law.yale.edu/18th _century/nworder.asp> or use the Library of Congress website in footnote 13 this chapter. Among the provisions of this ordinance were directives on how intestates' estates should descend in that area.

16   *JCC* 34:97–98, March 19, 1788.

17   *JCC* 33:695–696, October 22, 1787.

Knepper, *Ohio Lands Book*

Figure 1–3. The Seven Ranges and other surveys in Ohio.

Some of the veterans' assignees subsequently located their warrants in the Seven Ranges survey in eastern Ohio, but the veterans themselves, with some exceptions, generally did not locate in that area. Some veterans did hold their rights and used their warrants in the private company surveys of the Ohio Company Land Purchase and the Symmes Purchase in the Northwest Territory before the federal government finally opened the U. S. military tract in 1796. But many soldiers who had become impatient with delays and their own aging years had already opted to sell their warrants.

SEVEN RANGES SURVEY: The Seven Ranges, located in what is now eastern Ohio, was the first of the government surveys in the 1780s and also the only land surveyed by the government under the Continental Congress.[18] The Seven Ranges was not specifically a military tract; it was primarily open for private settlement.

THE OHIO COMPANY OF ASSOCIATES: This group, led by General Rufus Putman, purchased a tract from the federal government on July 24, 1787. Containing about 1,500,000 acres, the land was situated along the Ohio River west of the Seven Ranges. The purchase price of the Ohio Company's first tract of about 750,000 acres was paid at the time of the purchase. In 1792 the government allowed the company to repay by redeemed bounty warrants up to one-seventh of the amount due on over 200,000 acres of the second purchase.

The bulk of the Ohio Company's documents are located at the Marietta College Library in Marietta, Ohio. Among the items of interest is a "Register of Land Warrants" listing the name of the officer or soldier, rank, line of Army, number of acres, and number of the warrant. Some deeds transferring soldiers' interests and various other important documents are in the collection. Many of the items have been scanned and are available for viewing online.[19]

COLLECTION AT THE OHIO HISTORICAL SOCIETY LIBRARY: Though the Ohio Historical Society in Columbus, Ohio, does not hold the main collection of the Ohio Company of Associates, Tom Rieder, reference archivist, states that the Society does hold plat maps and transcribed tract and entry books from the Marietta Land office that include the names of the original proprietors of the Ohio Company Purchase, the location of their lots and tracts, and the names of the settlers in the Donation Tract and the locations of their lots. (The Donation

Manuscripts and Documents of the Ohio Company of Associates

---

18   Dr. George W. Knepper, *The Official Ohio Land Book* (n.p.: n.pub., 2002), 10, hereafter Knepper, *Ohio Lands Book.* An online version of *this book* is available at <www.auditor .state.oh.us/Publications/General/OhioLandsBook.pdf>.

19   Part of the Ohio Company of Associates collection has been digitized and can be viewed at the Marietta College website at <http://digicoll.marietta.edu/oca>.

Tract was 100,000 acres located along the northern border of the Ohio Company lands. In 1792 Congress authorized this land to be given in 100–acre lots to males eighteen or older, to create a buffer zone from Indian incursions. It was not bounty land.)[20]

After the close of the Ohio Company's Land Office in Marietta, remaining Ohio Company land was sold at the Marietta Land Office until 1840; after 1840, when the Marietta Land Office closed, the land was sold at the Chillicothe Land Office. The Society library holds tract and entry books and other purchase records that document those sales. The library also holds records that pertain to school and ministerial land sales in the Ohio Company Purchase.

THE SYMMES PURCHASE (ALSO KNOWN AS THE MIAMI PURCHASE): In 1787 Judge John Cleves Symmes, following the lead of the Ohio Company, petitioned the government for rights enjoyed by the Ohio Company. Symmes entered into a private contract with the United States in 1788 to purchase about one million acres. Unable to pay for that large tract, Symmes was forced into a reduction of between 300,000 and 400,000 acres when the land was patented in 1794. Located in the southwestern corner of the state between the Great and Little Miami Rivers, and bordering partly on the Ohio River, this land is a part of present-day Butler, Hamilton, and Warren Counties. Because of the large debt Symmes owed the government for this purchase, he was allowed to repay up to one-seventh of the sums due by locating bounty land warrants under the same terms as had been enjoyed by the Ohio Company of Associates.

The private survey of the Symmes tract is unusual in that the ranges run south to north, and fractional townships run west to east. The "Between the Miamis Survey" of United States congress lands north of this were surveyed by the government in the same manner as the Symmes Purchase so that confusion would be lessened. Sections were numbered in the manner set out in the 1785 Land Ordinance.

The Symmes tract was fraught with litigation and problems. Lines were inaccurate and in some cases land was sold that overextended the lines of the purchase. An accurate record of all the details of the warrants settled in the Symmes Purchase are not available as many of the personal papers of Judge Symmes were destroyed by a fire of his dwelling in Cincinnati on March 1, 1811.[21] Some records do exist in tract book entries and in the deeds of the county courthouses, and even in court cases in the affected counties as disputes arose.

Courtesy of the Ohio Historical Society
John Cleves Symmes

---

20   Knepper, *Ohio Lands Book*, 30.

21   Joan M. Dixon, *National Intelligencer & Washington Advertiser Newspaper Abstracts: 1811–1813* (Westminster, Md.: Heritage Books, Inc., 1997), 23.

RELATED MATERIAL FOR JUDGE SYMMES'S TRACT: The following should be examined by those interested in the Symmes tract:

- Beverly W. Bond, Jr., *The Correspondence of John Cleves Symmes* (New York: The Macmillan Company, 1926)
- *Symmes Purchase Records: a verbatim copy of the entry book, pamphlet and forfeiture records of John Cleves Symmes,* transcribed by Chris McHenry (Lawrenceburg, Ind.: C. McHenry, 1979)

The Cincinnati Historical Society Library at 1301 Western Avenue, Cincinnati, OH 45203, email at <library@cincymuseum.org> reports that it holds many manuscript items concerning Judge Symmes' tract, but its manuscript catalog is not all online. A personal visit to that repository is suggested.

UNITED STATES MILITARY DISTRICT (USMD)

Those veterans who held their rights and had not redeemed their federal warrants in either the Seven Ranges, the Ohio Company purchase, or the Symmes purchase, were finally able to surrender their warrants for land when Congress passed an act in 1796 to regulate grants for military service.[22] The area set aside for this purpose was located east of the Scioto River in the central part of the state. It embraced either in whole or in part the present-day counties of Coshocton, Delaware, Franklin, Guernsey, Holmes, Knox, Licking, Morrow, Muskingum, Noble, and Tuscarawas. After its formation the USMD was the only tract (with the exception of the South of the Green River tract in Kentucky and the Virginia Military District (VMD) in Ohio for Virginian veterans) in which the holder of a *federal* warrant for Revolutionary War service could locate his warrant until the scrip act of 1830. (See later in this chapter.)

The survey for the USMD departed from the six-mile survey parameters set out in the Land Ordinance of 1785. The USMD was surveyed in five-mile square townships, then subdivided into quarter townships of two and one-half square miles. Each quarter section contained 4,000 acres.

At first the law specified that sales in the military district had to be in no less than quarter townships but Congress soon realized that requiring the distribution of land in such large tracts was cumbersome and did not accomplish the government's goals. Instead of rewarding the soldier with a piece of land on which he could settle, the system with its delays and restrictions forced many to sell the warrant to an agent who could accumulate enough to enter a 4,000

DIVISIONS OF TOWNSHIPS IN U.S. MIL. DIST.

Figure 1–4. Quarter sections in the 5-mile surveys of the USMD.

---

22   1 *U.S. Stat.* 490, June 1, 1796. This should not to be confused with the Land Act of 1796, 1 *U.S. Stat.* 464–69 passed May 18, 1796, which revised and added to previous land acts for the public domain.

acre tract. Theoretically the agent, upon receiving the patent, could redistribute the land among the warrant holders. In actual practice speculators usually bought the warrants and later sold the acreage they accumulated which defeated the government's hope of encouraging veterans to settle on the frontier.

Congress relaxed the requirements in 1800 when a new law enabled veterans who still held their warrants to enter 100 acres.[23] Soon thereafter all warrant holders (including those who had acquired their rights by sale or assignment) were allowed to surrender their warrants for smaller parcels.[24]

DISTRIBUTION OF LAND IN THE USMD

The 1796 military bounty act provided that the Secretary of the Treasury should give public notice in the states and territories and then register warrants for nine months. After this period the priority of location of the registered warrants was determined by a lottery drawing. A warrant holder could then select the specific quarter township he desired. Those who failed to register within the specified time could make their selection from any land still available in the district.

Originally the lands in the USMD were to be distributed to the veterans by January 1, 1800. That proved impossible and extensions

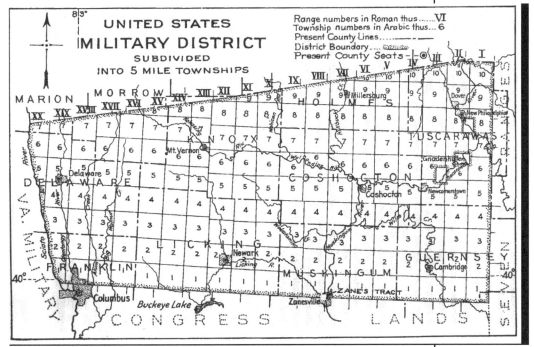

Figure 1–5.
USMD in Ohio. .

Knepper,
Ohio Lands Book

---

23   2 *U.S. Stat.* 14–6, March 1, 1800. This lowering of the tract size was only for original warrantees; not assignees.

24   2 *U.S. Stat* 155–56, April 26, 1802, and 2 *U.S. Stat.* 236–37, March 3, 1803, made further provisions for smaller lots.

were granted. To provide additional time to locate warrants, and also to grant warrants to soldiers who had made late applications or had not completed their claims, Congress passed the act of March 3, 1803, which was later amended by the act of 1806.[25] After 1806 Congress periodically extended the time limit necessary for registering and locating the warrants up to the time of the act of 1833.[26] Thereafter all the vacant land remaining in the district was subject to private sale.

THE APPLICATION FILES

NARA's M804 APPLICATIONS

When the government survey was completed and congress provided the veteran with a location for the fulfillment of the bounty land promise, the soldier or his legal representative or assignee could finally make application for the land. Any extant records of these applications are now among the records of NARA.

The 1788 act, passed twelve years after the initial resolution promising the land, allowed the secretary of war to issue warrants to eligible veterans after proof of fulfilling the requirements was submitted thus initiating an application file. Since evidence of service was required, the veteran's discharge certificate was sometimes included in that file. Most of the early Revolutionary War bounty land application files issued under the 1788 act were destroyed by a fire in the War Department in November 1800 and in the burning of Washington in 1814 during the War of 1812.[27] In the place of the lost bounty application files, a small reference card was later prepared by the War Department. The reference cards for missing bounty applications show the name of the veteran, his rank, his military or naval unit, warrant number, number of acres granted, date issued, and, where appropriate, name of the assignee (that is, the person or persons to whom the warrant had been assigned). These were placed in that veteran's envelope and are part of the National Archives Record Group 15 (RG 15) which have been preserved on NARA's microfilm publication M804, *Revolutionary War Pension and Bounty-Land Warrant Application Files.*[28]

FIRE

Two fires destroyed files at the War Department in 1800 and 1814.

Roll	Description
1	Aaron, William - Abbot, Ezra
2	Abbot, George - Abbot, William
3	Abbott, Aaron - Abbott, Moses
4	Abbott, Nathaniel - Abell, Thomas
5	Aber, Israel - Abston, John
6	Acart, Frederick - Ackler, Leonard
7	Ackley, Abraham - Acres, George
8	Acron, Gabriel - Adams, Bryant
9	Adams, Daniel - Adams, Ezekiel
10	Adams, Francis - Adams, Issacher
11	Adams, Jacob - Adams, Joel
12	Adams, John
13	Adams, Jonas - Adams, Luke
14	Adams, Mark - Adams, Phinehas
15	Adams, Reuben - Adams, Shubael
16	Adams, Silas - Adams, Titus
17	Adams, Walter - Adamy, John
18	Adare, James - Aderton, John
19	Adkin, Samuel - Adve, John

Figure 1–6. Example of roll listings from NARA's M804.

---

25   2 *U.S. Stat.* 236, March 3, 1803, and 2 *U.S. Stat.* 378, April 15, 1806.

26   4 *U.S. Stat.* 665, March 2, 1833.

27   An interesting website is <http://wardepartmentpapers.org>. This is a project of the Center for History and New Media, George Mason University with funding from the National Historical Publications and Records Commission and the National Endowment for the Humanities. It includes Papers of the War Department 1784–1804.

28   National Archives microfilm publication M804, Records of the Department of Veterans Affairs, *Revolutionary War Pension and Bounty Land Warrant Application Files, 1800–1900* (Washington, D.C.: National Archives and Records Service, 1974), RG 15, 2,670 rolls, DP. There is another NARA microfilm publication (M805) but it represents only selected records from these pension files.

The Descriptive Pamphlet (DP) accompanying M804 includes a roll listing. (See Figure 1–6.) It is easy to pick which of the 2,670 rolls is needed because the DP shows the beginning name and the ending name on each roll.

TIP For a complete alphabetical listing by surname of the Revolutionary War pension and bounty land applications in book form (which includes the state from which the soldier served and other limited information) see *Hoyt's Index*.[29]

As explained in the DP for M804, in 1912 a government project was completed that resulted in the consolidation of some of the pension

---

DESCRIPTIVE PAMPHLETS

Descriptive Pamphlets (DPs) are prepared by the National Archives to describe a microfilm series. The DP in most cases is reproduced at the beginning of the first roll of the series, though in some cases the microfilm copy is not as complete as the original printed copy. DPs can also usually be found at the National Archives' website <www.archives.gov>. Go to "Resources" and in the listing beneath it click on "A-Z Index." Then go to O and click on "Order Online," on the next screen on "Microfilm," and then "Order microfilm." In the order box there insert the microfilm number and then "Submit." The next screen will display the details. At the right of that screen note "View Important Publication Details" next to the "pdf" symbol. Click on that to view or copy the DP. If when entering the microfilm publication number a negative response is shown, try inserting an "A" after the microfilm number for sometimes NARA has split the series into several publications because of size. For example, to view details for M804 it will be necessary to enter M804A for rolls 1–200, M804B for rolls 201–400, etc. (These instructions were valid at the time of publication though in the future NARA could make changes on the website affecting the search path.) Most microfilm publications starting with "M" have Descriptive Pamphlets. NARA microfilm starting with "T" do not, though some of the "T" films do have roll listings.

---

and bounty land application files. Two or three files may have been merged. A widow's approved pension file, for example, could have been

---

29   National Genealogical Society, *Index of Revolutionary War Pension Applications in the National Archives, NGS special publication no. 40* (Washington, D.C.: National Genealogical Society, 1976), hereafter *Hoyt's Index* (named for one of its original compilers).

combined with the approved bounty land warrant application file. An approved pension file of a survivor could have been consolidated with the bounty land application of his heirs.

OFFICERS: Warrant records for approved officers' bounty land applications that were submitted before the War Department fire of November 1800 and are now missing are replaced by 10" x 14" cards that show the name of the state or organization for which an officer served, his name, the symbol "B.L. Wt." (Bounty Land Warrant) followed by the warrant number and the number of acres granted, the officer's rank, and issue date of the warrant, the notation "No Papers," and sometimes the name of a person other than the officer to whom the warrant was delivered or assigned.

These officers' reference cards for missing files were compiled about 1917 by the Bureau of Pensions from entries in a surviving register listing bounty land warrants issued to officers before November 8, 1800.[30]

FINDING AIDS FOR M804: To view all the images on NARA's M804 online go to <www.footnote.com> or to <www.ancestry.com>. These are subscription-based websites with access available in many librar-

Figure 1–7. Card for Capt. Alexander Rose from M804 showing "no papers" available.

ies and NARA facilities. These sources are especially helpful for their indexes. For example, the Footnote.com website not only includes every image in each file, but also attempts to index all names in each file, not just the name of the soldier.

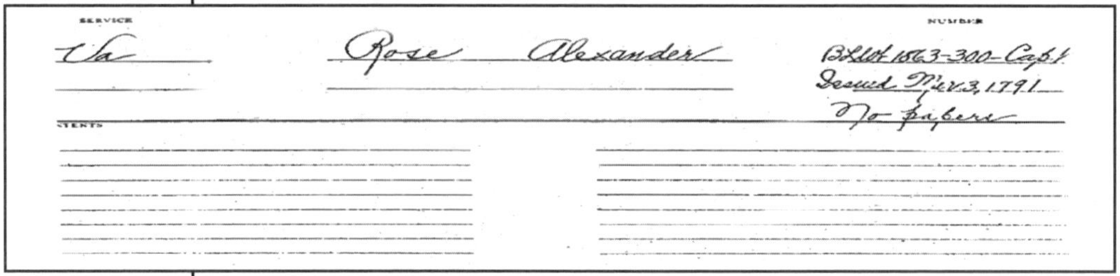

M805 is a microfilm publication of the selected papers from the revolutionary war pension files that appear on M804. These "selected" papers in each file were determined by NARA to be the key items. To summarize the difference: the M804 microfilm publication includes images of all papers in each soldier's file, both the "selected" and "non selected." M805 only includes the "selected" documents in each file.

---

30   Anne Bruner Eales and Robert M. Kvasnicka, *Guide to Genealogical Research in the National Archives of the United States*, 3rd edition (Washington, D.C.: National Archives and Records Administration, 2000), 182, hereafter Eales, *Genie Guide*, by which it is known colloquially.

Abstracts from the Revolutionary War pension files in M805 appear in a published book compiled by Virgil D. White.[31] This compilation does not abstract every paper in this microfilmed series but does abstract key details from each file. Those who have access to a copy of White's *Revolutionary Abstracts* will find that using that source helps to quickly determine if a particular serviceman received a pension. If so, then the full file can be accessed online as above noted or by obtaining a copy of the file using Form NATF 85 of the National Archives. (The form can be downloaded as a pdf or ordered online from NARA at <www.archives.gov/veterans/military-service-records/pre-ww-1-records.html>.

ISSUING OF WARRANTS

NARA's M829 Warrants

After an application was approved, a warrant was issued that evidenced the award of a certain acreage. Most of the warrant files issued under the act of 1788 were destroyed by fires in the War Department in 1800 and 1814 (as were the application files previously discussed).[32] The extant records relating to the warrants of the 1788 act have been reproduced as NARA microfilm publication M829, *U.S. Revolutionary War Bounty Land Warrants Used in the U.S. Military District of Ohio and Related Papers.* Warrant files show whether a warrant was assigned, where the land was located, and other details. Some selected remarks from the DP accompanying M829 follow (see also footnote 33):

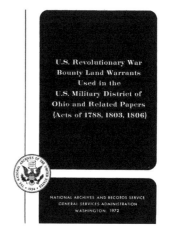

Title page of the Descriptive Pamphlet accompanying M829.

> The warrants and related papers reproduced in this publication are arranged by date of act and thereunder in numerical sequence. The first series includes U.S. military bounty land warrants issued under the act of July 9, 1788, which are numbered 1–14220.
>
> A warrant shows the date of issuance, the name and rank of the veteran, the State from which he enlisted, and when applicable the name of the heir or assignee. Because a warrant was assignable and was often sold by the veteran on the open market, a notation on the reverse of the warrant indicates subsequent transfers of ownership from the veteran to heirs or assignees.
>
> Most of the warrants from 1 to 6912 in this first series were destroyed during War Department fires in 1800 and 1814; generally the only existing documents in the files relating to these warrants are a few copies of patents granted for land claims. Beginning with warrant 6913 most of the actual warrants are intact. Those that are missing are presumed to be lost or not surrendered by the veteran or his heirs. Several warrant numbers that are included in a range of documents on a specific roll have cross–reference notations to see a warrant reproduced on another roll. In the few instances where a warrant was exchanged for scrip, a cross–

31 Virgil D. White, *Genealogical Abstracts of Revolutionary War Pension Files,* 4 volumes (Waynesburg, Tenn.: National Historical Publishing Co., 1990), hereafter White, *Revolutionary Abstracts.* Includes abstracts of all revolutionary pension/land bounty files on National Archives microfilm publication M805. Volume 4 is an all-name index to the first three volumes and therefore indexes many names in the documents other than solely the soldier's name.

32 *JCC* 34:307–8, July 9, 1788.

reference sheet among the records has been filmed to indicate the scrip application number and the appropriate act. The military bounty land scrip applications are in another series and have not been reproduced in this publication.

The second series comprises U.S. Revolutionary War bounty land warrants issued under the acts of March 3, 1803, and April 15, 1806. The warrants are numbered from 1 to 272 under the act of 1803 and continue from 273 to 2119 under the act of 1806. A series of 18 additional warrants issued under later acts is included: 1299, 2314, 2340, 2346, 2359, 2418, 2436, 2442, 2453, 2455, 2458, 2462, 2467, 2468, 2470, 2471, 2475, and 2479. These warrants are in this series although they were issued by authority of acts of January 17, 1835 (4 Stat. 749); July 27, 1842 (5 Stat. 497); and June 26, 1848 (9 Stat. 240). Presumably the remainder of the warrants issued under these three acts are no longer extant.

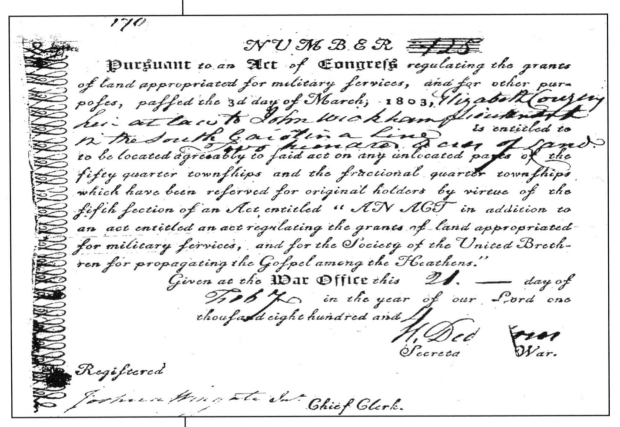

Figure 1–8. This warrant from M829 includes significant family information.

A warrant in the second series shows the date of issuance, the name and rank of the veteran, the State from which he enlisted, and the name of the heir or assignee. Most of the individual warrants present along with a certificate of location that indicates where the bounty land was located in the U.S. Military District of Ohio. Occasionally filed with a warrant are such related papers as an affidavit, a power of attorney, or a deed of conveyance showing transfer of warrant ownership. When there is no certificate of location with the warrant, a legal description of land location is usually provided on the front or reverse of the warrant by a series of numbers and dots, such as 23.1.2.8, indicating lot, quarter of section, township, and range, respectively. For this series, reference notations have been inserted to indicate if a warrant is missing or was exchanged for scrip.[33]

The records reproduced on M829 are part of the records identified as NARA's RG 49 Records of the Bureau of Land Management, which are now deposited in Archives I in Washington, D.C.[34]

SCRIP ACT: CONTINENTAL LINE AND VIRGINIA STATE LINE

Until the passage of the scrip act on May 30, 1830, the USMD was the only area where non-Virginia veterans holding federal bounty warrants for service in the Continental Line could take up their land.[35] Virginians who served in the Continental Line could take up their land in the Virginia Military District (VMD) in Ohio. Virginia State Line veterans (officers, soldiers, sailors and marines) were not allowed to locate their warrants in that Ohio location but could use their warrants in the South of the Green River military tract in Kentucky to the early 1790s, and in 1818–1820 were allowed to patent in the Jackson Purchase in western Kentucky.

Upon passage of the 1830 scrip act, all holders of warrants for Continental service (not just from Virginia but from all states) and all those who served in the Virginia Line could then exchange any unused warrants for scrip.

In 1832 Congress extended the time, and in 1833 the restriction on the area in which scrip warrants could be located was removed.[36] Warrants that had been exchanged for scrip could thereafter be used for any government land available for private sale. In 1835 additional acreage was again appropriated.[37] Another act allowing the exchange for scrip was approved in 1852.[38] At that time outstanding warrants were surrendered for scrip at the rate of $1.25 per acre, and Virginia relinquished all further claims to the VMD in Ohio.

The 1830 Scrip Act covered:
• **Virginia State Line**
• **Virginia Continental Line**
• **Continental Lines of other states**

---

33 National Archives microfilm publication M829, Records of the Bureau of Land Management, *U.S. Revolutionary War Bounty Land Warrants Used in the U.S. Military District of Ohio and Related Papers (Acts of 1788, 1803, and 1806), 1788–1806* (Washington, D.C.: National Archives and Records Administration), RG 49, 49 rolls, DP. These warrants were not orders for surveys. The 1785 Land Ordinance, as has been discussed, specified that the government had to first survey the area before even offering the land for purchase or as bounty rewards. Chapter Two will show that the warrants for the Virginia Military District in Ohio did order surveys; that was a different situation because the Virginia district was surveyed by metes and bounds after the warrantees first made their selections of land. In that Virginia system the warrant was the order for the survey.

34 The National Archives Research Center at 700 Pennsylvania Avenue, NW, Washington, DC 20408–0001 is designated as Archives I; the National Archives Research Center at 8601 Adelphi Road, College Park, MD 20740–6001 is known as Archives II.

35 *4 U.S. Stat.* 422–24, May 30, 1830.

36 *4 U.S. Stat* 578, July 13, 1832 and *4 U.S. Stat.* 665, March 2, 1833.

37 *4 U.S. Stat.* 770–71, March 3, 1835.

38 *10 U.S. Stat.* 143, August 31, 1852.

Those still holding warrants that had not been exchanged for scrip could not take up their land in any public domain location until a new act was enacted allowing them that privilege. In the meantime, they were restricted to either the USMD or, if they served from Virginia in the Continental Line, they were restricted to the VMD. Finally the act of 1842 was passed and all holders of federal warrants could take up their warrants anywhere in the public domain where public lands were subject to private entry.[39]

VIRGINIA SCRIP WARRANTS

The 1830 scrip act included the Continental line of all states.

SCRIP RECORDS OF VIRGINIA WARRANTS

When using the records of the National Archives be aware that there are separate consultants for the military records (RG 15 and various other Record Groups), and for the civilian records. The latter includes records of the Bureau of Land Management's General Land Office involving RG 49. Though they have separate responsibilities, these consultants are all housed in the same office in Archives I.

NARA's scrip warrants are among the records of the Bureau of Land Management's RG 49 and include a series designated "Applications for Military Bounty-Land Scrip."[40] The applications of veterans who exchanged their federal and their Virginia military bounty land warrants for scrip certificates are scattered among this series. The application file generally contains the original warrant together with correspondence and other papers. They include applications made under the following scrip acts:

> Acts of May 30, 1830, and July 13, 1832: 1–1994.
> Acts of March 2, 1833: 1–225.
> Act of March 3, 1835: 1–970.
> Act of August 31, 1852: 1–1689.

The consultants of RG 49 at Archives I have a slim volume titled "Alpha Index to Scrip Claims Acts of 1830, 1832, 1833, and 1835" and further marked as "Volume 35."[41] It provides the application number, volume, and page reference for applications. Through this researchers can locate a scrip application file by the surname of the applicant under those specified acts. For the act of 1852 see Brown, *Scrip Act 1852* which includes information on those who applied under that

---

39 5 *U.S. Stat.* 497, July 27, 1842.

40 Harry P. Yoshpe and Philip P. Bower, *The National Archives Preliminary Inventory of the Land Entry Papers of the General Land Office: Preliminary Inventory 22,* hereafter *Preliminary Inventory 22.* (1949: new edition, San Jose, Calif.: Rose Family Association, 1996). See 7, entry 4.

41 This is one of NARA's finding aids for *Preliminary Inventory 22,* 7, entry 4.

later act.[42] Brown's publication of the 1852 act applications includes some background information, and an alphabetical listing of applicants with their military designation and the application number. For example, Andrew Leitch is listed as "Maj VCL 337," that is, Major in the Virginia Continental Line. Using the provided application number of 337 it is easy to turn to the pages of file abstracts in the book and learn that there are several documents listed at New Orleans, Louisiana, Washington, D.C., and Prince William County, Virginia. Leitch's estate and will are mentioned. Also a notation that he was mortally wounded at the Battle of Harlem Heights in 1777, and that he died testate leaving a widow Margaret "Peggy." His daughter Sarah is shown, also her death date, and it is noted that she married John Addison. Their children are also listed. Clearly, this book is a source that could be helpful to researchers.

Because the 1830 scrip act included Virginians who served in their own state line as well as the Continental Line, this state was requested to furnish a statement of all outstanding warrants. Before the scrip could be issued to a Virginia applicant he was required to prove that the warrant had not been taken up in Kentucky or the Virginia Military District in Ohio. (Virginia's records will be discussed in more detail in the next chapter.)

FINDING AIDS: Revolutionary War

RG 49—LAND ENTRY

SMITH'S FEDERAL LAND SERIES: A valuable source for information on warrantees of the United States Military District is volume two of Smith's Federal Land Series.[43] This volume of the series applies only to land patented in the USMD, and patents issued under the various scrip laws after 1830 (as described earlier in this chapter). It does not include veterans who obtained state bounty land from the states they served (see Chapters Two and Three). This series from Smith is a monumental work and is far underused. The introductions to each volume are well worth reading.

It cannot be assumed that the warrantee named in Smith's *Federal Land Series* is a veteran. Smith did attempt to compare the warrant numbers with other source data and was able to identify many of

Federal Land Series

A CALENDAR OF ARCHIVAL MATERIALS
ON THE LAND PATENTS ISSUED BY THE
UNITED STATES GOVERNMENT, WITH
SUBJECT, TRACT, AND NAME INDEXES

Volume 2 · 1799–1835

FEDERAL BOUNTY-LAND WARRANTS OF THE
AMERICAN REVOLUTION

Clifford Neal Smith

Above is from the title page of a reprint in 2007 by Clearfield Company of Bowie, Maryland.

---

42   10 *U.S. Stat* 143, August 31, 1852. These have been published in Margie G. Brown, *Genealogical Abstracts, Revolutionary War Veterans Scrip Act 1852, Abstracted from Bureau of Land Management Record Group 49 National Archives Branch, Suitland* (1990; reprint, Lovettsville, Va.: Willow Bend Books, 1997, hereafter Brown, *Scrip Act 1852.*

43   Clifford Neal Smith, *Federal Land Series: A Calendar of Archival Materials on the Land Patents Issued by the United States Government, with Subject, Tract, and Name Indexes,* four volumes (Chicago: American Library Association, 1973), hereafter Smith, *Federal Land Series.* See volume 2 for the USMD.

the veterans in spite of the difficulties, but in many cases the name shown is an assignee rather than the veteran.

Use of Smith's publication could locate for researchers the land in the USMD. For example, if a search located a veteran's name and warrant number in *Hoyt's Index*, that soldier's name can be sought in the index of Smith's *Federal Land Series* volume 2. If it appears in this Smith's index, examine the page reference given. To use a specific example, *Hoyt's Index* lists: "Denniston, Thomas, N.Y., BLWt. 7030–100. Iss. 11/16/1791. No Papers." This indicates that the application file was destroyed in one of the Washington, D.C., fires. In the index to Smith's *Federal Land Series* volume 2, that name appears on page 11. That page reveals that the 100–acre Warrant #7030 of Thomas Denniston, a Private, was used on November 16, 1791, as part of a 4,000–acre tract registered by Godfrey Lauge or Lange. Further, that it was located in Range 2, Township 9. The entry in Smith's volume also indicates that data regarding that warrant was taken from Roll 1 of NARA's Record Group 49, microfilm publication M829, page 12. The researcher can now access M829 to ascertain if any further information is shown in that source.

Other uses for Smith's *Federal Land Series* will become apparent when the introduction to the volume is read.

PRELIMINARY INVENTORY 22: This is a finding aid for RG 49, Records of the General Land Office, which is out of date but is still useful is Yoshpe and Bower, *The National Archives Preliminary Inventory of the Land Entry Papers of the General Land Office*, known as PI 22.[44] Preliminary inventories provide researchers with descriptions of the holdings of individual record groups in the National Archives. Most of the items in this preliminary inventory have not been microfilmed but can be ordered in person for viewing by citing "PI 22" followed by the page and entry number of the item requested.

It is difficult to do research in the documents referenced in PI 22 from a distance since some of the series are quite large and not well indexed, if indexed at all. If it is not possible to go to Washington, D.C., in person it may be necessary to hire an onsite researcher in D.C. to peruse or copy the needed information.

THE TRANS-MISSISSIPPI WEST 1804–1912: Some of the material in PI 22 is now available in the newer guide of Kvasnicka, *The Trans-*

40		6 Jan 1800		A/1/042
By Whom Registered: Caleb Swan				
For Whom Registered: Caleb Swan				
Location: (4000 acres)		Mil – 5 5 – 2		
Based upon the following Army land warrants:				
Issued to		*No.*	*Date*	*Acres*
Frye, Frederick, Ens		708	1 Jul 1796	150
Frye, Nathaniel, Lt		707	13 Nov 1789	200
Laverswyler? [Saverswyler?]				
Mary, Ens		1284	10 Mar 1790	150
Catlin, Putnam, Fife Maj		5619	8 Jul 1790	100
Rix, Adam, Sgt		10248	10 Mar 1790	100
McLean, Arch[ibal]d, Pvt		9945	8 Jun 1790	100
Platt, Samuel, Surgeon's				
Mate		1721	30 May 1789	200
Footman, Peter, Pvt		8403	22 Jul 1796	100
Kellog, Solomon		6055	27 Aug 1792	100
Adkins, Jabez		5368	10 May 1798	100
Bailey, Louden, Sgt Maj		5481	7 Jul 1798	100
Allison, Richard, Sur-				
geon's Mate		44	20 Jun 1789	300
Allison, Richard, Lt		1429	20 Jun 1789	200
Strong, David, Capt		1951	17 Oct 1789	300
Dunn, Abner M., Lt		564	7 Sep 1790	200
Kearsey, John, Pvt		9765	20 Jun 1789	100
Redhair, Frederick, Pvt		10310	20 Jun 1789	100
Fennell? [Tennell?] Pat-				
rick, Pvt		9371	20 Jun 1789	100
Kingsbury, Jacob, Ens		1190	12 Sep 1789	150
Wood, Joseph M., Pvt		6150	20 Jun 1789	100
Orr, John, Sgt		10179	20 Jun 1789	100
Dixon, John, Pvt		9302	20 Jun 1789	100
Nace, George, Cpl		10143	20 Jun 1789	100
Dougherty, George, Fifer		9318	20 Jun 1789	100
Lattimore, Rich[ar]d, Pvt		9848	20 Jun 1789	100
Ford, Mahlon, Lt		2526	4 Aug 1790	200
Kellog, Josiah, Pvt		6056	27 Aug 1792	100
Swan, Caleb, Ens		1923	13 Nov 1789	150
Kellog, William, Pvt		6060	27 Aug 1792	100

Figure 1–9. Another example, this from a page from Smith's Federal Land Series, *volume 2, page 13. Using the explanation in the introduction, we see that the above is for the book's Serial entry number 120, the date is 6 January 1800, the source is NARA's microfilm publication M829 roll 1 page 42, and that it was registered by Caleb Swan for himself. Following that information is a list of all the individuals whose warrants were submitted to total the 4,000 acres.*

---

44 *Preliminary Inventory 22, 7, entry 4.*

Mississippi West 1804–1912.[45] This monumental work was ten years in the making. In particular, see Division "B" (Recorder's Division) pages 41–65 for much of that pertains specifically to military lands. Also see Division D Mail and Files Division which includes "Military Bounty Land Warrants and Related Records," and "Abstracts," pages 190–200. There is a second volume to the foregoing: *The Guide Supplement Containing State Lists and Other Appendixes.* This details by state the federal records regarding land. Kvasnicka, *Trans-Mississippi West 1804–1912* describes the many records in the possession of the federal government but is limited primarily to the states west of the Mississippi River. Because of this, PI 22 described above still can be used for the states east of the Mississippi.

To order records based on entries in Kvasnicka, *Trans-Mississippi West 1804–1912,* cite the book title, the page number, and the paragraph number (shown in boldface at the beginning of the description). If in the body of the description there is a reference in curly parenthesis, include that for it is the series number. For example, to request from this source a scrip file under the act of May 30, 1830, cite Kvasnicka, *Trans-Mississippi West 1804–1912,* Part IV, page 43, description 49.B8. NARA will then understand what is sought. If you order records from the same page 43, but from paragraph number 49.B10 (A register of letters received by Division "B," ...) you would note that it is followed by {UD 35A} which is the series number. Include that number when ordering.

RESEARCH IN THE LAND ENTRY FILES OF THE GENERAL LAND OFFICE RECORD GROUP 49: Another finding aid for RG 49 is Hawkins, *Research in the Land Entry Files of the General Land Office Record Group 49.*[46] This twenty page booklet is primarily directed to the larger collection of land-entry papers connected with federal land other than those awarded for military service but nonetheless does include information about the search path for surrendered warrant files based on bounty land. The booklet is available at no charge from NARA and also can be accessed in its entirety online (see footnote 46). The booklet clearly and succinctly describes the land entry files and should be of value to anyone seeking those records.

---

45   Robert M. Kvasnicka, *The Trans-Mississippi West 1804–1912. A Guide to Records of the Department of the Interior for the Territorial Period. Section 3: Records of the General Land Office.* Part IV, two volumes, the second being a supplemental guide. ([Washington, D.C.]: National Archives and Records Administration, 2007), hereafter Kvasnicka, *Trans-Mississippi West 1804–1912.*

46   Kenneth Hawkins, *Research in the Land Entry Files of the General Land Office Record Group 49* (Washington, D.C.: National Archives and Records Administration, 1997). This is available in its entirety online at <www.archives.gov/publications/general–info–leaflets/67 .html>.

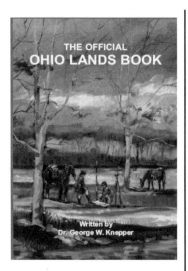

THE OFFICIAL OHIO LANDS BOOK: An indispensible booklet involving Ohio lands is *The Official Ohio Lands Book.*[47] Dr. George W. Knepper extensively rewrote some earlier publications on the subject and produced this helpful and attractive booklet amply illustrated in color. It covers all the varied surveys of Ohio including the original Seven Ranges, the Congress lands in different parts of the state, the two major ordinances of 1785 and 1787, the VMD, the USMD, the Firelands, the private company purchases, and more. It is an essential guide for anyone with a desire to understand the often confusing surveys of this state. For a copy go to <www.auditor.state.oh.us/Publications /General/OhioLandsBook.pdf>. (Those with a computer can use a CD-Rom version which is available by contacting The Auditor of State, 866 East Broad Street, Columbus, Ohio 43216–1140. Or contact their site's webmaster at <www.auditor.state.oh.us>.)

RELATED RECORDS

OHIO HISTORICAL SOCIETY LIBRARY: Tom Rieder, Reference Archivist mentioned previously in this chapter, provides the following additional useful information about the collection at their library:

> The Ohio Historical Society holds survey and purchase records from the Congress Lands that are part of the Ohio River Survey, the Between the Miamis Survey, the 8 Ranges East of the 1st Meridian Survey, and the Surveys of the 18 Ranges North and South of the Baseline and East of the 1st Meridian. The Library of the Historical Society also holds original and microfilm copies of Virginia Military District Entry and Survey Books. For the United States Military District, the Library holds original and microfilm copies of field notes and plats and microfilm copies of United States Military District Warrants used in the District to satisfy land claims. The Library also holds tract and entry books and other purchase records of the Chillicothe, Delaware, and Zanesville Land Offices that handled sales of unclaimed land in the Military District after 1812.[48]

OTHER REVOLUTIONARY WAR WARRANTS
Warrant Nos. 1299, 2314, 2340, 2346, 2359, 2418, 2442, 2453, 2458, 2462, 2467, 2468, 2470, 2471, 2475, and 2479 are a part of the series begun under the acts of March 3, 1803, and April 15, 1806, though issued on authority of the acts of January 27, 1835, ("An act to extend the time for issuing Military Land Warrants to the Officers and soldiers of the Revolution"), of July 27, 1842, and of June 26, 1848. Filed with the warrants are applications to locate lands, certificates of location, correspondence, and other papers. These are available at Archives I in the Land Entry Papers of the General Land Office, RG 49.[49]

---

47   Knepper, *Ohio Lands Book.*

48   Tom Rieder, Reference Archivist, Ohio Historical Society, Columbus, Ohio. E-mailed to the compiler on Friday, April 2, 2010.

49   *Preliminary Inventory 22*, 8–9, entry 11.

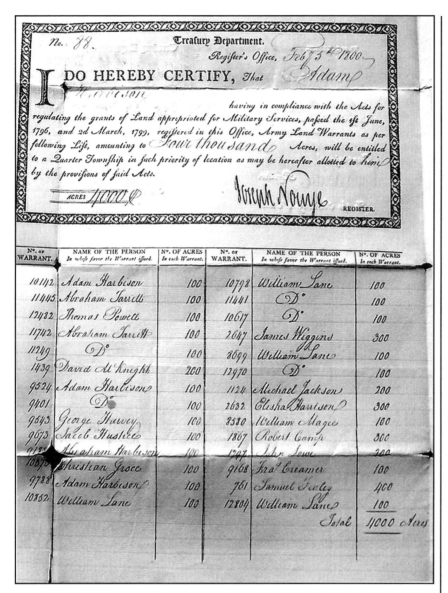

Figure 1–10. Treasury Certificate filed in compliance with acts of 1796 and 1799 for Adam Harbison. Note that it includes a listing of everyone who had a warrant used in this quarter section, totalling 4,000 acres.

TREASURY CERTIFICATES

These are certificates in compliance with the acts of 1796 and 1799, accompanied by certifications by the Secretary of the Treasury that persons registering their warrants in pursuance of these acts are entitled to patents. The date of patent and place of record are noted in each case.[50] These are at Archives I in the Land Entry papers of the General Land Office in RG 49. (See Figure 1–10.)

CANADIAN REFUGEE WARRANTS 1802–11

Warrants issued to Canadian refugees during the Revolutionary War were pursuant to the act of April 7, 1798, "An Act for the relief of the Refugees from the British provinces of Canada and Nova Scotia," and the act of February 18, 1801, "An Act regulating the grants of land

---

50 *Preliminary Inventory 22, 8, entry 7.*

appropriated for the refugees from the British provinces of Canada and Nova Scotia."[51] On the back of each warrant is a notation of the date of patent and the place of record. In addition, there is a bundle of powers of attorney and related documents under which locations were made and patents drawn. These are at Archives I in the Land Entry papers of the General Land Office in RG 49.

To summarize, this chapter presented information about federal bounty land for Revolutionary War service. That is not, however, the end of the story. Some states also awarded their own bounty land which will be discussed in Chapter Three. Before discussing that, though, Virginia needs to be considered in Chapter Two for that state had unique conditions involving both federal warrants for service in the Continental Line, and the rewards promised to the Virginia Line.

"This is not, however, the end of the story ... "

Points to Remember in this Chapter

- ✓ The Revolutionary War generated both federal and state bounty land (see Chapters Two and Three).

- ✓ Both officers and soldiers were eligible for bounty land for Revolutionary War service.

- ✓ The major location for Revolutionary War military bounty land was in the U.S. Military District in Ohio until 1830. Virginians on continental line could take up land in Kentucky or later in the Virginia Military District in Ohio. Those who served in Virginia's state line could take up their land in certain designated areas in Kentucky prior to the 1830 scrip act, but they could not locate their warrants in the VMD. (More about this in Chapter Two.)

- ✓ The scrip act for 1830 extended the available locations for settling the federal warrants for Revolutionary War bounty to Illinois, Indiana and Ohio. After the spring of 1833 restrictions on location were lifted for those who had exchanged their warrants for scrip warrants. The holders of the latter could use them anywhere in the public domain where there was land available for private purchase.

- ✓ The process to obtain federal bounty land started with the application file, was followed by the issuance of a warrant, and ended with a patent. (Virginians received a military certificate when the application was approved. This was followed by the issuance of a warrant for survey and culminated with a patent.)

- ✓ In spite of losses of some records, others involving the same warrant are likely to have survived.

---

51   *Preliminary Inventory 22*, 8, entry 8. The acts are found in 1 *U.S. Stat.* 547, April 7, 1798, and 2 *U.S. Stat.* 100–01, February 18, 1801.

2 REVOLUTIONARY WAR
Virginia

Virginia's process to claim and locate military land required different strategies. This colony promised bounty land as an inducement to enlist for service in Virginia's State or Continental Line. Originally the warrants were used for land on the south side of the Green River in what is now Kentucky though at the time was part of the Commonwealth of Virginia. By agreement in congress, if that land was found to be insufficient, Virginia was to have a tract situated northwest of the River Ohio. Virginia ceded its interest in its western lands in the Northwest territory to the United States Congress based on that promise.[1] This area became known as the Virginia Military District or VMD. However, only those Virginians who served in the Continental Line were eligible for the lands in Virginia's Ohio tract; Virginia State Line veterans were not.

In an act for "speedily recruiting the Virginia regiments on continental establishment" passed in October 1778, Virginia promised certain monetary and other benefits to 2,216 rank and file who enlisted for eighteen months. Those who enlisted for three years, or during the war, were entitled to certain monetary and supply benefits "together with the continental bounty of lands."[2]

Virginia's concern about adequate bounty land was based on an act passed by the Virginia General Assembly in May 1779 providing that every able bodied freeman who would enlist, "and who having enlisted to serve a particular period of time unexpired, will re-enlist to serve during the continuance of the present war, among the troops of this commonwealth, either at home or in the continental army ... " were to receive a designated allotment of clothing, pay and rations,

> The Virginia Military District was open to Virginia's Continental Line but not to Virginia's State Line. More of this later in this chapter.

---

1   William Waller Hening, *The Statutes at Large being a Collection of all the Laws of Virginia from the First Session of the Legislature, in the year 1619*, 13 volumes (New York: R & W. & G. Bartlow, 1823), hereafter referred to as *Hening* preceded by volume number and followed by the page number; 11 *Hening* 559–67, January 2, 1781. See p. 566 for the cession. See also 26 *JCC* 112, March 1, 1784 for Congress' acceptance of the cession.
2   9 *Hening* 588–592, October 1778.

and at the end of the war "every of the said soldiers, sailors, and marines" were entitled to a grant of 100 acres of any unappropriated land within the commonwealth.[3] The officers were to receive a grant of the like quantity of lands allowed to officers of the same rank in the Virginia regiments on continental establishment. (No bounty provision was made by this 1779 act for militia service; militia was covered by later federal acts.)[4]

Under the various acts Virginia warrants for varied acreage were allotted depending upon rank:

> Major General – 15,000 acres
>
> Brigadier General – 10,000 acres
>
> Colonel – 6,667 acres
>
> Lieutenant Colonel – 6,000 acres
>
> Major – 5,667 acres
>
> Captain – 4,000 acres
>
> Subaltern – 2,667 acres
>
> Noncommissioned officer enlisting and serving for war – 400 acres
>
> Noncommissioned officer enlisting and serving for three years – 200 acres
>
> Soldier or Seaman enlisting and serving for three years – 100 acres
>
> Soldier or Seaman enlisting and serving to end of war – 200 acres (in October 1780 increased to 300 acres)

Though the allotment to a soldier or sailor was at first 100 acres, under the act of 1779 those who served to the end of the war were to get 200 acres.[5] This act also provided that if any officer, soldier, or sailor had "fallen or died" in the service, his heirs or legal representatives would be entitled to receive the land. In subsequent resolutions it was noted and discussed that an increase for soldiers to 300 acres in the act of October 1780 had been overlooked. Further, that:

> Upon the whole, nothing seems clearer than that, all our soldiers who were in service at the passage of this act, who had already enlisted, or who might thereafter enlist by the first of April 1781, to serve during the war, and who continued to serve faithfully to the end of the war, are entitled to 300 acres of land, in lieu of all such

---

3 10 *Hening* 23–7; see also 10 *Hening* 50 *et seq.*, May 1779. Note that the wording in the act states "either at home or in the continental army" and thus it would appear to include Virginia's State Line.

4 3 *U.S. Stat.* 285–287, April 16, 1816, and 10 *U.S. Stat.* 701–02, March 3, 1855.

5 10 *Hening* 159–62, October 1779.

bounties given by any former laws. The former bounty, we have already seen was 200 acres.[6]

UNDERSTANDING SOME BASICS

Before proceeding some basics must be considered relating to Virginia's awards of bounty land. These will be discussed in more detail throughout this chapter.

1. Virginia's initial cession of its western lands included a provision that if bounty land promised in the South of the Green River tract within the commonwealth (that is, Kentucky) could not be satisfied then Virginia would have a tract northwest of the Ohio River in Ohio to satisfy promises to Virginia veterans. (The Ohio tract was later known as the Virginia Military District, or VMD.) The South of the Green River tract was open to Virginia's Continental Line and Virginia's State Line.

2. Though the Kentucky military lands included veterans holding warrants either for Virginia's State Line or its Continental Line, the VMD in Ohio was limited to those who served on Virginia's Continental Line.

3. When later patents were issued by the state of Kentucky in the Jackson Purchase in western Kentucky 1818–1820, it appears that only veterans who served in Virginia's State Line were eligible to locate there.

4. Virginia's application process included the issuance of a certificate to establish eligibility before the warrant to survey was issued. The application files for the certificates are in the custody of the Library of Virginia in Richmond. The warrant files that followed are held by the National Archives at Archives I in D.C.

5. The Virginia Military District in Ohio was surveyed by metes and bounds. This necessitated a difference in the process for other federal lands in Ohio were surveyed by regulations of the federal 1785 Land Act which required the survey to be completed before the land was disbursed. Therefore, while the United States Military District in Ohio was surveyed before the veterans or warrantees could make a claim and settle on it, in the Virginia Military District the veteran (or his heirs, assignee or agents) chose the land first and then it was surveyed.

6. After the scrip act of 1830 (see Chapter One), Virginians who had served as officers, soldiers, sailors, and marines of the Virginia State Line, or served in the Virginia Continental Line, could exchange their unused warrants for scrip and use them anywhere in Ohio, Illinois, or Indiana where there was federal land subject to private sale. After 1833, those holding a scrip warrant could use it anywhere in the public domain where there was federal land subject to private sale.[7]

The original thirteen colonies plus Tennessee, Kentucky, Maine, and later Texas, West Virginia, and Hawaii, are all considered "state-land" states and are not a part of the public domain. Of those, all are "metes and bounds" except for Texas which had its own system. The rest of the states not listed are "federal land "(public domain) states and subject to surveys by the rectangular survey system set out by the Land Ordinance of 1785 (revised in 1796). The government allowed Virginia, a "state-land" state to use their metes and bounds system in the Virginia Military Tract even though the VMD lay within the federal land in what became the state of Ohio. The Virginia warrantee chose his tract before the survey was made while those veterans subject to the rules of the federal land states had to wait until the government first surveyed the public domain land.

---

6   11 *Hening* 565, 1782–1784; also 10 *Hening* 331–32, October 1780.
7   4 *U.S.Stat.* 665, March 2, 1833.

7. All of Virginia's bounty land was either in the present-day state of Kentucky (which was then a part of Virginia) or Ohio (which was originally a part of the Northwest Territory). None of its bounty land was located within the bounds of present-day Virginia.

PROCESS OF CLAIMS

To prove their eligibility, Virginia veterans provided sundry documents. Often they obtained affidavits from their comrades or commanding officers, and submitted their discharge papers to help substantiate their claim. When a claim was proved, the governor's office issued a military certificate to the Register of the U. S. Land Office authorizing the Register to issue a warrant specifying the amount of land to be received and directing that the land be surveyed. The certificate was followed by the acquisition of a warrant which was needed before the survey could be started. The veteran then made his entry and a survey was made. Before Kentucky statehood, if the land was in the Kentucky military lands a patent was issued by the state of Virginia; after Kentucky statehood the patent was issued by Kentucky. If the land was in the VMD in Ohio, the patent was issued by the United States, not Virginia, because the Ohio lands were part of the public domain.

MILITARY CERTIFICATES

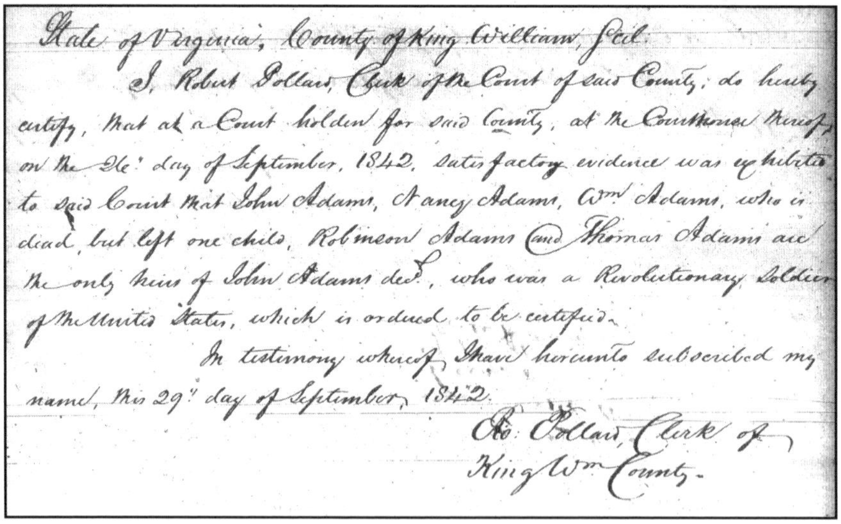

Figure 2–1. Military Certificates 1782–1876, LO 9055, Library of Virginia microfilm publication, reel 1, shows the value of these certificates. This one shown is dated 29 September 1842 in King William County, Virginia, and shows that John Adams, Nancy Adams, Wm Adams who is dead but left one child Robinson Adams, and Thomas Adams, are the only heirs of John Adams decd who was a Revolutionary Soldier of the United States.

Military certificate (LO 9166) from the same reel as above, presented evidence 6 January 1845 to the court of Princess Anne County, Virginia, that Edward Absalom, William Face, Margaret Gaskins, Mary Cavender, William Absolam and Henry Absolam were the only heirs at law of Edward Absalom deceased who was a private soldier in the continental line.

The value of these certificates can be seen!

MILITARY CERTIFICATES AT THE LIBRARY OF VIRGINIA

For information that is available on military certificates and related records for Virginia, start with the published *Virginia Land Office Inventory*.[8]

---

8   Daphne S., Gentry, revised and enlarged by John S. Salon, *Virginia Land Office Inventory*, Third edition (Richmond: The Library of Virginia, 2001). In particular, see pages 23–26.

The initial step of the process, the applications for bounty land, are available at the Library of Virginia in Richmond. For images of these application papers that were approved go to the website <www .virginiamemory.com/collections/collections_a_to_z> and then scroll to Revolutionary Warrant Bounty Warrants. The papers accumulated as proof of service are now part of the records of the Executive Department Office of the Governor (RG#3) and are called 'Bounty Warrants' if approved and 'Rejected Claims' if disapproved. These records are housed in the Archives at the Library of Virginia.

When applications were approved, military certificates (usually on printed forms) were issued. These certificates show the names of officers, soldiers, and sailors as well as details of their service in the Virginia State or Continental Lines. Included are rank and length of service. Certificates that were issued are numbered 1–9926 and cover the period July 14, 1782, to August 5, 1876.

The certificates and supplemental papers are filed in individual folders. Though the certificates can prove Revolutionary War service, the patent may have been issued in the name of others if the soldier sold his interest in the warrant. Bound registers contain information from the certificates and also notations that a warrant was issued for a stated quantity of land. The applications available as loose documents can be accessed on microfilm at the Library of Virginia or in digital form at their website.[9]

If the claim was not approved the application file for a military warrant was a "Rejected Claim." These have been digitized and are available for viewing at <http://lva1.hosted.exlibrisgroup.com/F /887S7YQCTIIIGQJRDSD7BPCAUGC HSHXTES77ST4GEKN71B2FU5-2374 ?func=file&file_name=find-b-clas60&local_base=CLAS60>. Or, use: < http://tinyurl.com/6bkjfy8>.

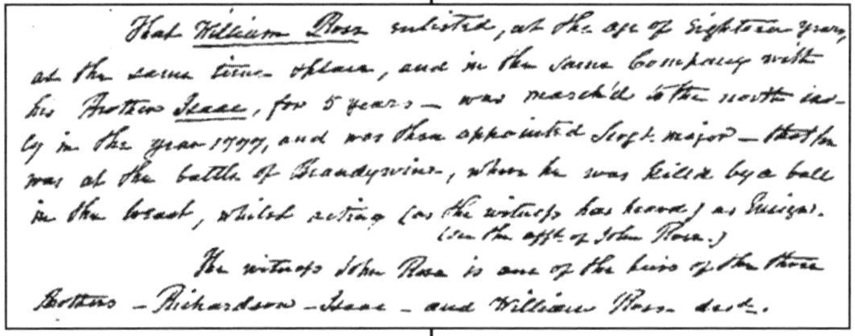

Figure 2–2. The above paragraphs are from the Richardson Rose rejected claim, accessed through the website shown to the left. The several documents in it actually document six brothers who served in the Revolutionary War. Three of them, Richardson, James and William died during the war, and three of them, George, John and Isaac, lived through it. The thirteen pages in this rejected file hold a wealth of family information, all readily available in the images at the website.

If the veteran died while in service or before the claim was made, his file was especially rich in genealogical information because the heirs submitted documentation proving they were the legal beneficiaries.

Also in the Library of Virginia is a "Register of Military Certificates Located in Ohio and Kentucky"; recorded copies of warrants 1–1320, 1328–5020, 8780–9969 (1782–1889), and other related papers.

---

9   *Virginia Land Office. Military Certificates A–Z.* Reels 1–38, available at the Library of
     Virginia in Richmond, Virginia. and at their website

"LOCATING" THE WARRANTS

Once the Virginia veteran obtained a military certificate he could apply for the bounty land warrant and proceed with the entry and survey. At first, as mentioned, he was limited to the tract in Kentucky.

Figure 2–3. This military warrant was located by accessing the website <www.sos.ky.gov /land/military>, then clicking in the left margin "Revolutionary War Warrants" and following links. The warrant was used for land in Kentucky based on services in the Virginia Continental Line.

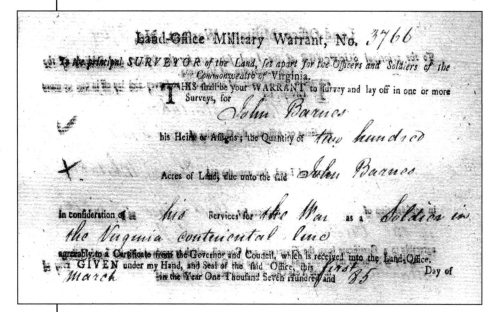

After the Virginia Military District opened in Ohio those holding warrants for Continental service could use their warrants in the VMD in that state.

VIRGINIA WARRANTS IN KENTUCKY

The best way to search for the Virginia warrants and patents in what is now Kentucky is to access the Kentucky Secretary of State's website at <www.sos.ky.gov/land/military>. A total of 4,748 warrants from the Virginia Military Warrants Register have been scanned. The website includes information regarding military warrants issued to Virginia veterans prior to Kentucky statehood June 1, 1792, and all Kentucky patents authorized by those warrants. The subsequent patents issued by the state of Kentucky are also on the website.

SOUTH OF THE GREEN RIVER TRACT: The act by Virginia on January 2, 1781, states that "in case the quantity of good lands of the southeast side of the Ohio upon the waters of Cumberland river, which have been reserved by law for the Virginia troops upon continental estalishment, and upon their own state establishment, should ... prove insufficient for their legal bounties, the deficiency shall be made up to the said troops in good lands, to be laid off between the rivers Scioti and Little Miamis on the north-west side of the river Ohio..."[10] As we will see on page 31 of the this chapter, the words "and upon

10   10 *Hening* 565, January 2, 1781.

28

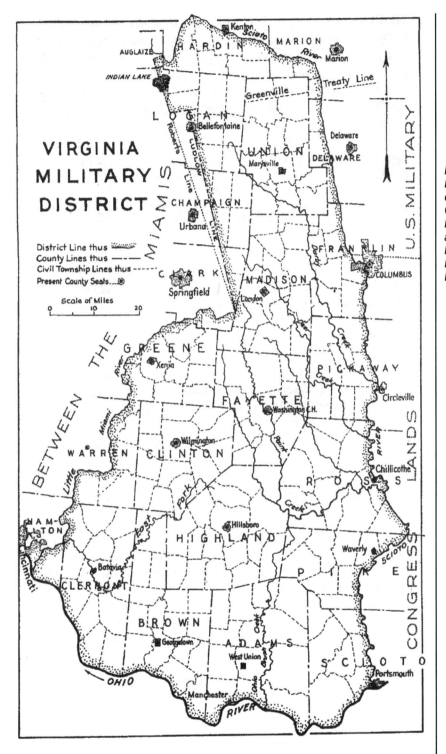

Figure 2–4. The Virginia Military District (VMD) embraces the counties of Adams, Brown, Clermont, Clinton, Fayette, Highland, Fayette, Madison, Union, and portions of Champaign, Clark, Delaware, Franklin, Greene, Hardin, Logan, Marion, Pickaway, Pike, Ross, Scioto, and Warren in Ohio.

Knepper, *Ohio Lands Book*

The Virginia Military District (VMD) of Ohio was surveyed by metes and bounds, but since it was land owned by the United States government, the patent issued from the U.S.

Marquis de Lafayette, from A. S. Barnes, *A Brief History of the United States* (New York: American Book Company, 1885). He is mentioned in the pension and bounty land applications of many veterans.

This western Kentucky land known as the Jackson Purchase was acquired under a treaty between the United States and the Chickasaw Indian Nation on October 19, 1818. Two years later, on February 14, 1820, legislation was passed by the Kentucky General Assembly establishing a rectangular survey system based on townships, ranges and sections and provided for it to be patented on military warrants for the officers and soldiers of the Virginia State Line.

their own state establishment" were later left out of the cession and thus the Virginia Military tract established in Ohio was open only to those of the Virginia Continental Line. It is clear, however, that the military tract South of the Green River tract was open to Virginia's Continental Line and its State Line. These records are available online at the Kentucky Secretary of State's website previously mentioned.

Some military surveys were made after statehood on June 1, 1792. According to Kandie Adkinson, Administrative Supervisor of the Land Office Division in the Office of Kentucky's Secretary of State, Kentucky does have some military patents beyond statehood in the Old Kentucky Patent Series. For example George Caldwell patented two tracts in the Military District, one surveyed in 1793 (#2932) and another in 1798 (#3443). The total of such entries is not known as they are not indexed at this time.

New legislation was passed by Kentucky on December 21, 1795, opening settlement in this South of the Green River military tract to non-veterans.[11]

An act to prevent illegal surveys in the South of the Green River tract was approved by the Kentucky General Assembly on February 12, 1798.[12] Any person who was guilty of making any survey on a military land warrant issued by Virginia on which an entry was not made on or before the first of May, 1792 (unless theretofore authorized by law) would forfeit and pay a penalty.

According to Kentucky's website, due to errors in patent series assignments, a number of patents in the South of Green River Series are located outside the region. Some are as far north as Pendleton County.

THE JACKSON PURCHASE: In 1818 the Jackson Purchase area in western Kentucky was acquired from the Chickasaw Indians.[13] In 1820 the Kentucky General Assembly approved legislation that instructed surveyors "of the lands set apart for the satisfaction of the legal bounties of the officers and soldiers of the Virginia line on state establishment ... to procure chain carriers and markers, and to survey without delay, all entries made in his office, prior to the first day of May, one thousand seven hundred and ninety-two, on warrants for military service

---

11   "An Act for the relief of the Settlers on the south side of Green River," in William Littell, *The Statute Law of Kentucky*, 1:349–52, December 21, 1795, available online at <www.sos.ky.gov/land/reference/legislation/greenriver/establish.htm>.

12   "An Act to Prevent Illegal Surveys on the South Side of Green River," in William Littell, *The Statute Law of Kentucky*, II:109-11, February 12, 1798, online at <www.sos.ky.gov/land/reference/legislation/greenriver/illegal.htm>.

13   Interestingly, surveys in the Jackson Purchase, contrary to other surveys of Virginia/Kentucky, were rectangular and not indiscriminate metes and bounds surveys.

aforesaid ..."[14] Included on the beforementioned Kentucky website are 242 patents authorized by Military Warrants issued to Virginia veterans. Links to scanned images of the patent files are at <www.sos.ky.gov/land/reference/legislation/wtrmilitary/jpclaims.htm>.

Information and listings for Virginia Revolutionary War warrants used to patent land in Kentucky are also included in Jillson's *Old Kentucky Entries* and Jillson's *Kentucky Land Grants*.[15]

VIRGINIA MILITARY DISTRICT IN OHIO (VMD)

By an act of 1781 the Legislature of Virginia resolved that it would yield to the Congress of the United States, for the benefit of the states, all right, title, and claim, which the Commonwealth had northwest of the river Ohio.[16] If the land that had been reserved for the Virginia troops upon continental establishment on the southeast of the Ohio (upon the waters of Cumberland river and between the Green River and Tennessee River) proved insufficient, the deficiences were to be made up in "good lands" between the rivers Scioto and Little Miami on the northwest side of the River Ohio in such proportions as had been engaged to them by the laws of Virginia. The cession as accepted was clear that the land to be reserved on the northwest of the River Ohio was for "Virginia troops upon continental establishment," but this was not without some dispute by Virginia.[17] It was asserted by Virginia that the resolution that was the basis of the cession had a transcribing error and that the words "and upon their own state establishment" were left out. There is, however, no indication that Congress accepted any revision of the cession to include those words.

Gaius Marcus Brumbaugh in his *Revolutionary War Records* lists many names with the heading "State and Navy Land Warrants, Military District of Ohio."[18] It appears that the heading is in error and that those listed did not take up land in the VMD because state line troops were not eligible for location in that district.[19]

> Virginia's bounty land warrants surrendered to the federal government are at NARA, not at the Library of Virginia. This important collection will be much easier to access when the Bureau of Land Management, Eastern States, finishes scanning the patents authorized by the act of August 10, 1790. The volume and page number of the patent which will be included at the website will enable researchers to request the surrendered warrant files from the National Archives.

---

14   "An Act for surveying the Military Claims west of the Tennessee River," *Acts of the Kentucky General Assembly*, December 26, 1820, online at <www.sos.ky.gov/land/reference/legislation/wtrmilitary/jpclaims.htm>.

15   Willard Rouse Jillson, *Old Kentucky Entries and Deeds: A Complete Index to All of the Earliest Land Entries, Military Warrants, Deeds and Wills of the Commonwealth of Kentucky* (1926; reprint, Baltimore: Genealogical Publishing Company, 1987), 313–97. See also: Jillson, *The Kentucky Land Grants: A Systematic Index to All of the Land Grants Recorded in the State Land Office at Frankfort, Kentucky, 1782–1924* (1925; reprint Baltimore: Genealogical Publishing Co., 1972).

16   11 *Hening* 564. 2 January 1781.

17   10 *Hening* 565–566 fn; 11 *Hening* 563–64, 566.

18   Gaius Marcus Brumbaugh, *Revolutionary War Records: Virginia* (1936; reprint, Genealogical Publishing Company, Baltimore, 1967), 323–86, hereafter Brumbaugh, *Revolutionary War Records.*

19   ibid. The introduction to the book indicates that the author did not personally examine all the records, which may account for the error.

Congress in March 1784 agreed to accept Virginia's cession with the condition of reserving land for the Virginia troops upon continental establishment, and other conditions.[20] This VMD district embraces Adams, Brown, Clermont, Clinton, Fayette, Highland, Fayette, Madison, Union, and portions of Champaign, Clark, Delaware, Franklin, Greene, Hardin, Logan, Marion, Pickaway, Pike, Ross, Scioto, and Warren Counties, Ohio.

The act enabling Virginia's officers and soldiers who served on Continental Establishment to obtain land in the Ohio tract was passed in 1790.[21] The VMD was opened by the act of 1794.[22] The metes and bounds system of surveys in this district brought considerable litigation during subsequent years when boundaries overlapped or small tracts were left unclaimed between survey lines.

To Summarize: The scrip act of 1830 (Chapter One) allowed Virginia veterans of the Continental Line, State Line, navy or marines, to exchange their unused warrants for scrip and take it up on any public domain land in Ohio, Illinois, or Indiana that was available for private purchase. The act of 1833 removed the restriction on location and the scrip could then be used anywhere in the public domain where land was available for private purchase. By an act of August 1852 Virginia agreed to surrender for scrip any remaining VMD warrants that were unused.[23] The process of settling outstanding scrip warrants continued for many years.

VIRGINIA WARRANT FILES AT NARA

NATIONAL ARCHIVES SERIES OF VIRGINIA WARRANTS

The National Archives has warrants that were surrendered for bounty land by Virginians for their Revolutionary War service.[24] (The *application* files preceding the issuance of the warrants are in the custody of the Library of Virginia in Richmond as previously discussed.)

This warrant series at NARA is titled "Virginia Military Bounty Land Warrants Surrendered to the Federal Government."[25] These boxes contain documents that were used to locate land tracts in the VMD in Ohio. A warrant file generally includes a surrendered warrant, land survey, power of attorney, certificate of location, an assignment statement, and an affidavit concerning the heirs of the veteran. The

20 26 *JCC* 112, March 1, 1784. See also 11 *Hening* 566 in which the copyist error in omitting "and upon their own state establishment" is discussed.
21 1 *U.S. Stat.* 182–4, August 10, 1790.
22 1 *U.S. Stat.* 394, June 9, 1794.
23 10 *U.S. Stat.* 143, August 31, 1852.
24 Eales, *Genie Guide*, 184–85.
25 *Preliminary Inventory 22*, 7, Entry 3.

file might also include the date and place of death, names of assignees and heirs, and places of residence. Sometimes an assignee who held several warrants combined them for use in one tract, or, a warrantee of one warrant may have used it to acquire more than one tract. The jacket of each file cites the volume and page number of the record copy of the patent located at the Bureau of Land Management, Eastern States, located in Springfield, Virginia. The NARA warrant files are arranged by the volume and page number of the patent.

NARA lists in their in-house information binder for RG 49 the following finding aids associated with the entry in PI 22.[26]

> a) An alphabetical index to names of warrantees that gives the warrant number.
> b) A register entitled "Virginia Military Warrants–Numerical–Continental and State Lines." This is arranged by warrant number and gives the survey number.
> c) A register entitled "Surveys for Land in Virginia Military District, Ohio," which is arranged by survey number and gives the volume and page number that identifies the case file.

If only the name of the warrantee is known, it is necessary to use all three finding aids in succession. The first two of these finding aids include entries for U.S. warrants and Virginia State Line warrants as well as Virginia Continental Line warrants. Basically, what is needed by NARA to find the file described in PI 22 Entry 3 (Virginia Military Bounty Land Warrants Surrendered to the Federal Government) is the volume and page of the patent. That information is available by accessing the register of "Surveys for Land ..." mentioned above in item c) as that includes the volume and page number which will identify the case file. But, as will be seen, item c) above cannot be utilized unless the survey number in b) is found. And, the survey number cannot be located unless the alphabetical index in a) is examined!

Surveyor's chains.

Some of the patents for the Virginia Military District have been scanned and are on the BLM website, but that series has not been finished at the time of this writing. Once it is completed, researchers will be able to get the volume and page number of the patent from that source which will simplify the search in NARA's Virginia warrant series. In the meantime, use the BLM website even if scanning has not been completed for the patent sought could be one that has already been scanned.

The names of warrantees have been published in Brumbaugh, *Revolutionary War Records*.[27] The Virginia warrants surrendered in the Virginia Military District of Ohio have been published in Smith,

---

26 ibid. These are also discussed in Eales, *Genie Guide*, 184–85.
27 Brumbaugh, *Revolutionary War Records*.

Federal Land Series, volume 4, and Bockstruck, *Revolutionary State Bounty*, both previously cited.

KENDRICK CASES

NARA also has eleven packages of warrants including surveyor's certificates as to warrant locations, requests for patents, powers of attorney, plats, notes, contracts, correspondence, and protests against surveys and the issuance of patents on warrants. Eleazer P. Kendrick, a surveyor of the Virginia Military District, Chillicothe, Ohio, is mentioned in many of these papers. To access the Kendrick Cases request from NARA the packages listed in PI 22, entry 19, RG 49.

Eleazer P. Kendrick

Following is an example of what might be found in the Kendrick Cases. From RG 49 [cited as above] Box 120, Folder 860, contains several documents including an affidavit:

> [Abstracted] At a Court held for Mason County [Kentucky} 14 April 1834, Samuel Strode and Ann Strode came into court and proved they were well acquainted with David Williams late an officer in the Virginia Line in the Revolutionary War, and with Thomas Williams late of the town of Washington–that the said David Williams and Thomas Williams were brothers and they had known them from their boyhood up to the time of their deaths–That David Williams died without children many years ago – that Thomas Williams died in the town of Washington about two years ago, leaving Thomas Williams, Sally Fox late Sally Williams and Elizabeth Faw daughter of Nancy Faw late Nancy Williams as heirs at law ...

The importance of the Kendrick Cases can be seen.

VIRGINIA RESOLUTION WARRANTS

Warrants issued under Virginia General Assembly resolutions authorized grants, usually to individuals who were especially deserving. They include the original warrants; affidavits and certificates as to service, death, and heirship; and plats and records of survey. The two boxes of this series have now been transferred to manila folders. They include, for example, copies of two wills from burned Virginia counties which had been copied before the fire to settle bounty claims.[28] It will be necessary to either go to Archives I personally or have a researcher examine them, since the Archives staff cannot undertake a search. Photocopies may be purchased if the folder is specifically identified.

To request these files for personal viewing specify the folders from PI 22, entry 5, RG 49.

---

28   *Preliminary Inventory 22*, 7, entry 5.

RICHARD CLOUGH ANDERSON PAPERS

Richard Clough Anderson was a Revolutionary War officer and land surveyor. In 1784 he went to Kentucky and lived in Jefferson County for the rest of his life while serving as chief surveyor of the lands allotted to Virginia patriots. The collection of Anderson's papers was obtained by the Illinois Historical Survey at the University of Illinois at Urbana-Champaign between 1911 and 1914. It contains 28 bound volumes and approximately 10,000 items of loose papers. The collection consists largely of material relating to Virginia's bounty lands in Kentucky and Ohio.

A description of the Richard Clough Anderson Papers is given on the Urbana-Champaign website at <www.library.uiuc.edu/ihx /rcanderson.htm>.[29] Many important items are included in this collection, among them maps, plats, patents, petitions, and other assorted materials. An inventory of the contents prepared by the Historical Records Survey of the Works Progress Administration (WPA) has been transcribed and appears at the website. Researchers of veterans who served from Virginia should find it worthwhile to peruse the contents of this valuable collection.

Another collection involving Richard Clough Anderson's surveys is at the Library of Virginia in Richmond.[30] It includes correspondence to Richard C. Anderson and his son-in-law Allen Latham. These letters were largely concerned with claims for land based on Revolutionary War service, especially the disposition of those claims. Considerable genealogical information appears, for often a descendant or acquaintance wrote to Anderson or Latham inquiring about the final disposition of the claim. While doing so they also provided details on the veteran's military service.

George Rogers Clark, pictured to the left, lived in a cabin similar to the reconstructed site of his home at the falls of the Ohio, Louisville, Kentucky. In 1809 Clark's medical condition forced his move to his sister's home, where he lived for several years. Clark's last years were fraught with illness, alcoholism, and debt, but his accomplishments in helping to open the northwest were major and never forgotten.

GEORGE ROGERS CLARK BOUNTY LAND TRACT

The May 1779 act (see footnote 2 this chapter) provided, among other things, that every soldier who enlisted into the corps of Vir-  ginia's volunteers commanded by Colonel George Rogers Clark and continued until the taking of several posts in the Illinois country would, at the end of the war, be entitled to a grant of 200 acres within the commonwealth. Later it was provided that every

---

29   The Illinois Historical Survey collection is housed in University Library, University of Illinois at Urbana–Champaign, 1408 W. Gregory Dr., Urbana, IL 61801. This inventory collection was produced in August 2000 by Mary Kay Coker for an independent study in archival description as part of her master's degree in library science. Her efforts in making the inventory available were guided by Dr. John Hoffman of the Illinois Historical Survey and Dr. Donald Krummel of the Graduate School of Library and Information Science.

30   This is part of the Library of Virginia website. Go to the website at <http://lva1.hosted .exlibrisgroup.com/F/?func=file&file_name=find-b-clas39&local_base=CLAS39lva.virginia .gov/WHATWEHAVE/bio/aboutAL.htm>.

freeman who would enlist, or who having enlisted for a period of time unexpired should reenlist to serve during the war for the defense of the country of Illinois would receive at the end of the war 100 acres. For a further discussion of the George Rogers tract see 11 *Hening* 561–62. The tract that was later laid off to fulfill this promise was on the northwest side of the Ohio River in what is now Clark, Floyd, and Scott Counties, Indiana. It has been known variously as the "Illinois Grant" or "Clark's Grant." Some records of the Illinois regiment have been published.[31]

FINDING AIDS

SMITH'S FEDERAL LAND SERIES. Volume Four (in two parts) of Clifford Neal Smith's *Federal Land Series* (previously cited) includes the survey number, acreage, survey book and page number citation, watercourse, county and township, warrant number and warrantee, patentee, and unidentified names. The introduction in this volume, pages vii through xx, gives important background. Smith's series is a remarkable work that greatly facilitates locating information on Revolutionary War warrants.

OTHER COLLECTIONS: A lesser number of documents can be located at the Henry E. Huntington Library, San Merino, California, at <http://catalog.huntington.org>. Then go to "Library," then "Online Library Catalog" and use their search box to insert keywords "Richard Clough Anderson." From the displayed selections select "Papers of Richard Clough Anderson, 1781–1892." (Also use the search box to enter keywords such as Virginia, bounty land, etc. for other items of interest.)

The Filson Historical Society in Louisville, Kentucky, has a number of interesting items in their collection. Go to their catalog at <www.filsonhistorical.org and use their search feature with subjects such as "Virginia Military District," "Bounty Land," etc.

Additionally, papers of private individuals can surface in a variety of locations. Consulting *The National Union Catalog of Manuscript Collections 1959–2009* at <www.loc.gov/coll/nucmc> may produce some of them.

The Library of Virginia is at 800 East Broad Street, Richmond, VA 23219; their website can be accessed at <www.lva.virginia.gov>.

OTHER COLLECTIONS

---

31   Printed material includes, among others, *A List of officers of the Illinois Regiment, and of Crockett's Regiment, who have received land for their services: a list of officers of the Illinois Regiment, who have not received lands for revolutionary services. A list of non–commissioned officers and soldiers of the Illinois Regiment, and the Western Army, under the command of General George Rogers Clarke [sic, Clark] who are entitled to bounty in land. A list of Captain Francis Charloville's Volunteers, entitled to two hundred acres of land each.* By Virginia Commissioner of Revolutionary Claims (Richmond, Va.: Virginia General Assembly, 1833).

The next chapter features a discussion of the other states that granted their own state bounty land for Revolutionary War service.

Points to Remember in this Chapter

- ✓ A study of the Virginia military land is complicated by the fact that Virginia's State Line and her Continental Line records are not all in the same location.

- ✓ Warrants for Virginian's Continental Line and State Line were at first taken up in Kentucky's South of the Green River military tract; in 1795 that tract was opened to non-military surveys.

- ✓ When the VMD opened in 1794, warrants for Virginia's Continental Line were taken up in the Virginia Military District of Ohio.

- ✓ In the 1818–20 period the Jackson Purchase in western Kentucky was available to those holding Virginia State Line warrants.

- ✓ The passage of the 1830 scrip act made it possible to take up federal and Virginia warrants in Illinois, Indiana, and Ohio.

- ✓ After the act of 1833 those holding scrip were not limited on location and could use the scrip anywhere in the public domain where there was land available for private purchase.

- ✓ Virginia relinquished rights to any remaining lands in the VMD in 1852 though claism on these scrip warrants were filed for many years thereafter.

3 REVOLUTIONARY WAR State Bounty

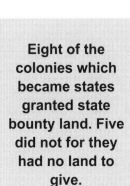

In addition to federal bounty land, states with sufficient land offered their own bounty land inducements for Revolutionary War service. Georgia, Maryland, Massachusetts, New York, North Carolina, Pennsylvania, South Carolina, and Virginia all promised land. Connecticut,[1] Delaware, New Jersey, Rhode Island, and Vermont did not. The amounts varied: the most generous to privates was North Carolina's grant of 640 acres. The least was fifty acres by Maryland to any recipient since this state had little surplus land. Massachusetts allowed 100 acres but limited its warrants to those soldiers who had not received 100 acres from the federal government. Virginia's generous policy was discussed in Chapter Two.

The archives of the states that made promises for state bounty land should be the first place to research for any original records that are extant. Additionally, there are various other sources (repositories, private collections, periodicals, books and others) with explanatory material.

One of the major sources for information on state bounty land, which includes a consolidated list of those who applied, is Bockstruck's *Revolutionary State Bounty*.[2] Accessing this book should be among the first steps for a researcher seeking information and documents awarded by states. Once the name is found in Bockstruck's index,

> **Eight of the colonies which became states granted state bounty land. Five did not for they had no land to give.**

---

1   The Connecticut State Legislature in 1792 set aside a tract on the western side of their Western Reserve in what became Ohio to compensate more than 1,800 Connecticut residents whose property had been damaged by the British during the Revolutionary War. This tract (also known as "Sufferers' Lands") was not bounty land. It was given as reimbursement to citizens for their losses, not for military service.

2   Lloyd DeWitt Bockstruck, *Revolutionary War Bounty Land Grants Awarded by State Governments* (Baltimore, Md.: Genealogical Publishing Company, 1996), hereafter Bockstruck, *Revolutionary State Bounty*. This informative resource includes names of recipients of state bounty land in states that made such grants.

note from which state the soldier served. If the soldier served from Virginia, examine Chapter 2 of this present book. If he served from another state, examine Chapter 3 and read about the laws and records of that state. That will assist in determining the next step to take to find the actual records.

For example, page 457 of Bockstruck, *Revolutionary State Bounty*, includes a listing:

Roundtree, Samuel. Va. Private. 18 Nov. 1818. 100 acres.

EXAMPLE

Since the state was Virginia, Chapter 2 of this present book was examined. Page 26 points to a link at <www.virginiamemory .co/collections/collections_a_to_z>. A search for the name Samuel Roundtree produced within seconds considerable information concerning his bounty application (see below). It is noted there that the applications for Virginia's state bounty are at the Library of Virginia's

---

URL (Click on link) http://image.lva.virginia.gov/cgi-bin/GetRev.pl?dir=0806/R0109&card=24
Document Images
Title Roundtree, Samuel.
Gen. note Rank: Soldier.
 Service: Army.
 Date: 1818.
Other Format Available on microfilm. Revolutionary War Bounty Warrants, reels 1-29.

Biog./Hist. Note The act of the General Assembly passed on June 22, 1779, which established the Virginia Land Office, also provided for the rewarding of lands promised as bounty for specified Revolutionary War military service. The purpose of the bounty land system was to encourage longer military service. In order to qualify for bounty land, a soldier had to serve at least three (3) years continuously in the State or Continental Line. Militia service did not count. Servicemen submitted various documents such as affidavits of commanding officers and fellow soldiers and discharge papers in order to substantiate their service record. When the claim was proved, the Governor's Office issued a certificate to the register of the Land Office authorizing him to issue a warrant. The first warrant was issued in 1782 and the last in 1876 as heirs of warrantees continued to seek lands for additional service. Land awarded as bounty was in the present-day states of Ohio and Kentucky.

Related Work: The papers accumulated as proof of service are now part of the records of the Executive Dept. Office of the Governor (RG#3) and are called 'Bounty Warrants' if approved and 'Rejected Claims' if disapproved. These records are housed in the Archives at the Library of Virginia.

Note Affidavit: Lewis Powers, Franklin County, Kentucky, as to service and heir.
Subject - Personal Roundtree, Samuel.
Subject - Topical Veterans -- Virginia.
Subject -Geographic Virginia -- History -- Revolution, 1775-1783 -- Sources.
Genre/Form Military records -- Virginia.
Added Entry Virginia. Governor's Office. Bounty warrants, 1779-1860.
 Library of Virginia. Archives.

---

website. From that website, links were followed to three pages of images which were listed. Each could be accessed to view and copy the actual documents.

The foregoing demonstrates how the information, starting in the example with Bockstruck's *Revolutionary State Bounty,* can be used to locate documents. Not all states have scanned their documents for online viewing, but if a state has not, ascertain where the records are located and contact that repository to obtain copies.

GEORGIA

Not everyone who received a bounty grant in this state was a Revolutionary War soldier. Fraud was a major problem, along with a system that at times was so disorganized that grants were made on both an original and duplicate warrant.

There were six "classes" entitled to bounty land, but only four were for military service.

The first of the classes was for those officers and enlisted men who served variously in the Georgia Line between January 7, 1776, and December 23, 1783. Next were the Minutemen, or officers and enlisted men of the three Minute Battalions formed June 3, 1777, and disbanded March 1, 1778. The third class was for State Militia, which had been created in February 1776. The militia was in state service rather than that of the Continental Congress. The fourth class were known as Refugees and had fled the state of Georgia when their homes were overrun by the British and who had subsequently enlisted in the service of South Carolina or North Carolina.

James Oglethorpe, governor and founder of Georgia. From William Cullen Bryant and Sydney Howard Gay, *A Popular History of the United States* (New York: Charles Scribners' Sons, 1881).

The fifth and largest class were citizens who received land for refraining from plundering. A sixth class was composed of deserters from the British. The awards of these two classes were not for military services.

GEORGIA'S PROCESS: The bounty land application process 1783–1785 started with a petition indicating the county in which the petitioner desired land and a voucher from the commanding officer under whom he had served. If accepted, a numbered certificate was issued, a survey and plat was made, and then a grant was issued.

The only step in which classification was required to be shown was in the issuance of the numbered certificate. By the time the grant was issued, this classification was not noted, and there is no way of knowing from the grant whether the recipient was a soldier, or a citizen applying under the 1781 act for not plundering.

Grants were to be made after February 22, 1786, unless applied for previously. A warrant issued before that date was allowed two years for a survey.

When the allotted time expired, the ungranted land was opened for other purposes. After sale was opened to other settlers, some of the clerks continued to write "bounty reserve" on the plats to indicate the land was located in the Bounty Reserve which further complicates efforts to determine which grants were issued to Revolutionary War soldiers.

The bounties granted by Georgia were to be tax-exempt for ten years. An act of February 25, 1784, increased the amounts of land by fifteen percent but removed the exemption.

The acreage granted under the original acts:[3]

> From 230 acres to 1,955 acres, Georgians were rewarded.

Private in Georgia Line – 230 acres
Private in Minute Battalions – 287½ acres
Private in Militia – 287½ acres
Refugee Private in Militia – 287½ acres
Seaman in Galleys – 287½ acres
Citizen – 287½ acres
Deserter from British – 287½ acres
Sergeant in Minute Battalions – 345 acres
Sergeant in Militia – 345 acres
Sergeant in Georgia line – 345 acres
Refugee Sergeant in Militia – 345 acres
Lieutenant in Militia – 460 acres
Lieutenant in Minute Battalions – 460 acres
Lieutenant in Georgia Line – 460 acres
Refugee Private in Militia (also Citizen) – 575 acres
Captain in Militia – 575 acres
Captain in Minute Battalions – 575 acres
Refugee Sergeant in Militia (also Citizen) – 632½ acres
Captain in Georgia Line – 690 acres
Refugee Lieutenant in Militia – 747½ acres
Major in Militia – 920 acres
Major in Minute Battalions – 920 acres
Major in Georgia Line – 920 acres
Refugee Captain in Militia – 977½ acres
Lt. Colonel in Georgia Line – 1035 acres
Lt. Colonel in Militia – 1035 acres
Lt. Colonel in Minute Battalions – 1035 acres
Colonel in Militia – 1150 acres
Colonel in Georgia Line – 1150 acres
Refugee Major in Militia – 1207½ acres
Brigadier General in Militia – 1955 acres

---

3   Alex M. Hite, "Georgia Bounty Land Grant," *Georgia Historical Quarterly* 38 (December 1954): 337–48. This is an excellent article explaining Georgia's bounty system.

FINDING AIDS: An online index to Revolutionary War veterans who were "fortunate drawers" in the 1820, 1827, and 1832 Land Lotteries is found on the Georgia Archives website at <http://sos.georgia. gov/archives/what_do_we_have/online_indexes/rev_war_veterans /default.htm>. The lists indexed in this database are on microfilm. Researchers should ask the archives's staff for assistance in locating the papers.

In addition to Bockstruck, *Revolutionary State Bounty* and Alex M. Hite's article, both previously cited, there are a variety of published works for this state including:

> *Revolutionary Soldiers' Receipts for Georgia Bounty Grants* (Atlanta, Ga.: Foote and Davies Company, 1928).

> Marian Hemperley, *Military Certificates of Georgia 1776–1800 on File in the Surveyor General Department* (Atlanta, Ga.: State Printing Office, 1983).

> Nicole O'Kelley and Mary Bondurant Warren, *Georgia Revolutionary Bounty Land Records 1783–1785* (Athens, Ga.: Heritage Papers, 1992).

The Georgia State Archives is located at 5800 Jonesboro Road, Morrow, GA 30260. Their website can be viewed at <www.GeorgiaArchives.org>.

Courtesy Carnegie Institution of Washington

Figure 3–1. Map of "Military Reserves 1778-1816" from Paullin and Wright's, Atlas of Historical Geography **(see footnote 20 this chapter). Not shown is Massachusett's military district in Maine, organized later. The west of the Tennessee River tract in Kentucky was not approved for Revolutionary War surveys until 1820.**

A carved
powderhorn

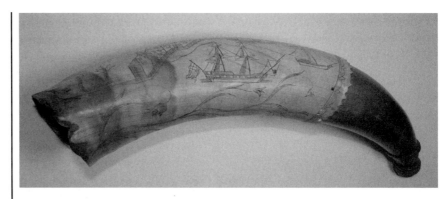

MARYLAND

By acts passed October 21, 1777, and later, a bounty of 50 acres of land was granted to each able-bodied recruit who enlisted and served for three years in the American Army, and 100 acres to each recruiting officer who enlisted twenty able-bodied men within certain specifications of the act.[4] Under an act passed in 1780 recruits who served during the war were entitled to 50 acres of land after the war, and were to be exempt from taxation for four years thereafter.[5]

In November 1781 lands in Washington County, Maryland, westward of Fort Cumberland (with some specified exceptions) were reserved for this use.[6] The General Assembly at its April session 1787 authorized the appointment of a person to lay out the reserves, in lots of 50 acres each. Francis Deakins was employed and returned a general plot of the area. Some 2,475 soldiers were entitled to bounty land. In addition, 100 lots were set apart to fulfill the promise to the recruiting officers. This total of 2,575 lots was set aside "in the most fertile part of the county" and contained in a section "beginning at the mouth of Savage river, and running with the present supposed boundary line of Maryland until the intersection of an east line to be drawn from the said boundary line, with a north course from the mouth of Savage river..." It was to be distributed by lot among the soldiers and recruiting officers, and their legal representatives.

In 1784 the Assembly appropriated further lands in Washington County, westward of Fort Cumberland.[7] In the winter of 1788 they directed that part of the remaining lots were to be distributed by lottery among the officers and their representatives of the Maryland

---

4   *Laws of Maryland, Made Since M,DCC,LXIII, consisting of Acts of Assembly under the Proprietary Government, Resolves of Convention, the Declaration of Right, the Constitution and Form of Government, the Articles of Confederation, And, Acts of Assembly since the Revolution* (Annapolis: Frederick Green, Printer to the State, 1787), 203:182, ch. VIII.

5   ibid. 203:245, ch. X. Passed between 12 June 1780 and 5 July 1780.

6   ibid. 203:296–99, ch. XX. November 1781.

7   ibid. 203:423-25, ch. LXXV. January 22, 1785.

Line who served to the end of the war, were killed, or who died of their wounds received in battle.[8]

Also included in the same act were those disabled from further service by wounds received, and in consequence retired, and heirs of those who died a natural death while in the service with the army. Each officer, or his representative, was to have four lots, the lots to be adjacent to those reserved for the soldiers.

FINDING AIDS: The website of the Maryland State Archives (shown below) contains a great deal of information to the land records of Maryland, including its patents. See also Jean H. Vivian, "Military land Bounties During the Revolutionary and Confederation Periods."[9] Other helpful information on Maryland bounty land appears at <http://www.msa.md.gov/msa/refserv/bulldog/bull89/html/bull89a.html>.

The Maryland State Archives is located at 350 Rowe Boulevard, Annapolis, MD 21401. Its website can be accessed at <www.msa.md.gov>.

MASSACHUSETTS\MAINE

By a resolution of March 5, 1801, Massachusetts allowed an award of two hundred acres of bounty land (or, in lieu of it, a sum of $20.00) to each non-commissioned officer and soldier who enlisted in the late war with Great Britain, who was returned as a part of this state's quota, who actually served the full term of three years, and who was honorably discharged. Also covered were the children and if there were none, the widow of such non commissioned officer & soldier.[10] On March 27, 1833, a similar resolution was passed, with the land to be taken up in number four of the second range, number two of the third range, in the county of Somerset, and number two of the seventh range in the county of Penobscot (now Maine).[11]

A further resolution extended the benefit of those non-commissioned officers and soldiers who had been honorably discharged before the

One of Massachusett's well-known figures of the Revolutionary War, Dr. Samuel Prescott. Though William Dawes and Paul Revere were stopped on their way to Concord on the night of April 19, 1775, Prescott made it through and alerted the countryside of the coming of the British. (From Minute Man National Historical Park, Massachusetts.)

---

8   *Laws of Maryland Made and Passed at a Session of Assembly, Begun and held at the city of Annapolis, on Monday the seventh of November, in the year of our Lord one thousand seven hundred and eighty-eight* (Annapolis: Frederick Green, Printer to the State, no. pub.), 294: 350–54, ch. XLIV.

9   Vivian, Jean H. "Military Land Bounties During the Revolutionary and Confederation Periods," *Maryland Historical Magazine* 61 (1966): 231–56.

10   *Acts and Resolves of Massachusetts 1800-1801* (1800; reprint, Wright & Potter Printing Company, State Printers, 1897), 217–19, January Session, ch. 139, March 5, 1801. Online at Google books <http://tinyurl.com/2dxr9ve>.

11   *Resolves of the General Court of the Commonwealth of Massachusetts Passed at the Several Sessions, Commencing, January, 1832, and Ending, April, 1834* (Boston: Dutton and Wentworth, Printers to the State, 1834), 448–49, March 27, 1833.

expiration of a term of three years because of disability.[12] An act in 1838 specified that the act of 1835 should be construed to extend the benefits to each non-commissioned officer and soldier and to the widow of those who "served in the army of the Revolution during the war in the line or lines of any other State as in the Massachusetts Line" provided they had not already received a grant of land or money in lieu thereof from any other state.[13]

On February 8, 1836, a resolution made an addition to the previous act of March 17, 1835.[14] It provided that whenever any officer or soldier (or his widow) entitled to the provisions of the previous resolve died or should die, the heirs of such officer, soldier, or widow would be entitled to the same lands in the same manner and proportions. A certificate was to be supplied from the judge of probate of the county where the deceased last dwelt, certifying the number and names of such heirs and in what degrees.

In March 1836 the two upper Indian townships in the county of Penobscot in Maine were appropriated (with some restrictions) to satisfy the claims for service.[15]

An award to commissioned officers of the Revolutionary War army who were inhabitants of Massachusetts proper or of the District of Maine, and "now" an inhabitant of the state, who had not already received a grant of land, or money in lieu thereof from the Commonwealth of Massachusetts, and each widow of such officer who at the time of his decease was an inhabitant of the State, was to receive 600 acres from a designated area in the county of Washington.[16] Each officer who was honorably discharged before the expiration of three years in conseqence of wounds received in service, or other bodily infirmity, and each widow of such officer, and the widow of each officer who died in the service within three years from the time of his entering, were also to receive a like grant of land.

---

12   *Resolves of the Fifteenth Legislature, of the State of Maine* (Augusta: William J. Condon, Printer to the State, 1835), 727–29, January 1835 Session, ch. 39, March 17, 1835.

13   *Resolves of the Eighteenth Legislature of the State of Maine, Passed at the Session which commenced on the third day of January, and ended on the twenty-third day of March, one thousand eight hundred and thirty-eight* (Augusta: Luther Severance, Printer, 1838), 341–42. January Session, ch. 86, March 23, 1838.

14   *Resolves of the Sixteenth Legislature of the State of Maine Passed at the Session Which commenced on the sixth day of January, and ended on the fifth day of April, one thousand eight hundred and thirty-six* (Augusta: Smith & Robinson, Printers to the State, 1836), 22, January Session, ch. 4, February 8, 1836.

15   ibid.: 44, ch. 49, March 16, 1836.

16   *Resolves of the Eighteenth Legislature of the State of Maine, Passed at the Session which commenced on the third day of January, and ended on the twenty-third day of March, one thousand eight hundred and thirty-eight* (Augusta: Luther Severance, Printer, 1838), 306–07, January Session, ch. 61, March 20, 1838.

Finding Aids: Piction Press has available on three series of CDs the Revolutionary War land bounty applications which originated in Massachusetts before Maine became a state in 1820, those applications which originated in Maine after 1820, and those in the records of the Hancock County, Maine Court of Common Pleas. This collection represents over twenty CDs.[17]

The Maine State Archives has an introduction to Maine's land grants and pension applications available at <www.maine.gov/sos/arc /archives/military/revintro.htm>. An alphabetical index by surname is provided, and a few of the files have been scanned and are available at the website. They plan to add more. In the meantime, copies of files not on the website are available for a nominal cost by ordering through the Maine State Archives, 84 State House Station, Augusta, ME 04333-0084.

The address of the Massachusetts State Archives is 220 Morrissey Blvd., Boston, MA 02125. Its website can be accessed at <www.sec .state.ma.us/arc/arcgen/genidx.htm>.

NEW YORK

Those eligible for New York's bounty land took it up in the Military Tract in the Finger Lakes region of central New York.[18] This included present-day counties of Cayuga, Cortland, Onondaga, and Seneca as well as parts of Oswego, Schuyler, Tompkins, and Wayne. The first act granting bounty lands in New York was passed on March 20, 1781.[19] Later additional land was purchased from the Onondaga and Cayuga Indian nations.

**Cayuga
Cortland
Onondaga
Senaca
and parts of
Oswego
Schuyler
Tompkins
Wayne**

According to *Atlas of Historical Geography* the military reserve's limits were as follows:

> ... all the Lands situate ... in the County of Tyron, bounded on the North by Lake Ontario, the Onondago [Oswego] River, and the Oneida Lake; on the West by a Line drawn from the Mouth of the Great Sodus or Asorodus Creek thro' the most westerly Inclination of the Seneca Lake; on the South by an East and West Line drawn thro' the most southerly Inclination of the Seneca Lake; and on the East by a Line drawn from the most westerly Boundary of the Oneida or Tuscarora Country on the Oneida Lake thro' the most westerly

---

17 For a full listing of the Picton Press listings go to <www.pictonpress.com/downloads /RevWar-listing.pdf>. These CDs are also available at various libraries.
18 *The Balloting Book, and Other Documents Relating to Military Bounty Land in the State of New York (*1825: reprint, Ovid: W. E. Morrison & Co., 1983), hereafter *The Balloting Book*.
19 "An Act for Raising Two Regiments for the defence of this state on bounties of unappropriated lands," *Laws of New York State*, 4th Session, Chap. 32, 1:351, March 20, 1781.

Inclination of the West Bounds of the Oneida or Tuscarora Country" (New York Session Laws, Ch. 11, July 25, 1782).[20]

It continues:

"This tract was reserved for the major-generals and brigadier-generals who at the time of their entering the military service resided in New York, for the troops of New York serving in the army of the United States and their legal representatives, and for such other persons as New York in the future should provide for an account of military service in the army of the United States."

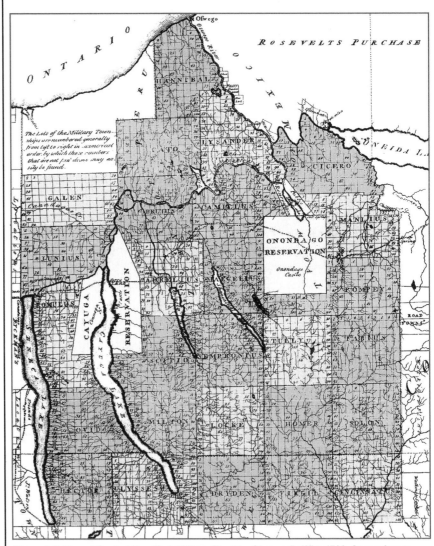

Figure 3-2. Map of Central New York Military Tract by Simeon DeWitt, 1793; from a larger map. DeWitt was Geographer and Surveyor General of the Continental Army during the American Revolution and later Surveyor General of the State of New York.

20   Charles Oscar Paullin and John Kirtland Wright, *Atlas of the Historical Geography of the United States* ([New York and D.C].: American Geographical Society of New York, 1932) Carnegie Institution of Washington Publication 401, 32, hereafter *Atlas of Historical Geography.*

The amounts promised by New York were:[21]

> Privates – 500 acres
> Non-commissioner officer – 500 acres
> Chaplain – 2000 acres
> Captain – 1500 acres
> Regimental surgeon – 1500 acres
> Subaltern – 1000 acres
> Surgeon's mate – 1000 acres
> Major – 2000 acres
> Colonel – 2250 acres
> Lieutenant colonel – 2250 acres
> Brigadier general – 4250 acres
> Major general – 5500 acres

FINDING AIDS: The New York State Archives' website provides information at: <www.archives.nysed.gov.> Access the online catalog, and then enter "bounty land" in the search box. According to this source, after the Revolutionary War ended, the legislature in 1784 passed a law providing for the administration of bounty land. As a result the "Old Military Tract" was laid out in northern New York but the land was not satisfactory. In 1789 another tract in central New York, referred to as the "New Military Tract," was designated and, the year following, the procedure was established for allocating that land. It is not known if anyone applied previously for land in the original tract. Many of the veterans sold their rights rather than take up the central New York land.

In the Secretary of State papers, New York Archives, are a number of other items involving bounty land, including the following:

> A0272. Applications for Land Grants ("Land Papers, 1st Series"), 1642-1803. 22 cubic feet (63 volumes). Volumes 37–63 cover grants of bounty land for Revolutionary War veterans. Documents included are claims giving the rank and unit of the officer or soldier, return of survey describing the land, certificate of location, assignments, and assorted powers of attorney, receipts, letters and affidavits. (Edmund Bailey O'Callaghan, comp. *Calendar of New York Colonial Manuscripts Indorsed Land Papers* (1864: revised reprint Harrison, New York: Harbor Hill Books, 1987) contains a name index to the foregoing. For the years 1785–1790 the following volumes contain name indexes to Revolutionary War veterans' claims: 37, 41, 43, 45, 46, 48. The above volumes are available on microfilm from the New York State Library.)

> A0447. Military Patents, 1764–1797. 4 cubic feet (8 volumes).

> A3123. Index and abstracts of patents for lands in the Military Tract, ca 1820. .3 cubic foot (1 volume).

> A3124. Abstract of Patents for Lands in the Military Tract, Including a Copy of the Balloting Book, 1790–1869. .3cubic foot (1 volume).

---

21 "Extract from the Journal of the Assembly of the State of New-York" in *The Balloting Book*, 6.

A0476. Register of Military Bounty Land Grants (The Balloting Book, and Other Documents Relating to Military Lands, in the State of New York, 1825), .2 cubic foot (1 volume).

A3307. Manuscript of Register of Military Bounty Land Grants (The Balloting Book, and Other Documents Relating to Military Bounty Lands in the State of New York, 1825), .5 cubic feet.

A3121. Geographical Index to Patents, ca 1786–1899. .6 cubic foot (1 volume).

A0451. Original Releases to the State, 1782–1929. 9 cubic feet (913 volumes) Arrangement: Chronological by recording date. Some volumes have name indexes. The first three volumes are pertinent to the Old and New Military Tracts.

Researchers should examine the cited New York Archives website for further details and other entries.

The New York State Archives is located at New York State Education Department, Cultural Education Center, Albany, NY 12230. Its website can be accessed at <www.archives.nysed.gov>.

NORTH CAROLINA/TENNESSEE

The land on which the bounty was settled for North Carolina veterans of the Revolution is not in present-day North Carolina, but in what became the State of Tennessee. The land was to be given to those who enlisted for the duration of the war; those with short enlistments did not receive the benefits of the bounty act.

The first of the bounty acts on April 16, 1780, provided for 200 acres for each soldier.[22] This was soon increased to 640 acres.[23] In addition, each was to receive a cash bounty, and a prime slave or cash in lieu thereof. In the spring of 1782 a graduated scale was enacted:[24]

Francis Marion, "The Swamp Fox." He was known for his surprise attacks on the British and his quick withdrawals, thus the name he was dubbed. Particularly prominent in North and South Carolina. A number of soldiers served under him and later applied for bounty land. For example, James Butler made an affidavit for pension 7 August 1833 from Rhea County, Tennessee, attesting to his service from North Carolina under General Marion (NARA M804, roll 436, file W338). Using the pension file as a start, Butler's descendants can conduct a search for any bounty land which may have been due to him.

Private – 640 acres
Non-commissioned Officer – 1,000 acres
Subaltern – 2,560 acres
Captain – 3,840 acres
Major – 4,800 acres
Lieutenant Colonel – 5,760 acres
Lieutenant Colonel Commandant – 7,200 acres
Colonel – 7,200 acres
Brigadier – 12,000 acres
Chaplain 7,200 acres
Surgeon – 4,800 acres
Surgeon's Mate – 2,560 acres

22 Walter Clark, editor, *The State Records of North Carolina* (Goldsboro, N.C.: Nash Brothers, 1906), vol. XXIV Laws 1777–1788, 337–39, ch. XXV.
23 *Acts of the North Carolina General Assembly, 1782*, 24:369.
24 ibid., 419–22, ch. III, April 13, 1782.

Though at first the bounty land warrant could not be assigned while the person was in service, the act of 1782 provided preemption rights.

An article by Paul V. Lutz is an interesting account of the various provisions North Carolina made for its troops and is the basis of many of the remarks in this present book.[25]

FINDING AIDS: The North Carolina State Archives has created a card index to land grants in what is now the state of Tennessee. Those that have been stamped "Military Warrants" are usually for grants that resulted from Revolutionary War bounty land acts. However, there are a few with such markings that were not the result of Revolutionary War service, but of service in other disturbances. There are also some not designated as bounty land that should have been so marked. A listing of grants have been microfilmed on National Archives microfilm publication M68, *List of North Carolina Land Grants in Tennessee, 1778–1791.*[26]

The grants themselves are microfilmed on *North Carolina Secretary of State Land Grant Office, Warrants, Surveys, and Related Documents (in the Tennessee territory), 1735–1757.*[27] This microfilm is available at the North Carolina State Archives, and at the Tennessee State Archives. From the latter's website at <www.tn.gov/tsla/history/manuscripts/mguide12.htm>:

Militia drum, Guilford Courthouse National Military Park, North Carolina. Drums were used as a means of communication; those seeking their ancestors who were drummers will find that many musicians were very young when they enlisted.

> This is a valuable collection of early land records for that part of western North Carolina which became Tennessee. These records of the North Carolina Land Office consist of the warrants, affidavits, plats and assignments of military land allocated to veterans of the North Carolina Continental Line for service in the Revolutionary War. The records are arranged by county or district where the grants were located and include the original military warrants on which the grants were based, plats showing the metes and bounds of each tract, and lists of the assignees to whom the warrants were sold by their original soldier-owners. These records represent the early stages of the process by which North Carolina soldiers, their heirs and assignees received land grants for military service in the Revolution. There is a name index to warrant holders.

More insight into bounty land grants by North Carolina are mentioned in Lloyd deWitt Bockstruck's "Revolutionary War Bounty

---

25 Paul V. Lutz, "A State's Concern for the Soldiers' Welfare: How North Carolina Provided for her Troops During the Revolution," *North Carolina Historical Review* 42 (July 1965): 315–18.

26 National Archives microfilm publication M68, Records of the Bureau of Land Management, *List of North Carolina Land Grants in Tennessee, 1778–1791.* DP. RG 49, 1 roll.

27 *North Carolina Secretary of State Land Grant Office, Warrants, Surveys, and Related Documents (in the Tennessee territory), 1735–1957.* North Carolina Department of Archives & History. 48 reels. TSLA Mf. 1177.

Land ..." Bockstruck includes a listing of men who opted to receive a grant of 300 acres of vacant land within Virginia or £120.[28]

The North Carolina State Archives is located at 109 E. Jones St., Raleigh, NC 27601. Its website can be accessed at: <www.archives .ncdcr.gov>.

The Tennessee State Library & Archives is located at 403 Seventh Avenue North, Nashville, TN 37243-0312. Its website: <www.tennessee.gov/tsla>.

PENNSYLVANIA

By a resolve of March 7, 1780, and a subsequent act of March 12, 1783, land was appropriated for the use of the officers and privates of the Pennsylvania Line who served to the end of the war. These became known as Donation lands. The amount alloted to each was based on rank. The Donation tract was located "beginning at the mouth of Mogulbughtiton creek; thence up the Allegheny river to the mouth of Cagnawagna creek; thence due north to the northern boundary of this state; thence west by the said boundary to the northwest corner of the state; thence south by the western boundary of the state to the northwest corner of lands appropriated by this act for discharging the certificates herein mentioned; and thence by the same lands east, to the place of beginning ..."[29]

Located just north of the Depreciation tract, the tract included parts of Armstrong, Butler, Lawrence, Forest, Venango, and Warren Counties. Depreciation land was set out at the same time as the Donation tract, but Depreciation was not bounty land.[30]

The 1783 act further designated that any prior rights, titles or claims to the described land, either obtained from Indians, late Proprietors, or any other person were null and void. The present applications were to be made within two years after peace was declared, and if any of the officers, non-commissioned officers or privates died before their respective applications then their heirs, executors or

Modern-day view of the site of the Battle of Brandywine, Chadd's Ford, Pennsylvania, where the ancestors of many researchers served.

---

28 Lloyd deWitt Bockstruck, "Revolutionary War Bounty Lands Awarded for Clearing the Road over the Cumberland Mountain into Kentucky County, Virginia in 1779," *Magazine of Virginia Genealogy* 45 (May 2007): 129–30. See also 10 *Hening* 143–44, act passed October 1779.

29 "An Act for the Sale of Certain Lands Therein Mentioned for the Purpose of Redeeming and Paying off the Certificates of Depreciation Given to the Officers and Soldiers of the Pennsylvania Line, or their Representatives, and for Appropriating certain other Lands therein Mentioned for the Use of the said Officers and Soldiers to be Divided off to them Severally at the End of the War," *The Statutes at Large of Pennsylvania from 1682–1801* (no pl.: State Printer of Pennsylvania, 1904), 11: 32–6, ch. MVII, March 12, 1783.

30 For a full treatment of Depreciation certificates and Donation lands, see Donna Bingham Munger, *Pennsylvania Land Records: A History and Guide for Research* (Wilmington, Del.: Scholarly Resources, Inc., 2000), 163–65.

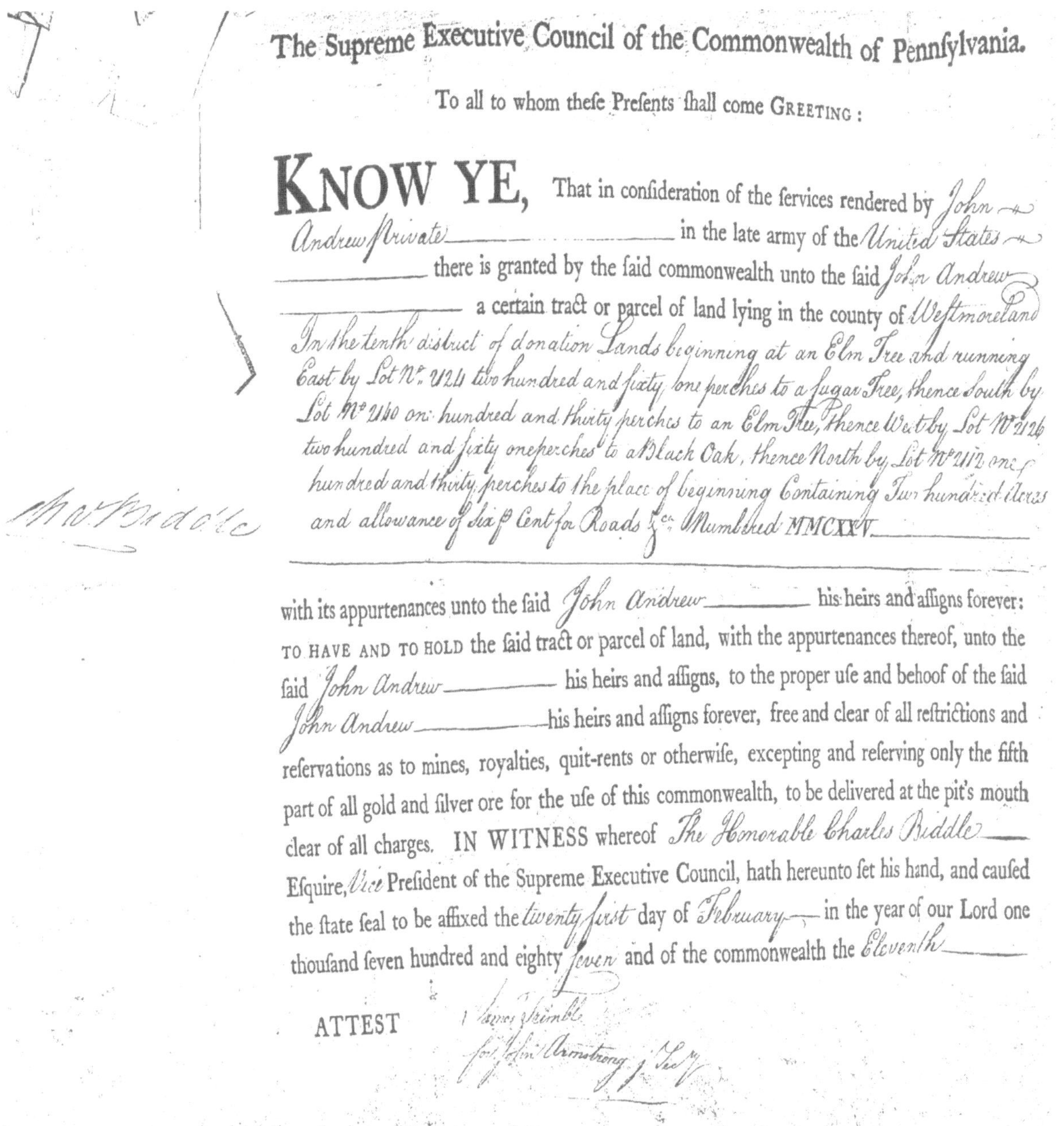

The Supreme Executive Council of the Commonwealth of Pennſylvania.

To all to whom theſe Preſents ſhall come GREETING :

KNOW YE,

That in conſideration of the ſervices rendered by *John Andrew Private* in the late army of the *United States* there is granted by the ſaid commonwealth unto the ſaid *John Andrew* a certain tract or parcel of land lying in the county of *Weſtmoreland In the tenth diſtrict of donation Lands beginning at an Elm Tree and running East by Lot No. 2124 two hundred and ſixty one perches to a Sugar Tree, thence South by Lot No. 2140 one hundred and thirty perches to an Elm Tree, thence West by Lot No. 2126 two hundred and ſixty one perches to a Black Oak, thence North by Lot No. 2112 one hundred and thirty perches to the place of beginning Containing Two hundred Acres and allowance of Six P Cent for Roads &c. Numbered MMCXXV*

with its appurtenances unto the ſaid *John Andrew* his heirs and aſſigns forever: TO HAVE AND TO HOLD the ſaid tract or parcel of land, with the appurtenances thereof, unto the ſaid *John Andrew* his heirs and aſſigns, to the proper uſe and behoof of the ſaid *John Andrew* his heirs and aſſigns forever, free and clear of all reſtrictions and reſervations as to mines, royalties, quit-rents or otherwiſe, excepting and reſerving only the fifth part of all gold and ſilver ore for the uſe of this commonwealth, to be delivered at the pit's mouth clear of all charges. IN WITNESS whereof *The Honorable Charles Biddle* Eſquire, *Vice* Preſident of the Supreme Executive Council, hath hereunto ſet his hand, and cauſed the ſtate ſeal to be affixed the *twenty firſt* day of *February* in the year of our Lord one thouſand ſeven hundred and eighty *ſeven* and of the commonwealth the *Eleventh*

ATTEST

Figure 3–3. From the Pennsylvania States Archives website, RG–17, Records of the Land Office, Donation Land Patents, [ca1785–1810], {series #17.169}, A, page 9 of images. These patents are primarily for Donation Land District 10, as well as a few other miscellaneous districts, that were surrendered to the Commonwealth in return for patents to land in other districts. Information given is the date of the patent, name of patentee, tract number, county, acreage, and a description of the tract boundaries.

administrators were permitted to make application within one year after the expiration of the allotted time. The intended recipients could not grant, bargain or sell their shares until the land was actually surveyed and laid off.

Further acts extended the time period for application, exempted the soldier from taxes, and granted sundry other benefits. A full treatment of the benefits and circumstances are set forth in William Henry Egle's *Virginia Claims ... with an Account of the Donation Lands of Pennsylvania.*[31]

Distribution of the Donation tract was by lottery, the first held October 1, 1786. A one-year limit was originally provided, but extensions kept the program open until April 1, 1810.

The Donation lands were to be surveyed into lots, and from that the following would be drawn:[32]

> General – four 500-acre lots
> Brigadier General – three 500-acre lots
> Colonel – two 500-acre lots
> Lt. Colonel – one 500-acre lot and one 250-acre lot
> Surgeon, Captain or Major – two 300-acre lots
> Captain – one 500-acre lot
> Lieutenant – two 200-acre lots
> Ensign or Regimental Surgeon's Mate – one 300-acre lot
> Sergeant, Sergeant Major, Quarter Master Sergeant – one 250-acre lot
> Drum Major, Fife Major, Drummer, Fifer, Corporal or private – one 200-acre lot

DONATION TRACT LANDS AWARDED TO PENNSYLVANIA OFFICERS AND SOLDIERS

Not all lots were claimed; the owners of those that were claimed received a patent from the state for their Donation land after the lots were drawn.

OTHER PENNSYLVANIA RECORDS: See the *Pennsylvania Archives*[33] for an interesting and complete account of the Donation lands of Pennsylvania. See also the *Pennsylvania Archives* for a listing of Donation or military tracts granted to soldiers of the Pennsylvania line.[34]

---

31 William Henry Egle, *Virginia Claims to Lands in Western Pennsylvania with an Account of the Donation Lands of Pennsylvania* (Baltimore: Clearfield Co., 2001), 576 et seq.

32 *Laws of the Commonwealth of Pennsylvania from the Fourteenth day of October, One thousand seven hundred, to the twentieth day of March, one thousand eight hundred and ten, Republished Under the Authority of the Legislature with Notes and References*, 4 volumes (Philadelphia: John Bioren, 1810), II: 290–94.

33 "An Account of the Donation Lands of Pennsylvania," *Pennsylvania Archives*, series 3 (Harrisburg, Pa.: Clarence M. Busch, State Printer, 1894), 3: 507–603.

34 "Donation or Military Tracts of Land Granted the Soldiers of the Pennsylvania Line," *Pennsylvania Archives*, series 3 (Harrisburg, Pa.: Clarence M. Busch, State Printer, 1896), 7: 657–795.

The website of the Pennsylvania Historical and Museum Commission at <www.phmc.state.pa.us> has links to several scanned Donation Land series including:

Revolutionary War flag, from John Bach McMaster, *A School History of the United States* (New York: American Book Company, 1897).

1. Indexes are located at the website: <www.phmc.state.pa.us/bah/dam/rg/di/r17DonationLandSeries/r17-174DonationLandRegister/r17-174MainInterface.htm>. The DONATION LAND REGISTER: ALPHABETICAL SURNAME INDEX, [ca.1794]. {series #17.174} provides the name of the claimant, the district and lot number, and the page number in the Numerical Listing (see: <www.phmc.state.pa.us/bah/dam/rg/di/r17DonationLandSeries/r17-174DonationLandRegister/r17-174AlphaIndexInterface.htm). The Numerical Listing provides the survey book, patent book and page numbers to locate the original records (see: <www.phmc.state.pa.us/bah/dam/rg/di/r17DonationLandSeries/r17-174DonationLandRegister/r17-174NumericTractInterface.htm). Using this index, the surveys of the individual tracts may be seen on the website at: <www.phmc.state.pa.us/bah/dam/rg/di/r17-114CopiedSurveyBooks/r17-114MainInterfacePage.htm>.
2. Donation Claimant Papers are at (www.phmc.state.pa.us/bah/dam/rg/sd/r17sdb.htm#17.168). While many of them are routine powers of attorney and legal documents, some contain information similar to pension applications. The Claimant Papers have been scanned and are available on the website.
3. Maps of the Donation districts are in the Land Office Map Collection (www.phmc.state.pa.us/bah/dam/rg/sd/r17sda.htm#17.522). Available are both original drafts and copies of the surveys of the district boundaries and the lots within each district. If the district and a lot number are known, the maps can provide a good idea of the location.

An example of the use of the above scans can be demonstrated by following an entry. In Bockstruck, *Revolutionary State Bounty,* the following was noted:

> **Rowland, John. Pa. [rank not shown]. 28 Feb. 1794. 200 acres to Walter Stewart, assignee.**

The scanned claimant papers cited in item 1 were accessed, and by use of the index, copies of the claim documents were found. These revealed that John Rowland assigned his interest to Frederick Beates, and that later the right was vested in Walter Stewart. The images could be printed from the website.

Finding Aids: The series of the published *Pennsylvania Archives* are available for viewing at <www.footnote.com>. This valuable resource includes many related Pennsylvania state land items, and military lists.

The Pennsylvania State Archives is located at the corner of Third and Forster Streets, Harrisburg, PA 17120-0090. It's website is: <www.phmc.state.pa.us>.

SOUTH CAROLINA

By an act passed in 1778 two hundred acres of land (including the one hundred acres allowed by Congress) was reserved for and granted in fee simple "to every South Carolina soldier who hath already enlisted or shall hereafter enlist to serve in either of the said regiments during the present war; provided he doth faithfully complete his term of service."[35] The act further provided that if the soldier "shall be slain in or depart this life during" the war, the heirs would be entitled to the land. All the lands in the forks between Tugaloo and Keowee rivers, up to the "new Cherokee boundary line" were reserved for this purpose.

An ordinance passed in the General Assembly in 1784 directed the commissioners to receive the entry of the respective officers and soldiers of the late South Carolina Continental Line, the officers on the staff, the three independent companies commanded by Captain Bowie and Captain Moore, and the officers of the navy of the states, and to issue warrants of survey.[36]

FINDING AIDS: Grants issued appear in four volumes now in the custody of the State Archives in Columbia, South Carolina. The four volumes have been retitled:

> Original Bounty Grant Vol. 1 is now Bounty Grants, Vol., 1, Control #84.
> Original Bounty Grant Vol. 2 is now Grants O., Bounty Book 2, Control #193.
> Original Bounty Grant Vol. 3 is duplicated in State Grants, Vol. 33, Control #226.
> Original Bounty Grant Vol. 4 is now Bounty Grants 1 duplicated in Grant Book Vol. 2, Control #195.

According to the South Carolina Department of Archives and History, the claims for Revolutionary War bounty land of that state do not exist. Fortunately the actual grants do exist and were originally located in four bound volumes. The Archives staff adds that these have not been scanned nor have they been filmed as a series per se. However, they were indexed and this index was printed in the *South Carolina Historical and Genealogical Magazine.*[37] This includes the names of recipients of grants recorded in the first three volumes mentioned above and an index to Bounty Grants recorded in the fourth volume.

Monument at King's Mountain National Park, South Carolina (on the North Carolina border). The act of 1855 (see Chapter Five) finally granted bounty land awards to these King's Mountain veterans. Those descended from ancestors who served from Tennessee and the Carolinas may especially find records for King's Mountain service.

---

35 Thomas Cooper, *Statutes at Large of South Carolina, Volume IV Containing the Acts from 1752, Exclusive, to 1786, inclusive* (Columbia, S.C.: A. S. Johnston, 1838) 410–13.
36 ibid., 27.
37 *South Carolina Historical and Genealogical Magazine* (1906), 7:173–78, 217–24.

The South Carolina Department of Archives and History is located at 8301 Parklane Road, Columbia, SC 29223. Its website can be visited at <http://archives.sc.gov>.

POINTS TO REMEMBER IN THIS CHAPTER

- ✓ Several states granted their own state bounty land for Revolutionary War service.
- ✓ The amount awarded to each officer or soldier differed in each state depending upon the availability of land the state owned.
- ✓ Some states did not have enough land to make awards.
- ✓ Only one state (Massachusetts) did not allow veterans to claim both the state award and the federal award.
- ✓ Always check the state archives for information on that state's bounty land.

4 WAR OF 1812 BOUNTY LAND

Even before the War of 1812 was officially declared, Congress had turned its attention to the question of bounty land to encourage upcoming enlistments. Unfortunate experiences with Revolutionary War warrants strengthened the legislators' resolve not to permit the assignment of warrants. Nor did they allow commissioned officers eligibilty for land bounty benefits. (In spite of a number of efforts by officers and congressmen to effect a change in the restriction against an award to officers it was not until 1850 that commissioned officers became eligible.)[1]

THE ACTS

The initial bounty award for this war was enacted in 1811.[2] Any non-commissioned officer or soldier who enlisted for five years was to receive a bounty of sixteen dollars plus 160 acres. If he was killed in action or died in service, his heirs could apply. Those eligible had to apply within five years of the war.

The 1812 act to fill specific numbers of regiments soon followed.[3] The provisions were much the same as in the 1811 act except that this one specified that the recruiting officer would receive $2.00 for each man he enlisted between the ages of eighteen and forty-five. It is further stipulated that the pay and bounty "shall be allowed and paid to each ... recruited as aforesaid ..." thus applying that age limit to the bounty award.[4] That law obviously caused problems, for in 1816 the age restriction for bounty eligibility was altered to allow men under eighteen and over forty-five to receive the awards.[5]

Once men outside the specified age-range enlisted and served Congress realized it was not equitable to deny them the tangible award of land for that service. Lifting the age restriction corrected the inquity, but not until after some hardships had been endured. (See Chapter 8.)

1   9 *U.S. Stat.* 520, September 28, 1850.
2   2 *U.S. Stat. 669*, December 24, 1811.
3   2 *U.S. Stat. 671*, January 11, 1812.
4   ibid.
5   3 *U.S. Stat. 285–87*, April 16, 1816.

Eligibility for bounty land was soon extended to the heirs of any non-commissioned officer or soldier in the volunteers who was killed in action.[6]

DOUBLE BOUNTIES: In order to further fill the ranks of the army, in 1814 each non-commissioned officer and soldier thereafter enlisted was entitled to 320 acres. These became known as "double bounty" warrants.[7]

LOCATING THE WARRANT

WAR OF 1812 MILITARY TRACTS

Three military districts were designated as locations for use of the warrants: two million acres to be surveyed in the territory of Michigan (specific location not specified), two million in the Illinois territory north of the Illinois river, and two million in the territory of Louisiana (present-day Arkansas) between the river St. Francis and the river Arkansas. The veterans were allowed to choose which territory they preferred: the usual preference was Illinois followed by Arkansas and then by Missouri which Congress had later substituted for Michigan. The applicants could not pick the actual tract; the choice was determined by lot.

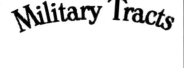

ACT OF 1842 LIFTS RESTRICTION OF LOCATIONS

Until 1842 the warrants for War of 1812 service could not be used for land outside the above designated districts. The 1842 act removed the restriction.[8] That act also provided that warrants were to be located within five years but subsequent acts granted extensions.[9]

ACT OF 1852 REMOVES RESTRICTION ON ASSIGNMENT

Until 1852 the warrants were not legally assignable though they could be inherited.[10] By fraudulent and clever maneuvers, however, many warrants ended up not in the hands of those for whom they were intended but in the control of speculators who proceeded to patent the land. Unsuspecting veterans were induced to sign blank powers of attorney or other legal documents that were subsequently used by agents and others for their own benefit. This resulted in large amounts of acreage held by speculators.

---

6   2 *U.S. Stat.* 676, February 6, 1812 repealed by 2 *U.S. Stat* 794-96, January 29, 1813, except the latter retained the benefit for those volunteers who were already in service.

7   3 *U.S. Stat.* 147, December 10, 1814.

8   5 *U.S. Stat.* 497, July 27, 1842.

9   9 *U.S. Stat.* 240, June 26, 1848 and 10 *U.S. Stat.* 267, February 8, 1854, extended the 1842 act above and the two 1835 acts, 4 *U.S. Stat.* 749, January 17, 1835 and 4 *U.S. Stat.* 70–71, March 3, 1835 (see Chapter One).

10   10 *U.S. Stat.* 3, March 22, 1852.

OPENING OF THE TRACTS

When the military tracts were ready to open around 1817 there were few settlers in the three designated areas. Some squatters had located, but long stretches of unoccupied land between neighbors was a formidable environment. For those coming from the settled states in the East it was such a daunting prospect that many veterans just sat on their rights and held their warrants, especially since they had no control over which specific lot would be drawn.

As each of the three territories where military tracts were located became states they were subject to provisions of the Enabling Acts for statehood. They agreed not to tax the military bounty lands for three years if the land remained in the name of the original patentee. The states also were not to tax other public lands for five years. This limitation on the states' sources for income lessened their ability to furnish improvements that might encourage settlement. However, interest in the military land finally began to grow, albeit slowly.

MICHIGAN TRACT. One of the three areas originally designated for the redemption of warrants was Michigan.[11] This changed when Edward Tiffin of the Surveyor General's Office, charged with surveying the Michigan land, rendered an unfavorable report dated at Chillicothe, Ohio, November 30, 1815. He stated that "it is with the utmost difficulty that a place can be found over which horses can be conveyed ... Taking the country altogether so far as it has been explored, and to all appearances, together with the information received in regard to the balance, it is so bad there would not be more than one acre out of one hundred, if there would be more than one out of one thousand, that would in any case admit of cultivation."[12] The fact that all the military lands were required by law to be fit for cultivation signaled the demise of the Michigan tract and spurred the passage in 1816 of legislation that authorized regions of Missouri and Illinois to be substituted.[13] Prominent Michigan leaders were incensed with the reasons advanced for the change. Led by Lewis Cass, an influential politician, they charged that the surveyors came to Michigan during one of its wettest seasons ever, were there for a short time only, and grossly misrepresented it. It took years for Michigan to overcome the negative impact on settlement.[14]

" ... it is so bad there would not be more than one acre out of one hundred, if there would be more than one out of one thoughsand, that would in any case admit of cultivation."

---

11   2 *U.S. Stat.* 728, May 6, 1812.
12   *Pioneer Collections: Collections and Researches made by the Pioneer Society of the State of Michigan,* 2nd edition (Lansing: Wynkoop Hallenbeck Crawford Company, State Printer, 1908), X:61–62.
13   3 *U.S. Stat.* 332, April 29, 1816.
14   Gates, *Public Land Law,* 249–70 includes an excellent treatment of the prevailing conditions in the military tracts.

In the place of the military district in Michigan, Congress substituted 500,000 acres in the Missouri Territory and 1,500,000 acres to be added to the previously designated area of Illinois.

ILLINOIS TRACT. The Military Bounty Tract in Illinois was surveyed in 1815–1816. The area included what are now the counties of Adams, Brown, Calhoun, Fulton, Hancock, Henderson, Knox, McDonough, Mercer, Peoria, Pike, Schuyler, Stark, and Warren. It also included parts of Henry and Bureau Counties, and the parts of Marshall and Putnam which are on the west side of the Illinois River. Of the three military tracts for War of 1812 veterans, this area garnered the most attention and the most settlers. In 1830, after Congress had allowed Arkansas veterans to exchange their certificates on unfit land for better lands, the like privilege for exchange was granted to Illinois and Missouri.[15]

FINDING AIDS: A valuable source for information on claims in the military tract of Illinois is Volkel, *Bounty Lands in Illinois.*[16] Pertinent details are given on each claimant, which should help the researcher to locate the bounty land application file and the surrendered warrant file (see Chapter Five).

Another source for Illinois records is the Illinois State Archives in Springfield, Illinois. In particular, examine in their collection the U.S. General Land Office Records for Illinois, Record Series 952.000 at <www.sos.state.il.us/departments/archives/di/952_002.htm#A1>. This details a large number of listings for Illinois' federal land records including a few that deal specifically with papers relating to military land claims. Some are not indexed but could reveal interesting items. See for instance the following; others can be located by visiting the website.

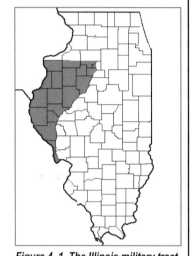

Figure 4–1. The Illinois military tract.

952.344: RECEIVER'S REGISTER OF MILITARY LAND SCRIP OR U.S. TREASURER'S RECEIPTS RECEIVED. January 1, 1840– December 31, 1844. 1 partial vol. No index.

This is a chronological list of military bounty land scrip or U.S. Treasurer's receipts surrendered in partial or total payment for land purchased. Entries for each include name of purchaser, number of certificate or receipt, cash value of scrip or receipt, legal description of tract purchased, and Receiver's receipt number. May 31, 1849. 1 partial vol. No index.

15   4 *U.S. Stat. 383*, March 23, 1830.
16   "Lands in Illinois to Soldiers of the Late War," House Document 262, 26th Congress, 2nd Session, 1840 [Serial set #369]. Reprinted as Lowell M. Volkel, *War of 1812 Bounty Lands in Illinois.* Introduction by James D. Walker (Thomson, Ill.: Heritage House, 1977), hereafter Volkel, *Bounty Lands in Illinois.*

952.353: MONTHLY ABSTRACT OF LAND LOCATED ON MILITARY LAND WARRANT CERTIFICATES. October 1, 1849–ca. May 1855. Fair copy: 2 vols. Rough copy: 1 partial vol. No index.

These are monthly lists of tracts entered pursuant to acts of Congress of February 11, 1847; September 28, 1850; March 22, 1852; and March 3, 1855, granting military bounty land. Entries include Register's and Receiver's numbers, number and date of warrant, number of acres, name of warrantee, legal description of tract entered, date located, name of person by whom located, and occasional notes of withdrawn or suspended warrants.

952.354: REGISTER OF MILITARY LAND WARRANTS RECEIVED. July 1–November 29, 1848. 1 partial vol. No index.

Entries for each warrant received include number and date of warrant, name of warrantee, date of location of land, legal description of tract, and name and residence of person actually making location.

952.355: ABSTRACT OF EXPIRED OR CONDITIONAL MILITARY LAND WARRANT LOCATIONS. November 17, 1847-May 31, 1849. 1 partial vol. No index.

This list of expired or unpaid conditional locations on military land warrants includes number and date of warrant, name of warrantee, date of location, legal description of tract, and name and residence of person actually making location.

The Illinois State Archives is located at the Norton Building, Capitol Complex, Springfield, IL 62756. The mailing address is 901 Southwind, Springfield, IL 62703-5125. Its website can be accessed at <www.cyberdriveillinois.com/departments/archives/services.html>.

ARKANSAS TRACT. This tract was found to contain so much inferior land that selections did not start until 1820. So extensive were difficulties that in 1826 Congress agreed to the exchange of both patented and unpatented land that was "unfit for cultivation" for any good land between the St. Francis and Arkansas Rivers provided that the warrantee still held a title with no encumbrances.[17]

The Arkansas Exchange Certificates resulting from the new legislation are part of NARA's Land Entry Papers of the General Land Office in RG 49 and consist

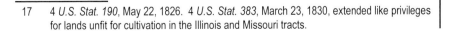

Some settlers of the frontier from *Frank Leslie's Illustrated Newspaper*, December 15, 1860; Col. D. H. Huyett.

---

17   4 *U.S. Stat. 190*, May 22, 1826. 4 *U.S. Stat. 383*, March 23, 1830, extended like privileges for lands unfit for cultivation in the Illinois and Missouri tracts.

of a number of certificates for Batesville and Little Rock, Arkansas, and Quincy and Springfield, Illinois.[18] They are register's certificates issued under the act of May 22, 1826, "An Act authorizing certain soldiers of the late war to surrender the bounty lands drawn by them, and to locate others in lieu thereof." Files include correspondence, affidavits supporting assertions that tracts originally located were unfit for cultivation, and relinquishments.

FINDING AIDS: According to Russell P. Baker, retired archivist of the Arkansas History Commission, there is a microfilm publication that specifically deals with the military tract in that state and a published book that indexes the names.

1. Arkansas History Commission. Little Rock, Arkansas, General Microfilm Collection, State Land Office Records, Roll 32, Military Bounty Land Grants—War of 1812, item one on Reel 32. A list of War of 1812 veterans who received federal land grants in Arkansas records contain the name of the veteran, the legal description of the property included in the grant, and the certificate number. There is no index with these records. (See below.)
2. Katheren Christensen's *[Index to] Arkansas Military Bounty Grants* lists the name of the veteran, the certificate number, and the county in which the land is located.[19] There is a full name index. It does not contain the legal description of the land.

Those interested in the military district in Arkansas should contact the Arkansas History Commission, One Capitol Mall, Little Rock, AR 72201 or visit its website at <www.ark-ives.com>.

MISSOURI TRACT. This tract of 500,000 acres was added when Michigan was removed in 1816. It consisted of Townships 53–55 in Ranges 16–23 inclusive, except lands within these limits lying south of the Missouri River. The area included Randolph, Macon, Chariton, and Carroll Counties. The distance of this tract, almost 100 miles from the Missouri River and 174 miles from St. Louis made it the least desired of the three military tracts. Gates in *Public Land Law* states that "there seems to be a conspiracy of silence concerning the experience of settlers and warrant holders in the Missouri tract for the usual indexes of state histories and state historical societies offer no information that would throw light on the question."[20]

"there seems to be a conspiracy of silence concerning the experience of settlers ..."

---

18 *Preliminary Inventory 22*, 8, entry 10.
19 Katheren (Mrs. Paul) Christensen, *[Index to] Arkansas Military Bounty Grants [War of 1812]* ([Hot Springs]: Arkansas Ancestors, 1971).
20 Gates, *Public Land Law*, 270.

In 1830 an act provided that claimants who had received bounty land that was unfit for cultivation could exchange it for land that was fit.[21]

FINDING AIDS: An excellent booklet titled *Missouri's Public Domain* was published by the State of Missouri.[22] It appears that this is out of print and it may be somewhat difficult to locate a copy for perusal but it is worth the effort. The publication explains the various tracts of the public domain including Missouri's military tract and accompanies the text with maps.

The following sources for Missouri should also be consulted:

> Dunaway, Maxine, compiler, *Missouri Military Land Warrants, War of 1812.* Springfield, Mo.: Maxine Dunaway, 1985.
> *Military Land Warrants in Missouri, 1819.* Denver, Colo.: Stagecoach Library for Genealogical Research, 1988.

The Missouri State Archives holds an alphabetical index to War of 1812 military lands of north Missouri. Their physical address is 600 West Main Street, Jefferson City, MO 65101. Mail requests should be sent to PO Box 1747, Jefferson City, MO 65102. The website can be accessed at <www.sos.mo.gov/archives>.

THE WAR OF 1812 APPLICATION FILES

APPLICATIONS NOT ALL IN THE SAME SERIES

The application files for bounty land based on War of 1812 service are not all a part of the same series of records. Basically, there are three sets of applications that should be used when searching. Two of the three series include bounty land application files that have been combined with pension files:

1. NARA's OLD WAR INDEX TO PENSION FILES (T316):[23]
   This is an index to the "Old War" series of pension files that applies chiefly to service in the Regular Army, Navy, or Marine Corps and, in some cases, others. This included deaths or disabilities of the War of 1812, Mexican War, Indian Wars, and sometimes Civil War. If the soldier died during War of 1812 service or was disabled, the pension file (with some possible bounty land documents included) may be in the Old War

Library of Congress
General Andrew Jackson at the Battle of New Orleans. Descendants of Tennesseans in particular may find their ancestor served with Jackson at this or other disturbances.

---

21 4 *U.S. Stat.* 383, March 23, 1830.
22 Gary W. Beahan, *Missouri's Public Domain: United States Land Sales, 1818–1922* (Jefferson City: State of Missouri Office of Secretary of State Records Management and Archives Service) Archives Information Bulletin Vol. II No. 3, July, 1980, hereafter *Missouri's Public Domain.*
23 National Archives microfilm publication T316, Records of the Department of Veterans Affairs, *Old War Index to Pension Files, 1815–1926,* RG 15, 7 rolls.

series. NARA microfilm publication T316 is only the index; the files are still textual but can be ordered online or by mail by using NARA's Form NATF 85.[24] A published version of the index in book form is available.[25]

Only a few of these Old War pension files may have bounty land documents, nonetheless, they should be checked.

2. NARA's INDEX TO WAR OF 1812 PENSION FILE (M313):[26] The general pension laws for the War of 1812 were enacted in 1871 and 1878.[27] Many soldiers had died by those dates but if a widow survived she may have initiated a pension, or, if not, minor children may have done so. If there was an "unindexed" bounty application (see Chapter 5) that involved War of 1812 service, in most cases that file was removed from the unindexed applications and combined with papers of the pension file.[28] Therefore this M313 index should not be overlooked; some files could include bounty land applications. At this time the pension files indexed in M313 are available only in textual form, though a major project is underway to microfilm or digitize them. The cost is high and it will require some time to accumulate sufficient funds.

Once a name is found in either index mentioned above, use NARA's Form NATF 85 to order a photocopy of the file. It can be ordered by mail using the address on the form, or the file can be ordered online at <www.archives.gov>.

The third series, "Unindexed" Bounty Land Application files for the War of 1812 and other conflicts, will be discussed in Chapter Five.

TIP In searching for a War of 1812 bounty land application, cover all bases by checking: 1) the War of 1812 pension files indexed on M313, 2) the Old War pension files indexed on T316, and 3) the unindexed bounty land files (described further in Chapter Five).

ARC

The National Archives Archival Research Catalog (ARC) is the online catalog of NARA's nationwide holdings in the Washington, D.C., area, regional archives and presidential libraries. ARC provides valuable resources such as titles; record groups, collections, series, and other descriptive information; the extent of the holdings; hierarchy; location of the records; and more. To learn more about ARC go to <http://www.archives.gov/research/arc/topics/genealogy/index.html#part1>. Access their search tool at <www.archives.gov/research/arc>.

---

24 For information on these textual files: National Archives and Records Service, "Case Files of Pension Applications Based on Death or Disability Incurred in Service Between 1783 and 1861 ("Old Wars"), compiled ca. 1815–ca. 1930, documenting the period ca. 1783–ca. 1930, ARC Identifier 1105306 / MLR Number NM22 23, NM22 27, view description at <http://arcweb.archives.gov>, then enter "Old War pension" in the search box.

25 Virgil D. White, *Index to War of 1812 Pension Files*. 2 volumes. (Waynesboro, Tenn.: National Historical Publishing Co., 1992).

26 National Archives microfilm publication M313, Records of the Department of Veterans Affairs, *Index to War of 1812 Pension Application Files*, RG 15, 102 rolls, DP.

27 16 *U.S. Stat.* 411, February 14, 1871. The act in 20 *U.S. Stat.* 27, March 9, 1878, supplemented the 1871 pension act.

28 See also Virgil D. White, *Index to War of 1812 Pension Files*. 2 volumes. (Waynesboro, Tenn.: National Historical Publishing Co., 1992) for a published version.

THE WARRANTS

THE EARLY WAR OF 1812 WARRANTS (M848)

Warrants for the War of 1812 differed from those of the Revolutionary war in that the warrants issued under acts 1811–1816 were not

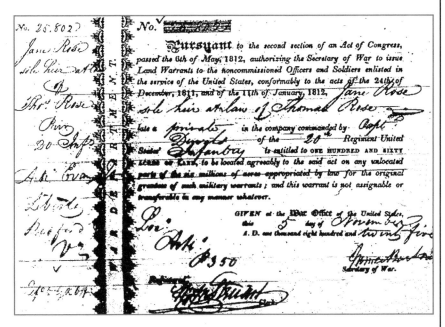

Figure 4–2. From M848, a warrant showing in the margin that Jane Rose was the heir at law of Thos. Rose.

actually delivered to the veteran but were retained by the General Land Office.[29] After his application was accepted, the veteran received notification that a warrant had been issued in his name. Most of the warrants for early acts were kept in bound volumes in two series, one for 160-acre warrants and one for 320-acre warrants. The warrants, stubs, and indexes are available in NARA microfilm publication M848 *War of 1812 Military Bounty Land Warrants, 1815–1858.* The indexes appear on roll 1. However, only a partial index was available for Illinois when these were filmed.[30] Two series of General Land Office (GLO) copies of notifications, which are further discussed below, are part of the holdings of the National Archives. From NARA's DP of M848:

> The warrants reproduced in this microfilm publication are originals from both series [i.e. 160 acres and 320 acres], with two exceptions. First, warrants 1 to 2519 under the act of 1812 (160 acres) and warrants 1 to 79 under the act of 1814 (320 acres) were detached from the volumes and are now included in the two series of notifications mentioned above. For these warrants the record kept on stubs remaining in the volume is reproduced. The information on the stubs includes warrant number; veteran's name, rank, and regiment; and in many cases date of

NARA's method of titling microfilm publications should be explained. NARA's microfilm publication M848, for example, shows 1815–1858. Those are not the dates of service, but the dates within which the warrants were issued. This method of titling the microfilm by dates of application or issuance rather than by date of service applies to most of NARA's other military related microfilm publications as well.

---

29   Eales, *Genie Guide,* 185.

30   National Archives microfilm publication M848, Records of the Bureau of Land Management, *War of 1812 Military Bounty Land Warrants,* 1815–1858. RG 49, 14 rolls, DP.

location and the citation from the Abstracts of Military Bounty Land Warrant Locations. The Abstracts, which were kept by the GLO, are chronological lists of locations of sites for which patents (documents conveying title to land) were granted on the basis of bounty land warrants.

The second exception is that warrants 27116 to 28085 under the act of 1812, and warrants 1077 to 1101 under the act of 1814, are neither in bound volumes nor in the two notification series, and their location, if they have not been destroyed, is unknown. In the case of warrants 27116 to 28085 under the 1812 act, copies from Records of the Veterans Administration, Record Group 15, have been filmed.

The warrants contain the following information: (1) name of the veteran; (2) his rank on discharge from military service; (3) his company, regiment, and branch of service; (4) date the warrant was issued; and (5) usually the date the land was located and the page on which the location is recorded in Abstracts of Military Bounty Land Warrant Locations. They are arranged according to warrant number and are in chronological order. For warrants appearing in this microfilm publication, issue dates of the first series (act of 1812, 160 acres) extend from August 19, 1815, to June 2, 1858, and for the second series (act of 1814, 320 acres) from August 23, 1815, to April 1, 1839.

Four indexes, applying to both series, have been included on roll 1. They are (1) "Alphabetical Index of Missouri Patentees," in which entries are arranged alphabetically by name of patentee and include date of patent, warrant number, warrantee's military rank, company in which he served, and legal description of the land (in terms of township, range, section, and fraction of section); (2) Index of Arkansas Patentees, in which entries are arranged alphabetically by first letter of surname of patentee and contain GLO patent book citation (the patent books remain in the custody of the Bureau of Land Management, successor agency to the GLO), legal description of the land, and warrant number; (3) Partial Index of Illinois Patentees, containing entries only for those whose surnames begin with letters "C" and "D" each entry including the veteran's name, company and regiment of service, warrant number, and Abstract citation; and (4) Index of Patentees Under the Act of 1842, in which entries are arranged alphabetically by first two letters of surname of patentee and include GLO patent book citation, legal description of the land, and warrant number.

No complete index for Illinois patentees has been found among the GLO records ... resolution of the U.S. House of Representatives on April 6, 1839, required the GLO to prepare a list of names of veterans to whom patents were issued for land in the Military Bounty Land District in Illinois for service in the War of 1812 ... [the list] was transmitted to the House July 21, 1840, and published as H. Doc. 262, 26th Cong., 1st sess.[31]

RELATED RECORDS

Canadian Volunteer Warrants

Canadian Volunteer Warrants were issued to Canadian volunteers pursuant to the act of March 5, 1816.[32] These were citizens of the United States who before the War of 1812 were living in Canada and who during the war joined the armies of the United States as volunteers and were slain, died in service, or continued until honor-

The River Raisin, near present-day Monroe, Michigan, where Tecumseh, a bold Indian leader who fought with the British, lost his life.

---

31   This list is available in many large libraries and was also used in Volkel, *Bounty Lands in Illinois.*

32   3 *U.S. Stat.* 256–57, March 5, 1816.

ably discharged. Each colonel was entitled to 960 acres, each major to 800 acres, and each non-commissioned officer, musician, or private to 320 acres. Bounties also extended to the medical and other staff according to their pay. The warrants could be taken up on any unappropriated lands within the Indiana Territory.

Documents in the Canadian Volunteer files include powers of attorney, assignments, correspondence, notations of the tracts located, date of patent, and the place of record. In addition, there are miscellaneous papers including correspondence regarding locations and issuance of patents, warrant numbers, date, acreage, to whom granted, to whom assigned, location of tract, date of locations, and by whom location was made. These records are in the Land Entry Papers of the General Land Office in Record Group 49 at Archives I in Washington, D.C., and can be obtained in person or by requesting them in a letter. Cite the reference and give details of the soldier's name and other known data.[33]

To read an interesting assessment of the Canadian grants see Treat, *National Land System,* pages 250–53.[34] Calling it "one of those ill considered acts which continually crept into the statutes" Treat explains the problems that were generated by this legislation. Congress amended the law the following year, and thus the law was in force for only one year.

In the next chapter unindexed bounty land application files and the surrendered warrant files are discussed. These are among the most informative of all records involving bounty land.

> "one of those ill considered acts which continually crept into the statutes"

POINTS TO REMEMBER IN THIS CHAPTER

✓ At first only non-commissioned officers or soldiers were entitled to bounty land in the War of 1812. In 1850 commissioned officers also became eligible.

✓ Transfers were restricted; warrants could not be sold or assigned though they could be inherited. This restriction was lifted in 1852.

✓ Three tracts were set out: Michigan, Illinois, and Lousiana Territory. Michigan lands were declared unfit for settlement, and additional land in Illinois and a tract in Missouri were substituted in 1816. The Louisiana Territory land was located in present-day Arkansas.

---

33 *Preliminary Inventory 22,* 8, entry 9.
34 Payson Jackson Treat, Ph.D., *The National Land System* (New York: Russell & Russell, 1910), hereafter Treat, *National Land System.*

✓ In 1842 restrictions on location were lifted and outstanding warrants could be used anywhere in the public domain where there was land available for private settlement.

✓ To locate bounty application files for War of 1812 check the indexes on M313 *War of 1812 Pensions* and T314 *Old War Pensions*. Also check the unindexed bounty land applications (see Chapter Five).

✓ To locate warrants for War of 1812 check M848 *War of 1812 Bounty Land Warrants and Pension*. Also search the surrendered warrants (see Chapter Five).

UNINDEXED BOUNTY, etc.

Though a number of acts were passed between the end of the War of 1812 and 1847, those acts were not intended to induce new service but to expand, continue, or revise benefits from the conflicts through the War of 1812. It was not until the impending War with Mexico in that new legislation was again considered to encourage enlistments. Additional acts of 1850, 1852, and 1855 granted awards to veterans who served in the War of 1812, Indian Wars, Mexican War, and sundry other disturbances. The government acted generously, granting land for service in just about any disturbance from 1790 forward. An additional act in 1856 (amending the 1855 act) included the Revolutionary War.

Some veterans ineligible under previous acts were eligible under the 1856 act for the required length of service was reduced. Or, they were given additional land under the new laws.

IMPORTANT TO GENEALOGISTS

The series known as the "unindexed bounty land application files" is based on voluminous files that are still only textual (that is, in their original form and not microfilmed or digitized).[1]

This series of applications is part of National Archive RG 15, Records of the Department of Veterans Affairs, 1773–2007.[2] They are among the most genealogically valuable files relating to military service. More often than not some gems, such as proofs of marriage, death

---

1   For information on the textual collection: National Archives and Records Service, Record Group 15: Records of the Department of Veterans Affairs, 1773–2007, "Bounty-Land Warrant Application Files, compiled ca. 1800–ca. 1900, documenting the period ca. 1790–ca. 1900," ARC Identifier 567388/ MLR Number A1 26, A1 4, see description at <http://arcweb.archives.gov>.

2   Evelyn Wade, comp. *Preliminary Inventory of Bureau of Pensions Correspondence and Pension and Bounty-Land Case Files Relating to Military Service Performed Between 1775 and 1861*, NM 22 (Washington, D.C.: National Archives and Records Administration, 1964).

records, names of former spouses, Bible records, physical descriptions, and other jewels are found. At times they can even provide a connection to an earlier soldier from another state. For example, John Taylor's bounty land application from Grant County, Wisconsin, based on his Black Hawk War service verifies, by his own statement, that he was the same John Taylor who had served from Randolph County, Illinois, twenty years earlier.

THE 1847-1855 ACTS

Following is information pertaining to each of the acts passed from 1847 forward based on service prior to 1855.

THE ACT OF 1847: MEXICAN WAR

The price of purchasing government land had decreased since the War of 1812, thus bringing into question the lure of bounty land for recruiting purposes. Nonetheless Congress believed that promises of bounty land to induce enlistments in the War with Mexico would be effective. No matter what, they reasoned, land was always prized and its reward would therefore encourage men to join.

The act of 1847 provided that each non-commissioned officer, musician, or private, whether in the regular army or regularly mustered volunteers who served no less than twelve months was entitled to 160 acres.[3]

If the soldier was killed, died of wounds or sickness incurred in service, or was discharged before the expiration of his term because of wounds or sickness, he (or his heirs) were eligible for the acreage. (Volunteers, however, were only to receive their benefit if they were actually marched to the seat of war but the records show that exceptions existed. The Regular Army did not have such an exclusion.)

Congress determined that the warrants for the Mexican War were not to be assignable. The experience surrounding the warrants issued for War of 1812 service imbued these legislators with a legitimate concern that speculators would defraud soldiers by encouraging them to transfer their rights before even receiving them. In an attempt to prevent anyone from circumventing the wishes of Congress the new law stated that any sale or transfer of the soldier's rights before the issuance of the warrant was null and void. In spite of the efforts to prevent assignments, records disclose that again unscrupulous attorneys and speculators found other ways to bypass the regulations. The unindexed bounty land application files do show a number of assignments for Mexican War veterans even before the act of 1852 specifically permitted them.

Adapted from George W. Kendall, *The War Between the United States and Mexico, Illustrated*, published in 1851. Those whose ancestors served in this war will enjoy the illustrations at <www.loc.gov/rr/print/list/picamer/paMexican.html>.

---

3   9 *U.S. Stat.* 123–26, February 11, 1847.

A clause was also included in the new 1847 legislation providing that though the land could be taken up anywhere government land was subject to private entry, the warrant could be used only if there was no preemption right or actual settlement and cultivation of the land. Previous clashes between the soldier's desire to locate a warrant and a squatter's right to preempt land on which he had made improvements prompted this restriction.

SCRIP OFFERED

The soldier who was eligible for bounty land for his Mexican War service had the option of foregoing the receipt of a warrant and accepting instead treasury scrip for $100.00. Soldiers and volunteers who joined after the war started and served for less than twelve months were entitled to 40 acres or $25.00 in scrip. In the event of the soldier's death during service, the heirs were entitled to the benefits: first the wife, if no wife then the children, if none then the father, and then the mother.

Evidence of the soldier's choice between the monetary amount or the warrant for acreage should appear in his unindexed application file. For example, papers in the file titled "Milton B. Rose #1847 SC 691-$100. Priv., Capt. John Jones, 1st Reg. Ga. Vol., Co. E" indicate that Rose received treasury scrip in lieu of land and that it was sent to his agent, Wm. Christy, in New Orleans.

Gates in *Public Land Law* points out that the certificates for Mexican War service differed from those of earlier acts because the scrip under the 1847 act was issued in dollars, not acres, and was acceptable for any payment due the government.[4]

It will be seen when accessing NARA's T317, *Index to Mexican War Pension Files*, that the index refers to files which in some cases include bounty land papers.[5] However, there was no effort by the government to actually combine all of the land bounty applications from the unindexed series based on Mexican War service with the pension files of that war as was done for the War of 1812 (see Chapter Four). Researchers should therefore check both series, that is, the unindexed bounty land application files (1812, 1847–1855) and the Mexican War pension index (T317), for bounty land records of ancestors who served in that war. Though the index to the pension files has been microfilmed as noted above (T317) the actual pension

---

4   Gates, *Public Land Law*, 271.

5   National Archives microfilm publication T317, Records of the Department of Veterans Affairs, *Index to Mexican War Pension Files, 1887-1926* (Washington, D.C.: National Archives and Records Service, n.d.), RG 15, 14 rolls.

applications have not been microfilmed; they are still in their original textual form.[6]

THE ACT OF 1850

Under the act passed in the fall of 1850, each of the surviving non-commissioned officers, musicians, or privates, whether regulars, volunteers, rangers, or militia, who performed military service in any regiment, company, or detachment in the war with Great Britain

> Sept. 28, 1850. CHAP. LXXXV. — *An Act granting Bounty Land to certain Officers and Soldiers who have been engaged in the Military Service of the United States.*
>
> 1852, ch. 19.
>
> *Be it enacted by the Senate and House of Representatives of the United States of America in Congress assembled,* That each of the
>
> Certain classes of persons in the military service surviving, or the widow or minor children of deceased commissioned and non-commissioned officers, musicians, or privates, whether of regulars, volunteers, rangers, or militia, who performed military service in

Figure 5–1.
From the act of 1850.

declared in 1812, or in any of the Indian Wars since 1790, and each of the commissioned officers engaged in the War of 1812, were entitled to lands.[7] Not only was the act generous but finally, after years of futile attempts by officers to be included as eligible recipients of bounty land for their War of 1812 service, they, too, would benefit by an award of land.

Those eligible who had engaged to serve twelve months or the duration of the war and actually served nine months were to receive 160 acres; those who engaged to serve six months and actually served four months were to receive 80 acres; and those who engaged to serve "for any or an indefinite period" and actually served one month received 40 acres. If captured, the time in captivity was added to actual service.

These warrants under the 1850 act could be taken up anywhere there was government land subject to private entry (as were the bounties under the act of 1847) and similarily, they were not assignable by law though they could be inherited by the widow. (Her heirs, however, were not eligible to apply for the warrant for it was to be issued in her favor, and ensue to her benefit but not to her heirs.)

Further restrictions stated that the warrant could not be used for any land on which there was a preemption right or an actual settlement and cultivation except with the consent of the settler satisfactorily proven to the proper land officer. Benefits were also not to accrue to any person who was at the time a member of Congress.

---

6   For information on this textual collection see National Archives and Records Service, Record Group 15: Records of the Department of Veterans Affairs, 1773–2007, "Case Files of Mexican War Pension Applications, compiled ca. 1887–ca. 1926, documenting the period ca. 1846–ca. 1926", ARC Identifier 1104361 / MLR Number NM-17 10, NM-17 11, <http://arcweb.archives.gov>.

7   9 *U.S. Stat.* 520–21, September 28, 1850.

The new legislation also set out that "no patent issued under this act shall be delivered upon any power of attorney or agreement dated before the passage of this act, and that all such powers of attorney or agreements shall be considered and treated as null and void." It is clear again that Congress by this means strove to avoid some of the pitfalls of earlier legislation and the massive land speculation that arose.

THE ACT OF 1852

For those still holding their warrants, the act of 1852 finally made all warrants assignable.[8] This was inevitable, for many had found ways to circumvent the law, while those still holding their warrants because of restrictions in the law were not able to benefit from the award of land unless they chose to personally settle on the property. This new act also allowed those holding warrants to use them for preemption rights at the rate of $1.25 per acre. If the land they desired was of higher value, they could pay the difference.

Another benefit accrued: in cases where the militia, volunteers, or state troops were called into service and were paid by the United States subsequent to June 18, 1812, the 1852 act provided that they, too, were entitled to the provisions of the act of September 28, 1850. (They were not, however, to again benefit if they had already received their bounty land.)

If any company, battalion, or regiment in an organized form marched more than twenty miles to the place where they mustered into service

---

"That all warrants for military bounty lands which have been
or may hereafter be issued ... are hereby
declared to be assignable."

---

during one of the wars specified in previous acts awarding bounty land or were discharged more than twenty miles from that place, the 1852 act provided that they were to be allowed one day for every twenty miles in calculating time served.

THE ACT OF 1855

The 1855 act made all those who fulfilled the requirements of previous acts awarding bounty land eligible for 160 acres (providing they were not deserters or dishonorably discharged) and reduced the

---

8   10 *U.S. Stat.* 3–4, March 22, 1852.

KNOW all Men by thefe Prefents, that I
of the County of   and State of   have this
day bargained and fold, and by thefe prefents do bargain, fell and affign over to
                 of the county of   and State of
all my right, title, and intereft in and to   acres of Land,
due me in confideration of my fervices in the army of the United States, to the end
of the late war with Great-Britain, under the command of
agreeable to an act of Congrefs, and I do moreover requeft, order and direct Henry
Knox, Efquire, Secretary at War for the time being, or his fucceffors, to iffue to
                 his heirs or affigns, in his or their own name as
affignee of me, the faid   a warrant for the land aforefaid,
and on receipt of the fame, I do hereby ratify and confirm any receipt or other inftru-
ment in writing, that he the faid   may neceffarily fign,
or procure to be figned, in touching the premifes aforefaid, as fully as I could do, if
I was perfonally prefent. IN Teftimony whereof, I have hereunto fet my hand and
feal this   of   179

Sealed and delivered }
in the prefence of }

to wit :

THIS day   came before us
Juftices of the Peace for the   aforefaid, and acknowledged the
foregoing bargain of fale and Power of Attorney, to be his hand and feal, act and
deed, and for the purpofes therein mentioned. Given under our hands this
day of   179.

Figure 5–2a. A form for assignment provided by the federal government to veterans and their agents. However, the assignment could be less formal; a written statement, usually on the back of the warrant, would suffice.

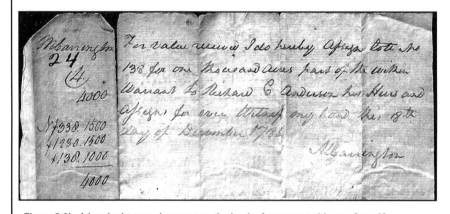

Figure 5-2b. A handwritten assignment on the back of a warrant, this one from M. Covington to Richard C. Anderson as appears in the Kendrick files, NARA RG 49, Box 120, dated 18 December 1784. See Chapter 2 page 33.

service requirement to no less than fourteen days. In some cases this meant an increased number of acres was due, and since it lessened the required time of service more veterans were now eligible.

The 1855 act extended land bounty benefits to a number of groups not covered under earlier acts.[9] The list of those now eligible included:

- commissioned and non-commissioned officers, musicians, and privates
- regulars, volunteers, rangers, or militia
- every officer, commissioned and non-commissioned, seaman, ordinary seaman, flotilla-man, marine, clerk, and landsman in the navy or in any of the wars in which the country has been engaged since 1790
- each of the survivors of the militia, volunteers, or State troops of any State or Territory called into service and regularly mustered thereon, whose services have been paid by the United States
- wagon-masters and teamsters who may have been employed under the direction of a competent authority in time of war in the transportation of military stores and supplies
- officers and soldiers of the revolutionary war, or their widows or minor children
- volunteers at the invasion of Plattsburg 1814
- Battle of King's Mountain (Revolutionary War)
- Battle of Nickojock [Nickajack], against "savages of the South"
- chaplains of the army who served in wars
- volunteers at the attack on Lewistown, in Delaware, by the British fleet, War of 1812

The act of May 14, 1856, amended the above act of 1855.[10] When an applicant had already received part of the 160 acres, the act allowed the use of that evidence to prove eligibility for the balance of the 160 acres. The 1856 act also clarified that the 1855 act was to embrace officers, marines, seamen, and other persons engaged in the naval service during the Revolutionary War, and their widows and minor children. Provisions also would extend to the volunteers with the armed forces subject to military orders for the space of fourteen days in any of the wars specified in the first section of the act of 1855.

Warrants issued under the acts of 1855 and 1856 were assignable.

EXTENSIVE COVERAGE

9   10 *U.S. Stat.* 701–2, March 3, 1855.
10   11 *U.S. Stat.* 8–9, May 14, 1856.

THE APPLICATIONS

In addition to applications under the 1847-plus acts described in this chapter, the unindexed bounty land series includes a number of applications under the act of 1812 (and perhaps sundry other early acts for bounty land) that had not yet been located.

Also, some previously ineligible War of 1812 veterans became eligible under the provisions of later acts. According to the DP for M848:

> Some War of 1812 veterans, including both commissioned officers and noncommissioned officers and soldiers, received warrants under acts of 1850 (9 Stat. 520), 1852 (10 Stat. 3), and 1855 (10 Stat. 701), which were general acts applying to veterans of several wars. Warrants issued under these acts are not included in... [M848]...."[11]

Therefore, the unindexed bounty application files consist mainly of applications under acts of 1847–1855 and some warrants, still unlocated, under the act of 1812 and other early acts.

An example of an unindexed bounty land file designation under the act of 1812:

ABRAHAM ROSE #12-160 WT 9175.
[That is, Abraham Rose for War of 1812 service (as designated by the "#12"), under act of 1812 received warrant #9175 for 160 acres.]

Arrangement of Files: The unindexed bounty land applications are arranged alphabetically in legal-size manila files. This series consists of approximately 360,000 bounty land application files in 6053 boxes. Each box contains a number of files, each marked with the range of names within that box, submitted by veterans or their heirs based on service between 1790 and 1855. The majority of the claims are based on service in the War of 1812, Indian Wars, and the Mexican War.

Those who visit Archives I in Washington, D.C., can personally examine these application files by completing an in-house request form provided by the consultants for RG 15. Copies of the files can also be ordered by mail on NARA's Form NATF 85 or ordered online at <www.archives.gov>. (Indian applications discussed later in this chapter are arranged separately.)

INDEX IN PREPARATION

At the time of this writing, volunteers at NARA are working on an index by soldiers' names to the unindexed bounty land application

---

11   See Chapter 4 footnote 30. This is NARA's microfilm publication M848 on warrants under early acts for the War of 1812.

files. These are voluminous records—it will be a long-term project. When completed, the index will be a tremendous finding aid, creating for researchers a resource to readily determine if the soldier or his

First Name	Middle	Last Name	Rank		War	Unit	State	Act / Warrant Number	Rejected	Indian
James		Baxter	Private	1812		VA Militia, Capt. Rostin, Col. Buckner	VA	55-316822	Yes	No
James		Baxter	Private	1812		VA Militia, Capt. Thomas Royston, Col. Brannon	VA	50-116640	Yes	No
James		Baxter	Private	1837		GA Vols., Capt. Rogers	GA	52-160-542	No	No
James		Baxter	2nd Lieut	1837		MO Vols., Capt. Robert Mitchell, Col. Wilson	MO	55-296659	Yes	No
James		Baxter	Private	1847		4th Regt. TN Vols., Capt. J.T. Council	TN	47-160-53717	No	No

Figure 5–3. From the Unindexed Bounty Land Application files index in preparation at NARA.

heirs applied and to provide the specific ordering information. The index completed to date is available to researchers on a computer at Archives I in Washington, D.C.

The new index includes:

> First Name, Middle, Last Name, Rank, War, Unit, State, Act/Warrant Number, Rejected [Yes or No], Indian [Yes or No]

Example of a listing:

> James Baxter, [Rank] Private, [War] 1812, [Unit] VA Militia, Capt. Thomas Royston, Col. Brannon, [State] VA, [Act/Warrant Number] 80–116640, [Rejected] Yes, [Indian] No

REJECTED APPLICATIONS

A claim could be rejected for any number of reasons: not enough service under the act, not enough proof, evidence of fraud, etc. Later, more information could change the status to an approved application. Though the files in these cases are usually combined, occasionally they are not, and two files may exist.

> **TIP** In some instances there are two files for the same soldier for reasons other than the rejection of one of the applications. Perhaps the claim lay idle for some time and a new file opened when additional information was submitted. Other reasons may have also occasioned the opening of a second file.

RICH IN FAMILY DETAILS

The importance of applications under the acts from 1847–1856 cannot be overstated. They are rich in details that can help the genealogist. Every effort should be made to identify and obtain these textual unindexed bounty land files. Also to be considered: it is more likely that an unindexed bounty land application might be found than a pension file. For example, for War of 1812 service the first general pension law was not passed until 1871. If the soldier died in 1858 and his widow in 1860, likely there is no pension file. Yet, this soldier almost certainly filed for bounty land under the unindexed bounty acts when restrictions eased and benefits were expanded. That application file with all its data could be no further away than the filing of the form to obtain a copy. Each file differs, but most do not disappoint researchers eager for details of their families.

TIP If the veteran or his representatives filed for a War of 1812 pension under the 1871 act, any previously filed unindexed bounty land application file in most instances was combined with that pension file. However, exceptions do exist so it is best to check both series, that is, the unindexed bounty land application files and the pension files for that war. (See Chapter Four.)

TITLE OF FILE: When the application file is ordered, the title of the Bounty Land file usually is entered by the National Archives on a duplicate copy of Form NATF 85, then returned to the submitter with the copies. This title or a variation thereof will be similar to this example:

WT 109655-160-55

Interpreting the above file number: 109655 is the warrant number, 160 represents the number of acres awarded under this warrant, and 55 is the year of the act, that is, 1855. All of this information is needed to obtain the surrendered warrant case file showing where the land was located (see later in this chapter).

Many traveled to their new home taking family and belongings in wagons. Adapted from *Frank Leslie's Illustrated Newspaper*, May 16, 1885.

TIP If the application file refers to the awarding of more than one warrant for the soldier, the title of the application file generally refers only to the *latest* of those warrants. For example, Bennet Rose's application produced a warrant #15855 for 80 acres under the act of 1850. When his widow applied for the additional land due under later acts, her warrant was #42167 for 80 acres under the act of 1855, and therefore the file is titled WT 42167-80-55. Note both warrant numbers when examining the application file so that both of the surrendered warrant files can be ordered.

SURRENDERED WARRANT FILES

The warrants issued as a result of applications in the unindexed bounty land series are sometimes referred to by NARA as the "unspecified warrants," since the warrants could be used anywhere in the public domain where land for private entry was available.

Surrendered warrant files should be sought when the researcher wants to determine the disposition of a particular warrant. They are part of NARA's RG 49, the Land Entry papers of the General Land Office. The surrendered warrant file can be obtained by submitting RG 49's Form NATF 84 or ordering and viewing the files in person in Washington, D.C.[12] Either way, the information provided must include the following in order for NARA to retrieve the file:

- warrant number
- acreage
- act

Figure 5–4. A surrendered warrant for 120 acres issued to Elizabeth Foland.

Though the surrendered warrant files usually include only a few papers, nonetheless the information is of value in showing if the soldier or an assignee took up the warrant, when and to whom the warrant was assigned, and the legal description of the land located. In the case of the death of the soldier, the file may disclose his heirs. In some cases, relationships may be shown such as widow or minor heirs at law. And importantly, the original warrant should be in the file. Copies make wonderful mementos for the family.

TIP Use separate forms for each request. NARA will not fulfill requests for two different surrendered warrant files on the same NATF 84 form, even if both warrants are mentioned in the same application file. Fill out one form for *each* surrendered warrant file being requested.

---

12   Form NATF 84 can be obtained online at <www.archives.gov> or at any National Archives facility. Mail the completed request form to: Archives I Reference (NWCT1F-Land), Textual Archives Services Division, National Archives and Records Administration, 700 Pennsylvania Avenue, NW, Washington, DC 20408-0001.

INDIAN BOUNTIES

INDIAN BOUNTY LAND APPLICATIONS

Section 7 of the act of 1855 specifically states that "the provisions of this act, and all the bounty-land laws heretofore passed by Congress, shall be extended to Indians, in the same manner, and to the same extent, as if the said Indians had been white men."[13] Thus, the provisions of all the bounty land acts accrued to Indians under this act. Indians had often served along with colonists and later with United States soldiers. This act assured that they would finally get the same benefits.

An interesting series of applications specifically for Indians is available in textual form at the National Archives. According to an excellent article by Mary Frances Morrow in *Prologue*, the 1855 act that extended bounty land to Indians entitled those veterans from the Revolutionary War era to 1855 to warrants that could be exchanged for public lands.[14] A few earlier acts had specified bounty lands for Indians, but this act marked the first time land was made available on a large scale. This collection consists of forty-five boxes of envelopes, around a hundred per box. The name of the veteran is given, along with his grade, service date, company commander, tribal affiliation, and the warrant number and number of acres.

The applications are still in original form and are part of Entry 27 described in National Archives' Preliminary Inventory NM-22, "Case files of bounty land warrant applications of Indians based on service between 1812 and 1855."[15]

A knowledge of the Indian name will facilitate the search for a file.

According to Morrow's *Indian Bounty* the applications, arranged alphabetically by the veteran's name, are primarily transcriptions of Indian names "such as In-to-yo-ye, Ish-tar-yi-see, or Soks-set-he-ne-ha. Whenever second names appear, the order is by the first name. For example, Ne-har-locco Harjo is filed under N."

Inside the envelope is an application, usually a printed form with the appropriate blanks filled in by the Indian agent.

Morrow, *Indian Bounty* continues:

---

13   10 *U.S. Stat.* 701–02, March 5, 1855.

14   Mary Frances Morrow, "Indian Bounty Land Applications," *Prologue* (Washington, D.C.: National Archives), 25 (Fall 1993) no. 3, available at <www.archives.gov/publications /prologue>, hereafter Morrow, *Indian Bounty.*

15   National Archives and Records Service, Record Group 75, Records of the Bureau of Indian Affairs, 1793–1999, "Abstract List of Indian Applicants for Military Bounty Lands, compiled 1855–1882," ARC Identifier 2113317 / MLR Number PI-163 545. See also: *Preliminary Inventory of the Records of the Bureau of Indian Affairs,* (PI-163), Entry 545.

The form typically gives the name of the veteran and establishes the veteran's eligibility for bounty lands through military service in a particular war. There is confirmation of the veteran's service in the form of statements and signatures of witnesses. The claimant might be the veteran, his widow, or a minor heir. Different forms were used for each according to specifications by the Office of Indian Affairs. The form established the right of the claimant to the benefits of the veteran.

If the veteran was known by an Indian name, that name was used in preparing the index. This makes accessing these applications difficult. The tribes represented are principally the Five Civilized Tribes but others are also included. Researchers should thoroughly read the cited Morrow, *Indian Bounty* article. There are some indexes and abstracts included in Record Group 75. Additionally, these Indian bounty applications are being indexed at the National Archives in the same project as those for the unindexed bounty land files described previously in this chapter.

NO BOUNTY LAND FOR SERVICE RENDERED AFTER 1855

There is no bounty land for Civil War service, or for any service rendered after 1855.[16] Acts later than 1855 extended the time period for applying or otherwise modified previous acts, but these additional acts refer to service prior to 1855; they did not create awards for service performed after that date.

In the next chapter we look at Patents, the final step in the process to obtain military land from the government.

POINTS TO REMEMBER IN THIS CHAPTER

✓ Application files under acts of 1812 and 1847–1855 and perhaps a few sundry other early acts (other than those covered in *War of 1812 Bounty Land Warrants and Pension* M848) are referred to as "unindexed bounty land applications" and are part of RG 15, Records of the Veterans Administration.

✓ The unindexed applications are textual only (not microfilmed or digitized) but can be ordered either online or by mail using National Archives Form NATF 85.

✓ An index prepared by volunteers at the National Archives for both the unindexed application files and the Indian bounty application files is in progress. The partial index is available for viewing at Archives I in Washington, D.C.

---

16   It should be noted that under a supplemental act of the Homestead Act of 1862 passed on June 8, 1872 (17 *U.S. Stat.* 333), Union veterans were given credit for the time they served in Union service. This should not be considered bounty land, for the land itself was not awarded for service rendered.

Unindexed Bounty, etc.

    ✓ The files showing the location of the warrants are called surrendered warrant files. These are in the Land Entry files General Land Office in RG 49 in Archives I, Washington, D.C.

    ✓ If the warrant was sold, assigned, or inherited, the patent will be in the name of a person other than the veteran.

6 FEDERAL LAND PATENTS

Once the military bounty warrant was surrendered and the land office verified that all requirements had been met, a patent was issued by the federal government. This was the final step in obtaining the land due from the government to a veteran or his representatives or assignees. After the patent was issued, subsequent sales or transfers of the tract went through the normal channels of local records such as deeds, inheritance and other transfer documents. (States who offered bounty land in the Revolutionary War issued their own grants or patents. Those records are generally available in the states' archives.)

The Bureau of Land Management Eastern States (BLM-ES) in Springfield, Virginia, embarked several years ago on a project to scan the patents to provide the images online. Since that time they have not only worked diligently on that goal but are adding surveys and field notes. In developing the website and scanning the documents, BLM has created display screens that contain information of considerable help to researchers.

This monumental BLM project involving the scanning of 1135 volumes of patents of military bounty land (in addition to many more of non-military patents) is nearing completion. The images can be viewed at <www.glorecords.blm.gov>.

There is no Final Certificate preceding the issuance of a federal military patent. To retrieve a surrendered warrant file for federal military patents, the warrant number, act, and acreage are necessary. (Non-military patent case files require a Final Certificate number to obtain the case file.)

THE SEARCH

Knowing some search strategies on how to conduct an online search for a patent involving a military warrant will increase the success rate. Every type of search that could be conducted won't be demonstrated, but a few should show what can be found.

TIP Before beginning, it is helpful to read the Glossary at the BLM website at <www.glorecords.blm.gov/Visitors/Glossary.asp>.

Following an Example

First, we'll start at the BLM homepage at <www.glorecords.blm.gov>. Note that at the top of the screen (See Figure 6–1) are three tabs: "Land Patents," "Survey Plats and Field Notes," and "Land Status Records." For our present purpose start with the "Land Patents" search (see Figure 6–2). I chose to enter the state of Missouri, and the surname of ROSE, and at the bottom checked the boxes for

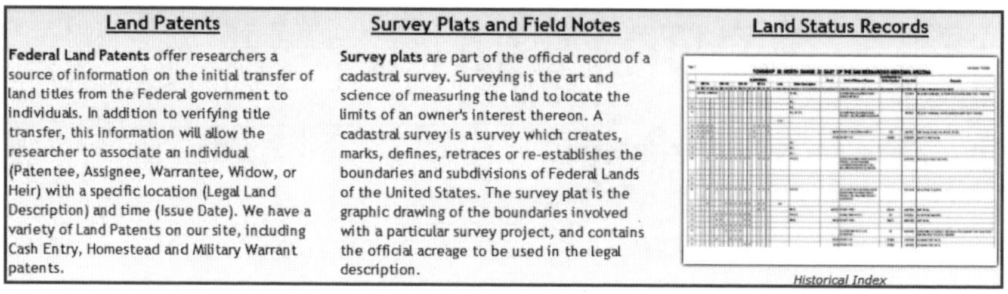

Figure 6–1. Shown are the three tabs found on the home page, that is, "Land Patents," "Survey Plats and Field Notes," and "Land Status Records."

Land Patents	Survey Plats and Field Notes	Land Status Records
Federal Land Patents offer researchers a source of information on the initial transfer of land titles from the Federal government to individuals. In addition to verifying title transfer, this information will allow the researcher to associate an individual (Patentee, Assignee, Warrantee, Widow, or Heir) with a specific location (Legal Land Description) and time (Issue Date). We have a variety of Land Patents on our site, including Cash Entry, Homestead and Military Warrant patents.	**Survey plats** are part of the official record of a cadastral survey. Surveying is the art and science of measuring the land to locate the limits of an owner's interest thereon. A cadastral survey is a survey which creates, marks, defines, retraces or re-establishes the boundaries and subdivisions of Federal Lands of the United States. The survey plat is the graphic drawing of the boundaries involved with a particular survey project, and contains the official acreage to be used in the legal description.	*Historical Index*

"select patentee" and "select warrantee." (I could have chosen just one of these.) After scrolling though multiple pages of Roses from

Figure 6–2. Clicking "Land Patents" brings forth this screen in which "Missouri" and the last name ROSE were entered. (Note the "Show Advanced" link in the upper right, to be discussed later.) Towards the bottom left both the "search patentee" and the "search warrantee" were checked.

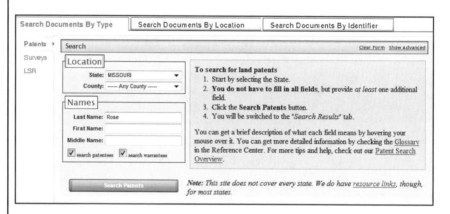

the Missouri listings (Figure 6–3), I examined those that name my demonstration target Thompson Rose and then chose the first one. It shows Thompson Rose (see Figure 6–4) as patentee, and Owen Ragon as warrantee.

Figure 6–3 shows a partial list of results for the above search. It includes either a patentee or a warrantee with the surname of ROSE. The MW part of the accession number indicates it was a patent based on a military warrant.

Image	Accession	Names	Date	Doc #	State	Meridian	Twp - Rng	Aliquots	Sec. #	County
🗎	MW-0269-284	[P] ANDERSON, OLIVER, [P] ROSE, JOHN M, [W] PATTERSON, IVER D	12/10/1859	38893	MO	5th PM	041N - 030W	W½NW¼, Lot/Trct 1	4	Bates
							041N - 030W	W½SW¼	4	Bates
🗎	MW-0227-007	[P] BAILEY, HORACE T, [W] ROSE, RUTHERFORD	11/1/1859	43608	MO	5th PM	026N - 007E	W½SE¼	26	Butler
							026N - 007E	NE¼SE¼	26	Butler
							026N - 007E	NE¼SW¼	26	Butler
🗎	MW-0316-190	[P] BONSELL, EDWARD, [W] ROSE, GEORGE P	5/10/1860	35452	MO	5th PM	067N - 024W	E½NE¼	33	Mercer
							067N - 024W	W½NW¼	34	Mercer
🗎	MW-0909-390	[P] BROCK, JOHN W, [W] ROSE, VINCENT D	6/16/1856	16870	MO	5th PM	066N - 036W	W½NW¼	35	Nodaway
🗎	MW-0269-333	[P] BROWN, JAMES W, [W] ROSE, VINCENT D	12/10/1859	39233	MO	5th PM	042N - 021W	W½SE¼	13	Benton

TIP To the left of each name is a small box. It may not be easily readable in these screen shots, but these boxes have either a P for Patentee or a W for Warrantee

	MW-0118-070	P	ROSE, THOMPSON, RAGON, OWEN	11/1/1858	32576	MO	5th PM	064N - 028W	N½SW¼	10	Harrison
	MO4730 .227	P	ROSE, THOMPSON	4/2/1857	16521	MO	5th PM	064N - 028W	N½SE¼	14	Harrison
	MO4770 .049	P	ROSE, THOMPSON	7/1/1857	21562	MO	5th PM	062N - 028W	NW¼SE¼	15	Harrison
	MO4810 .192	P	ROSE, THOMPSON	5/5/1859	21561	MO	5th PM	064N - 028W	SE¼NW¼	14	Harrison
	MO4670 .342	P	ROSE, THOMPSON	3/10/1856	16522	MO	5th PM	064N - 028W	NE¼SW¼	15	Harrison

Figure 6–4 shows part of a continuing page for the many Rose entries, this one showing listings for Thompson Rose, our demonstration target.

Clicking on the first listing of Thompson Rose in Figure 6–4 produced Figure 6–5. This shows the Document Number as 32576, acreage as 80, Land Office as Plattsburg, No US or Mineral reservations, and importantly, the Authority as the March 3, 1855, "Scrip Warrant Act of 1855 (10 Stat. 701)" thus providing us with the act under which this patent were issued. It also discloses that Thompson Rose was locating his own bounty land warrant for Thompson Rose was not the warrantee. The warrantee was the veteran, Owen Ragon, who had assigned the warrant to Thompson Rose. Rose then became the patentee. Note in Figure 6–8 that the legal description of the property is given. We're going to need that later.

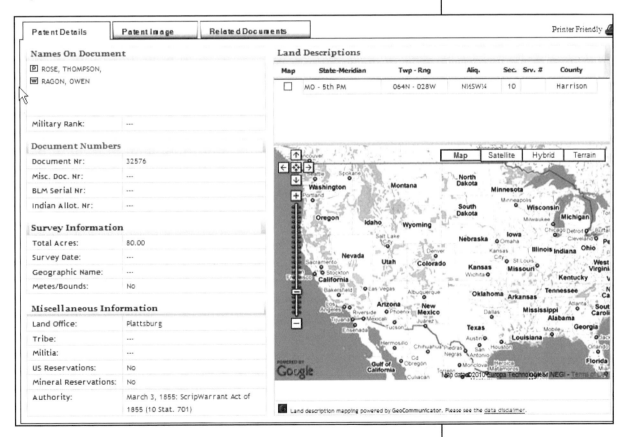

Figure 6–5 showing screen with "Patent Details" on the left, and a map on the right. Note that along the very top, to the right of the tab showing "Patent Details," are additional tabs for "Patent Image" and "Related Documents." Note too the legal description above the map. If we add a check mark in the box above the map just before "MO - 5th PM" we'll get a new map screen showing where the section is located, though it will not include the aliquot parts (such as NW ¼ of the SW ½, etc.).

70

THE UNITED STATES OF AMERICA,

To all to whom these Presents shall come, Greeting:

WHEREAS, In pursuance of the Act of Congress, approved March 3, 1855, entitled "An Act in addition to certain Acts granting Bounty Land to certain Officers and Soldiers who have been engaged in the military service of the United States," there has been deposited in the GENERAL LAND OFFICE, Warrant No. *32576* for *80* acres, in favor of *Owen Ragan a private in Captain Maloney's Company, of Tennessee Militia, War of 1812*

with evidence that the same has been duly located upon *the North half of the South West quarter of Section ten, in Township sixty-four of Range twenty eight in the district of lands subject to sale at Plattsburg, Missouri, containing eighty acres.*

according to the Official Plat of the Survey of said Lands returned to the GENERAL LAND OFFICE by the SURVEYOR GENERAL *the said warrant having been assigned by the said Owen Ragan to Thompson Rose, in whose favor said tract has been located;*

NOW KNOW YE, That there is therefore granted by the UNITED STATES unto the said *Thompson Rose, as assignee as aforesaid and to his heirs*

the tract of Land above described: TO HAVE AND TO HOLD the said tract of Land, with the appurtenances thereof, unto the said *Thompson Rose, as assignee as aforesaid and to his*

heirs and assigns forever.

In testimony whereof, I, *James Buchanan* PRESIDENT OF THE UNITED STATES OF AMERICA, have caused these Letters to be made Patent, and the Seal of the General Land Office to be hereunto affixed.

GIVEN under my hand, at the City of Washington, the *first* day of *November* in the year of our Lord one thousand eight hundred and *fifty-eight*, and of the Independence of the United States the *eighty third*

BY THE PRESIDENT, *James Buchanan*

By *J. J. Albright* .... Sec'y.

J. N. Granger .... Recorder of the General Land Office.

Figure 6–6. The patent gives the the legal description and also the volume and page number of the recorded patent. The image can also be printed with the citation displayed.

Now let's take a look at an image of the patent. In Figure 6-5 "Patent Image" was shown as the second tab. Click on it, and see the patent, Figure 6–6.

FINDING NEIGHBORS: This time we want to search for neighbors of Thompson Rose. From the home page click on Land Patents and in the Note at the bottom that this time we only filled in "Patentee" for we know that Thompson Rose in the patent we searched was the patentee and not the warrantee. At the top upper right click on "Show Advanced." The resulting screen is shown in Figure 6–8. Note that at the bottom there are several choices. We fill in the Land Description from the information at the top of Figure 6-5, that is, Section 10 in township 64 North, Range 28 West, and Land Office as Plattsburg.

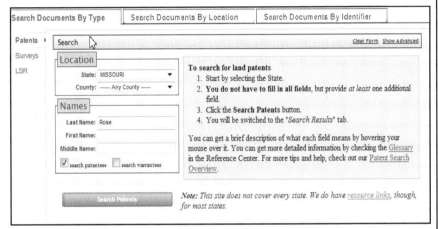

Figure 6–7 showing the search for the patent.

After completing that form click on "Search Patents" at the bottom of Figure 6-8 and now view what is displayed in Figure 6-9.

We now see that among the neighbors in Section 10 (where Thompson Rose's land was located) is a Timothy Rose. It seems likely because of the surname that he is related. The details of Timothy's patent can

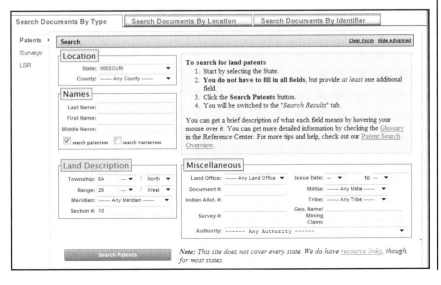

Figure 6–8. This screen adds items at the bottom for the legal land description and various other choices to be selected. The land description for Thompson Rose's tract was entered, taken from the top of Figure 6–5 showing his tract as Section 10 in Township 64 North, Range 28 West.

Figure 6–9. Thompson Rose and his neighbors in Section 10, township 64 North, Range 28 West.

Image	Accession	Names ⊤	Date	Doc #	State	Meridian	Twp - Rng	Aliquots	Sec. #	County
🖹	MO4820 .111	🅿 CRAFT, RUFUS F	5/5/1859	24630	MO	5th PM	064N - 028W	NE¼SE¼	10	Harrison
🖹	MO4850 .297	🅿 CRAFT, RUFUS S	4/2/1860	23668	MO	5th PM	064N - 028W	S½SE¼	10	Harrison
							064N - 028W	SE¼SW¼	10	Harrison
							064N - 028W	NE¼NW¼	15	Harrison
🖹	MW-0317-065	🅿 DEARMOND, JOSEPH, 🅿 ROSENFELD, ZACHARIAH, 🆆 PERKINS, JEREMIAH	10/1/1860	44115	MO	5th PM	064N - 028W	SW¼SW¼	10	Harrison
							064N - 028W	NW¼NW¼	15	Harrison
🖹	MW-0259-126	🅿 HARDIN, WILLIAM, 🅿 ZIMMERMAN, PRAGET, 🆆 ZIMMERMAN, JACOB	12/1/1859	33877	MO	5th PM	064N - 028W	S½NE¼	10	Harrison
🖹	MW-0259-363	🅿 MCBANE, ANDREW J, 🆆 PRATER, JOHN	12/1/1859	83049	MO	5th PM	064N - 028W	S½NW¼	10	Harrison
							064N - 028W	NW¼NW¼	10	Harrison
🖹	MW-0118-070	🅿 ROSE, THOMPSON, 🆆 RAGON, OWEN	11/1/1858	32576	MO	5th PM	064N - 028W	N½SW¼	10	Harrison
🖹	MO4820 .268	🅿 ROSE, TIMOTHY	5/5/1859	24924	MO	5th PM	064N - 028W	NW¼SE¼	10	Harrison
🖹	MW-0112-164	🅿 SHUMARD, THOMAS P, 🆆 MARTIN, WILLIAM B	8/16/1858	33517	MO	5th PM	064N - 028W	S½SW¼	3	Harrison
							064N - 028W	NE¼NW¼	10	Harrison
🖹	MW-0257-168	🅿 SHUMARD, THOMAS P, 🆆 HORNBACK, ISAAC	3/28/1859	12127	MO	5th PM	064N - 028W	N½NE¼	10	Harrison

be searched for any additional clues, and he can be further sought in other records such as census, county courthouse, etc.

This ability to check for neighbors is a valuable research tool. We can extend the proximity search by eliminating the Section number; we will then turn up all neighbors who had land specifically in Township 64 North Range 28 West, not just those in Section 10.

ALL ROSES LISTED IN THE PLATTSBURG LAND OFFICE

Let's try another search. This time we want to know the names of everyone with the surname of Rose who had a land patent in the Plattsburg Land Office (where records of Thompson Rose's land were registered). In the basic search screen (Figure 6–10) we fill out some minimal information: State as Missouri, last name as Rose, and we check the boxes for search patentee and search warrantee.

Figure 6–10 shows the completed form to start the search for those whose records are in the Plattsburg Land Office.

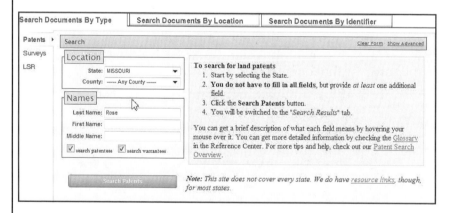

Clicking on "advanced search" in the upper right in Figure 6-10 displays a screen shown in Figure 6–11 which offers a variety of choices. We'll fill in "Plattsburg" for the Land Office.

After clicking on Search Patents at the bottom of Figure 11, the screen in Figure 6–12 is displayed. It lists numerous Roses, the list only partially shown here. In addition to Thompson Rose and Timothy

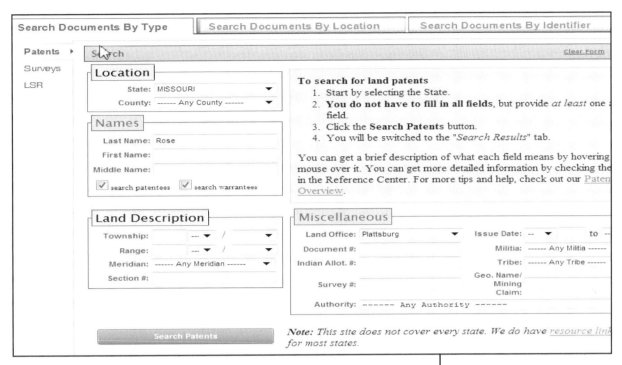

Rose, the list includes Fanny Rose, Erastus Rose, Alfred Rose, Baron D. Rose, Henry Rose, Charles Rose, Emsley Rose, Ezra Rose, and a number of others. Any of these Roses listed in the same Land Office District could be related to Thompson Rose. A similar search was conducted using the form in Figure 6–11, this time showing the county of Harrison instead of the the larger Land Office of Plattsburgh district. That search revealed nineteen Rose listings, eight of which were for Thompson Rose and several for Timothy Rose.

Figure 6–11 demonstrating a search for Roses in Plattsburg Land Office records.

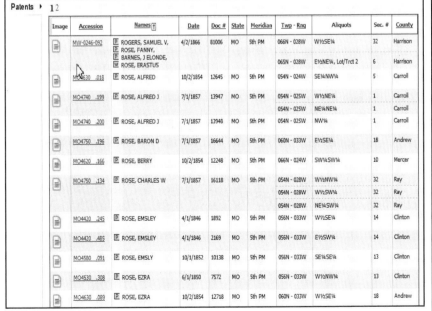

Figure 6–12 showing only a partial list of those Roses in the same Plattsburg Land Office District as Thompson Rose lived.

SEARCH BY AUTHORITY, ETC.

This time in the advanced search, scroll down to "Authority," and pick "Scrip Warrant Act of 1855" from the pull-down menu and click on "Search." Search results include those who specifically had patents under that 1855 bounty land act. They are not reproduced here, but this type of search can be generated with any of the items listed under "authority." At the time of this writing, the BLM had included on the new website only a fraction of the authorities listed on the original website. The expanded list may be completed when you read this.

PLOTTING THE LAND

An amazing feature on the new BLM website is the ability to plot the location of a patent within seconds. For example, I decided to plot the tract of land Nancy Rose had patented in Alabama. First, by searching patents I found the following for Nancy Rose (Figure 6-13). Two transactions were located but the one of interest was in Lauderdale County.

Figure 6–13. The search for the Nancy Rose patent in Alabama.

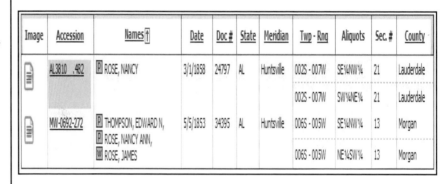

Clicking on the accession link for Nancy Rose of Lauderdale County produced a screen shown in Figure 6–14. Notice the detail it provides in the map of the area, and the additional information it offers.

Click the box beside the first land description to view the location of the section where Nancy's land was located and we'll find that is now displayed in Figure 6–14.

Note that a box appears where the section is located on the map. The box to the left of Figure 6–14 indicates the total acreage, that it is in the Huntsville Land Office, and the act under which the entry was made.

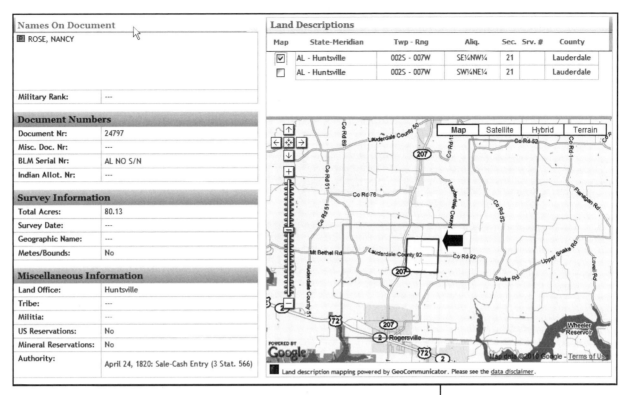

Figure 6–14 above. Note the x at the top right next to "Al - Huntsville ..." This was a blank box before I checked it. Immediately after being checked, the plot appeared in the middle of the Lauderdale County County Road 82. Though the plotting does not have the capability of adding the aliquot parts (for example, in this case, Southeast 1/4 of Northwest 1/4, it does show the location of Section 21 so that the researcher knows the land was located within that area. (The arrow has been added.)

LOCATING AN ADDRESS

Another amazing feature is the ability to import many mailing addresses into a map of the area where it is located. For example, I wanted to locate 6385 Fuqua Rd., Rogersville, AL. I first accessed the home page and clicked on the middle tab "Search Documents by Location." A screen was then displayed as shown in Figure 6–15:

Land Patents	Survey Plats and Field Notes	Land Status Records

Figure 6–15 is the home page. Click on the middle tab.

After I clicked on the middle link, a screen was shown (see Figure 6–16) though without the address filled in. The address was entered, and presto! The map displayed the location on Fuqua Road. Further, to the left there now appears the legal description showing that it is in Section 9, Township 3 South, Range 7 West, Huntsville Principal Meridian. (Again, aliquot parts are not displayed.)

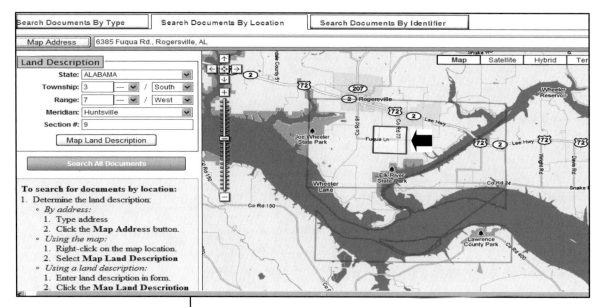

Figure 6–16 showing bar with "Map Address" and "Enter address." The 6385 Fuqua Road address was entered and within moments the map was displayed with the legal description to the left and the tract shown in a box in the map on the right. (Arrow added.)

MICHIGAN SURVEY SEARCH

Scanning of surveys and field notes is a long-term project and is only partially completed. But, to get an idea of how to search the surveys, we'll do a search on a military warrant in Michigan. As the surveys become available in more locations, researchers may find the surveys of the land owned by their family.

On the BLM home page, click on "Search Documents by Type," and in the search box insert Michigan for the state, last name of "Rose," and the first name of, let's say, "David." From the list that is displayed in Figure 6–17, click on the second listing of David Rose of Kent County, Ionia Land Office, Document 7594.

Figure 6–17. Three warrants were in the list displayed. The first one lindicates by the "MW" in the accession number that it is a Military Warrant.

Image	Accession	Names	Date	Doc #	State	Meridian	Twp - Rng	Aliquots	Sec. #	County
	MW-0760-252	P ROSE, DAVID, W ROSE, DAVID	1/2/1854	7594	MI	Michigan-Toledo Strip	009N - 011W	NE¼SE¼	18	Kent
	MI0810 .153	P ROSE, DAVID	8/18/1837	25286	MI	Michigan-Toledo Strip	003S - 002E	S½NE¼	13	Jackson
	MI2610 .257	P ROSE, DAVID M	10/10/1839	3271	MI	Michigan-Toledo Strip	004N - 007W	W½SW¼	28	Barry

We now have Figure 6–18. Note the legal description just above the map in Figure 6–18 and jot it down. (In this case, 9 North, 11 West, Section 18.) Next, access the homepage and click on "Survey Plats and Field Notes." Fill in what you know from the legal description, that is, state, county, township and direction, range and direction, and the meridian. We won't pick a specific type of survey - we'll just see what comes. After filling in the form, click "Search Surveys" at the bottom to perform the search.

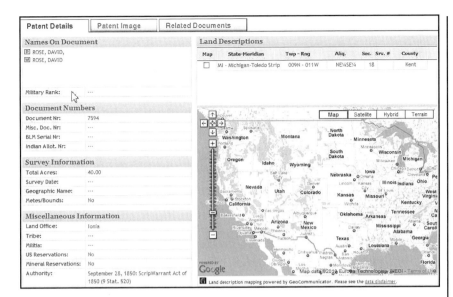

Figure 6–18. This displays essential information on the land and survey to the left; the legal description is shown above the map.

Below in Figure 6–19 is the result, showing in this case two surveys. There could be many more on another tract.

Survey	Approved / Accepted	State	Meridian	Twp - Rng	Boundaries / Subdivisional	County	Field Notes
Original Survey	3/12/1839	MI	Michigan – Toledo Strip	009.0N - 011.0W	N, S, E, W	Kent	Plat Image	
Original Survey	3/12/1839	MI	Michigan – Toledo Strip	009.0N - 011.0W	Subdivisional		Plat Image	

Figure 6–19. Two surveys are shown. Clicking on them will bring up further details including, if they are available, the plat image and field note images.

Clicking on the first link in Figure 19, Original Survey, a screen with tabs for Survey Details, Plat Details, Plat Image, and Field Note Images appears. These items are not available in all instances. Experiment with each, and in many cases you will access considerable information about the tract of land.

As noted, not all states have surveys available, but many will be added as the BLM is able to do so. In some cases external links to other sites containing the field notes will be provided. Watch for progress on this feature.

Experiment with Searches

There are many other variations to searches that can be conducted. For example, in Figure 6–4 we had only tried searching Thompson Rose as a patentee. If we searched for him by checking "Warrantee" and without designating a state we would have found two military warrants for Thompson Rose for service as a Lieutenant in the Virginia militia. He assigned his rights in both those patents. and instead took out a non-military patent on the tract we've already discussed earlier in this chapter.

The opportunities for search in the BLM patents are varied. Try using the information gleaned from the application file in a variety of BLM searches.

Aliquot
parts are used
to represent the
exact subdivision of
a section of land in the
rectangular survey
system, for example
SW ¼ of NW ½
Section 10 is
an aliquot
part.

✓ The last step in the process to obtain bounty land is the patent issued by the U. S. Government. Check the BLM website at <www.glorecords.blm.gov>.

✓ If the warrant was sold, assigned, or inherited, the patentee will be a person other than the veteran.

✓ In searching the BLM GLO patents, try entering the name of the person sought as Patentee, and, then separately, as Warrantee.

✓ Not all military patents are scanned and online at the time of this writing, but they may be when you read this.

✓ Surveys and field notes are being added, but it will be a long process.

FINDING AIDS, etc.

Some of the finding aids mentioned previously and some additional sources are discussed here in further detail.

ARCHIVAL RESEARCH CATALOG (ARC)

The Archival Research Catalog (ARC) is the online catalog of NARA's nationwide holdings in the Washington, D.C., area, and their Regional Archives and Presidential Libraries. To learn more about this system go directly to: <www.archives.gov/research/arc/about-arc.html>.

According to NARA's website there are currently 2,720,765 cubic feet of holdings described in ARC. This breaks down to:

- 520 Record Groups
- 2,365 Collections
- 102,598 Series
- 292,887 Items
- 3,265,988 File Units

Most of the records described in ARC are not related to bounty land. but the ARC search can be narrowed to those that could be useful by inserting the words "bounty land" in ARC's search box at <www.archives.gov/research/arc>. Many pages concerning bounty land documents will be listed for access. Click on any of those links to determine whether that series of records might be useful. ARC is a helpful tool to supplement our knowledge of these important records.

The goal of NARA's ARC is to eventually include all the finding aids of the National Archives.

A National Archives Record Group (RG) represents a major archival unit that comprises the records of a large organization such as a Government bureau or independent agency.

PRELIMINARY INVENTORY 22 (PI 22)

Harry P. Yoshpe and Philip P. Brower's *Preliminary Inventory 22*[1] was published in 1949 but nonetheless is useful. Kvasnicka *Trans-Mississippi West* (see later in this chapter) replaces PI 22 with updated material but only for those states which are west of the Mississippi River. Virginia and other east of the Mississippi River states are not covered so we still depend upon PI 22 for information on those records. For our purposes in discussing military lands, Entries 1 through 19 of PI 22 are pertinent. They are reproduced here in their entirety. The numbers to the right are entry numbers in PI 22 and should be cited when requesting records:

When ordering these listed records specify that they are from PI 22, and include the page number and the entry number (shown here on the right of each series.)

WARRANTS ISSUED UNDER ACT OF JULY 9, 1788. 7 ft. <u>1</u>
Warrant Nos. 6913–14220 (Warrant Nos. 1–6912 are missing, having been
destroyed when the British captured and burned much of Washington
in 1814).

WARRANTS ISSUED UNDER ACTS OF MAR. 3, 1803, AND APR. 15, 1806. 5 ft. <u>2</u>
Warrant Nos. 1–2500. Warrants issued under the act of 1803 include
Nos. 1 to 272. Warrants issued under the act of 1806 begin with number
273, as the same numbered series was continued. Warrants issued under
these acts could be exchanged for land scrip under the scrip acts
of 1830, 1832, 1833, 1835, and 1852. In cases where this was done,
the original warrants will be found in entry 4. Applications for Military-Bounty-Land
Scrip.

VIRGINIA MILITARY-BOUNTY-LAND WARRANTS SURRENDERED TO
THE FEDERAL GOVERNMENT. 20 vols. 14 ft. <u>3</u>
These are arranged according to the volume and page number of the
patent record in the General Land Office covering patents issued in
satisfaction of Virginia Military Warrants. Military-bounty-land warrants
located in Virginia, or in that part of Virginia which later became
West Virginia and Kentucky, were surrendered to the State of Virginia,
or to the State of Kentucky after its admission to the Union. Virginia
warrants exchanged for scrip are found in the series listed below
as *Applications for Military-Bounty-Land Scrip*, entry 4.
Many Virginia warrants are also to be found in the series *Virginia
Resolution Warrants.* entry 5, and Virginia Military Warrants
- Kendrick Cases," entry 19.

APPLICATIONS FOR MILITARY-BOUNTY-LAND SCRIP. 35 ft. <u>4</u>
These applications were made under the following acts:
Acts of May 30, 1830, and July 13, 1832: 1–1994.
Act of Mar. 2, 1833: 1–225.
Act of Mar. 3, 1835: 1–970.
Act of Aug. 31, 1852: 1–1689.
This series contains applications to exchange both Federal and Virginia
military-bounty-land warrants for scrip. The application file usually
contains the original warrant which it was desired to exchange for
scrip, together with correspondence and other papers.

VIRGINIA RESOLUTION WARRANTS. 2 pkgs. 6 in. <u>5</u>
Warrants issued under resolutions of the Virginia General Assembly
authorizing grants in addition to those already made. Included are

---

1   See Chapter 1, footnote 40.

the original warrants; affidavits and certificates as to service,
death, and heirship; and plats and records of survey.

LISTS OF FEDERAL REVOLUTIONARY-BOUNTY-LAND WARRANTS PRESENTED
FOR REGISTRY. 2 in.   <u>**6**</u>
These lists (1799–1800) were presented for the purpose of being registered
under the acts of June 1, 1796, and Mar. 2, 1799,
for locations in the United States Military Reserve in Ohio: 1–199. Each
list includes citations of the warrant numbers, persons in whose names
the warrants were issued, acreages, by whom and for whom presented
for registration, and a statement to the effect that the warrants
belong to the subscriber.

TREASURY CERTIFICATES. 2 in.   <u>**7**</u>
Certificates as to compliance with the acts of 1796 and 1799, accompanied
by certifications by the Secretary of the Treasury that persons registering
their warrants in pursuance of said acts are entitled to patents.
The date of patent and place of record are noted in each case.

CANADIAN REFUGEE WARRANTS. 1802–11. 2 pkgs. 4 in.   <u>**8**</u>
Warrants issued to Canadian refugees during the Revolutionary War
pursuant to the act of Apr. 7, 1798, *An Act for the relief of
the Refugees from the British provinces of Canada and Nova Scotia,*
and the act of Feb. 18, 1801, *An Act regulating the grants of
land appropriated for the refugees from the British provinces of Canada
and Nova Scotia.* On the back of each warrant is a notation of
the date of patent and the place of record. In addition, there is
a bundle of powers of attorney and related documents under which locations
were made and patents drawn. These packages of warrants bear the notation
Ohio Vol. 214, pp. 1–166.

CANADIAN VOLUNTEER WARRANTS. 1 FT.   <u>**9**</u>
Warrants nos. 1–285, issued to Canadian volunteers in the War of 1812
pursuant to the act of Mar. 5, 1816, An Act granting Bounties
in Land and extra Pay to certain Canadian Volunteers. Warrants
include powers of attorney, assignments, correspondence, notations
of the tracts located, date of patent, and the place of record. In
addition, there is a package of miscellaneous papers including correspondence
regarding locations and issuance of patents; *List of Canadian
Volunteer Warrants issued by War Dep't. Received 1st March 1820,*
citing the original claimant, rank, corps or regiment, and number
and date of warrant; and returns of locations in that part of the
District of Vincennes included with the Territory of Indiana, pursuant
to the act of 1816, citing warrant number, date, acreage, to whom
granted, to whom assigned, location of tract, date of location, and
by whom location was made.

EXCHANGE CERTIFICATES. 4 in.   <u>**10**</u>
Batesville, Ark.: 1–33; Little Rock, Ark.: 1–36; Quincy, Ill.: 1–
7; and Springfield, Ill.: 1. These include Register's certificates
issued under the act of May 22, 1826, *An Act authorizing certain
soldiers of the late war to surrender the bounty lands drawn by them,
and to locate others in lieu thereof,* to the effect that patents
for earlier locations had been relinquished and new locations made
in lieu thereof, and patents for new locations. Files include correspondence,
affidavits that tracts originally located are unfit for cultivation,
and relinquishments.

REVOLUTIONARY WARRANTS. 1 in.

11

    Warrant Nos. 1299, 2314, 2340, 2346, 2359, 2418, 2442, 2453, 2458, 2462, 2467, 2468, 2470, 2471, 2475, 2479. These warrants are a part of the series begun under the acts of Mar. 3, 1803, and Apr. 15, 1806, though issued on authority of the acts of Jan. 27, 1835 (*An Act to extend the time for issuing Military Land Warrants to the Officers and soldiers of the Revolution*), of July 27, 1842, and of June 26, 1848. Filed with the warrants are applications to locate lands, certificates of location, correspondence, and other papers.

PAPERS RELATING TO REVOLUTIONARY-BOUNTY-LAND SCRIP. 1 pkg. 2 in.

12

    These papers relate to scrip issued under the Act of Aug. 31, 1852 including correspondence and other documents regarding assignments and locations of scrip requests for approval of such assignments, and certificates of death and heirship.

DOUBLE-BOUNTY WARRANTS ISSUED UNDER ACT OF MAY 6, 1812. 2 ft.

13

    320-acre warrants: 1–1101.

WARRANTS ISSUED UNDER ACTS OF DEC. 24, 1811, JAN. 11, 1812, MAY 6,1812, AND JULY 27, 1842. 41 ft.

14

    60-acre warrants: 1–28085.

WARRANTS ISSUED UNDER ACT OF FEB. 11, 1847. 244 FT.

15

    40-acre warrants: 1–7585.
    160-acre warrants: 1–80689.

WARRANTS ISSUED UNDER ACT OF SEPT. 28, 1850. 396 ft.

16

    40-acre warrants: 1–103978.
    80-acre warrants: 1–57718
    160-acre warrants. 1–27450.

WARRANTS ISSUED UNDER ACT OF MAR. 22, 1852. 129 ft.

17

    40-acre warrants: 1–9070.
    80-acre warrants: 1–1699.
    160-acre warrants: 1–1223.

WARRANTS ISSUED UNDER ACT OF MAR. 3, 1855. 516 ft.

18

    10-acre warrants: 1–4.
    40-acre warrants: 1–542.
    60-acre warrants: 1–359.
    80-acre warrants: 2–49491.
    100-acre warrants: 1–6.
    120-acre warrants: 1–97096.
    160-acre warrants: 1–115783.

VIRGINIA MILITARY WARRANTS-KENDRICK CASES. 11 pkgs. 1 ft.

19

    Consist chiefly of Virginia military-bounty-land warrants and including surveyor's certificates as to warrant locations, requests for patents, powers of attorney, plats, notes, contracts, correspondence, and protests against surveys and the issuance of patents on warrants. Eleazer P. Kendrick, surveyor Virginia Military District, Chillicothe, Ohio, figures prominently in these papers.

KVASNICKA *Trans-Mississippi West 1804–1912*

This tremendous undertaking by Robert M. Kvasnicka, published in 2007 in two volumes (the second being a supplemental guide), is mentioned in Chapter 1.[2] The paragraphs are numbered, for example, 49.A.30 with "49" being the record group number, "A" the division designation, and "30" the paragraph number. The listings of particular interest to those seeking bounty records are pages 41–65 (Division "B" Recorder's Division) and pages 190–200 (Division "D" Mail and Files) of the first volume.

Division "B" (Recorder's Division) contains a number of records important to bounty land research. Laws are cited, descriptions are included, as well as other related items of importance. Many letters were written and received concerning bounty land.

These volumes by Kvasnicka provide researchers with an understanding of what is available and how to cite a record for retrieval in NARA's RG 49. For an example, the following is from page 47.

> 49.B24. Volumes 10–29 of the series of letters sent relating to Revolutionary War and War of 1812 military bounty land warrants 1821–78 (29 vols., 6 ft.), [UD 45], are specifically labeled "Military-Late War with Great Britain," but volumes 1–9 also include letters concerning bounty land warrants issued for service in the War of 1812. The letters are addressed to officials of other Government departments, attorneys and agents, and private persons, as well as to land office officials in several States and Territories, including Arkansas, Iowa, and Missouri, concerning lands located in those areas. Record copies of form letters sent transmitting patents on military bounty land warrants, ca. 1817–25 (8 vols., 10 in.), [UD 108], to private persons and to Registers of local land officers cover lands located in Arkansas, Illinois, and Missouri Territories. The form letters, including warrant numbers and legal land descriptions, are arranged by Territory and thereunder chronologically with the letters for Missouri Territory (1 vol.) covering the period December 5, 1820, to April 19, 1825. Each volume is indexed by name of addressee.

The above could be helpful to researchers seeking information on veterans who served in the Revolution and the War of 1812. If ordering information from the above, state it is from Kvasnicka's *Trans-Mississippi West,* and include page number, the paragraph description number of 49.B24, and the series number shown in curly brackets, in this instance either UD 45 or UD 108.

Pages 190–200 from Division "D" Mail and Files in the book contain a number of items from Warrants, Case Files, Indexes, and Registers are included. These are potentially of use in the search of an ancestor. For example, on page 195 in paragraph 49.DM61:

> 4. "Suspension Docket of Military Bounty Land Warrants Issued Under the Act of 1850," 1850–1858 (1 vol., 1 in.), [UD 2212]. The entries are arranged in sections for 40 acres and 80 acres, and thereunder numerically by warrant number. They give date of letter, warrant number, name of locator and land office, and remarks.

---

2   See Chapter 1, page 17, and also footnote 45 on page 17.

A Monumental New Guide

The above-listed items involve warrants that had been suspended; these would not be readily found in other sources.

Researchers should peruse all of the descriptions on pages 41–65 of Kvasnicka's book to see if any of the items appear to be pertinent to their search.

COMPILED MILITARY SERVICE RECORDS (CMSR)

From the Revolutionary War through the Mexican War (the last war which is pertinent to a bounty land search) the National Archives has Compiled Military Service Records (CMSR). These records were "carded" by extracting information from a variety of sources: payrolls, muster rolls, hospital registers, etc. Those involving the same soldier were then combined and inserted into a jacket with the name and a few identification details. These CMSR are available, arranged alphabetically by surname. The index to each series for the different wars has been microfilmed. The actual records have not been microflmed (with the exception of the Revolutionary War and the 1784–1811 period) but the indexes are a starting point to determine if the man served.

Some men who served in this period were not eligible for bounty land or did not apply. However, for those seeking the possibility of finding an ancestor who was entitled to bounty land the CMSR could be a good place to search for a record that discloses if the ancestor even fought in one of those wars. If so, the CMSR listing would provide valuable details specifying the company, time period, etc., to initiate a search for the bounty land records.

The following is a listing of the CMSR for the various wars in which veterans were entitled to bounty land benefits:

Figure 7–1 is a card from a CMSR of the Revolutionary War.

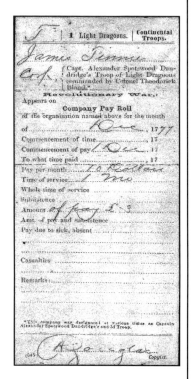

Revolutionary War
M860. *General Index to Compiled Military Service Records of Revolutionary War Soldiers.* 58 rolls. DP. [The records have been microfilmed on M881.]

Post Revolutionary War
M694. *Index to Compiled Service Records of Volunteer Soldiers Who Served From 1784 to 1811.* 9 rolls. DP. [These records have been filmed on M905.]
See also: Virgil D. White, *Index to Volunteer Soldiers, 1784–1811* (Waynesboro, Tenn.: National Historical Publishing Co., 1987).

War of 1812
M602. *Index to Compiled Service Records of Volunteer Soldiers Who Served During the War of 1812.* [In spite of the title it includes some regular army.] 234 rolls.

Indian Wars (prior to Civil War)
INDEXES to Compiled Military Service Records of Volunteers. (May be an occasional regular army man listed, especially if he served in both the volunteer corps and the regular army.)

M629. *Index to Compiled Service Records of Volunteer Soldiers Who Served during Indian Wars and Disturbances.* 42 Rolls. Each card shows soldier's name, rank, unit, and the war or disturbance.

Note: Virgil D. White's published *Index to Volunteer Soldiers in Indian Wars and Disturbances, 1815–1858* (Waynesboro, Tenn.: The National Historical Publishing Co., 1994) only includes those names listed in M629 above.

M244: Ala., Creek War 1836–37
M243: Ala., Cherokee Removal 1838
M245: Ala., Fla. War 1835–58
M1086: Fla., in Fla. War 1835–58
M907: Ga., Cherokee Disturbances and Removal 1836–38
M239: La., Fla. War 1836
M241: La., War of 1837–38
M258: N.C. Cherokee Disturbances and Removal 1837–38
M908: Tenn., Cherokee Disturbances and Removal, and Field and Staff of the Army of the Cherokee Nation 1836–39

Mexican War
M616. *Index to Compiled Service Records of Volunteer Soldiers ... During the Mexican War.* 41 rolls.

Some compiled service records are on: M863 Miss.; M1028 Pa.; M638 Tenn.; M278 Tex.; M351 Mormon Organizations. For the rest use NATF 86.

T317. *INDEX to Mexican War Pension Files 1887–1926.* 14 rolls. Service 1846–48. (Includes some enlisted men.)

See also: Virgil D. White, *Index to Mexican War Pension Files* (Waynesboro, Tenn.: National Historical Publishing Co., 1989).

Regular Army (Enlisted men)
(Check these sources for service in 1855 or earlier.)
M233. *Register of Enlistments in the U. S. Army, 1798–1914.* 81 rolls. [An index to M233 is available in an online database at <www.ancestry.com>. Included are images from the registers.]
See also:
Loose Enlistment. Textual. RG 94 PI 17 *Preliminary Inventory...of the Adjutant General's Office.*
Two series: 1798-July 14, 1894 and July 15, 1894-October 31, 1912. Cite: RG 94, PI 17 Entry 91
A third series: Cite RG 94 PI 17 Entry 19 (this is a smaller series)

Remember that not all of the men listed in the above applied for bounty land. But a significant number of them did so which makes the CMSR a good place to initiate a search.

AMERICAN STATE PAPERS (ASP)
The *American State Papers* consist of thirty-eight published volumes of legislative and executive documents of Congress covering the period 1789 to 1838.[3] The volumes are arranged into ten classes or series which include:

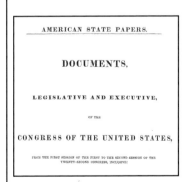

I.   Foreign Relations
II. Indian Affairs

---

3   *American State Papers: Documents, Legislative and Executive, of the Congress of the United States.* Washington, D.C.: Gales and Seaton, 1832+. See particularly series VIII, *Public Lands,* 8 volumes and series IX, *Claims,* 1 volume. Hereafter, *American State Papers.*

The collection contains 6,278 documents published in the various volumes from 1831 to 1861. Not all of the classes are complete for the 1789–1838 period. Every volume contains an index and all but one has a table of contents. The volumes that are especially helpful to those searching bounty land records are series eight (Public Lands) and series nine (Claims).

Fraudulent Claims: An example of the usefulness of the *American State Papers* is an entry in Volume 1 1789–1809, page 827, of the Public Lands volume online at <http://memory.loc.gov>. The Committee on Public Lands in the 10th Congress, 2d Session, Report No. 157, took up the case of several persons, Job Sheldon, William Irwin, and Richard Long. They were soldiers of the Revolution and in consequence of their services they were entitled to military bounty lands but they were defrauded of their rights. The land warrants that were issued supposedly to satisfy them for their services instead went to unauthorized others who made application, without their knowledge. Cases of this type posed a difficult problem for Congress for in their opinion Congress had to rely on the public record and could not issue second warrants. They denied the petitions. This example presents only one of many reasons why a bounty land claim could end up on the pages of these volumes.

Figure 7–2, from American State Papers, 10th Congress, 2d Session, No. 157, Public Lands: Volume 1, page 827 of the online version at the Library of Congress website. In the published volumes (footnote 3, this chapter) see Public Lands: Volume 1, page 911.

1809.]   MILITARY BOUNTY LAND WARRANTS.   827

10th Congress.   No. 157.   2d Session.

MILITARY BOUNTY LAND WARRANTS FRAUDULENTLY OBTAINED.

COMMUNICATED TO THE HOUSE OF REPRESENTATIVES FEBRUARY 27, 1809.

Mr. Jeremiah Morrow, from the Committee on the Public Lands, to whom were referred the several petitions of Job Sheldon, William Irwin, and Richard Long, made the following report:

The petitioners state that they were soldiers in the revolutionary war, and in consequence of their services entitled to military bounty lands, out of which they have been defrauded; land warrants having issued to satisfy them for their services before they made application, without their knowledge, and to persons not authorized to receive them.

The petitioners pray that an inquiry may be instituted in order to devise a mode of relief.

The committee cannot doubt but that, in some instances, the soldiers of the revolutionary war have been defrauded out of their bounty lands. But they believe that it is now as difficult to provide a safe remedy for such wrongs, as it was formerly to adopt regulations entirely to prevent them; had a degree of evidence been required by law to be produced by persons claiming bounty lands, so as entirely to have prevented impositions, the effect must have been to render it difficult, and, in some instances, impracticable, for persons rightfully entitled to have substantiated their claims. It is not the opinion of the committee that the regulations on the subject were insufficient or defective, or that the Government are accountable for the frauds that may have been committed.

The committee are informed that numerous applications are made at the War Office for land warrants on claims which it appears by the records have been already satisfied. To authorize a second warrant to be issued whenever it is alleged by the original claimant that the first had not issued by his order, or to his assignee, would be to sanction the principle that the public record is not conclusive evidence; the admission of which principle would expose the public to extensive impositions. Nor do the committee believe a legislative provision necessary to afford a remedy in the cases stated by the petitioners, inasmuch as the military land warrants are designated by numbers; they can ascertain the number of the warrants issued on their respective claims, the person to whom issued, and the lots on which they have been located, and, by resorting to a court of competent jurisdiction, obtain full and complete relief against the fraud practised upon them. From the foregoing view of the subject, the committee respectfully submit the following resolution:

Resolved, That the petitioners have leave to withdraw their several petitions.

The images for the *American State Papers* are available at the Library of Congress website.[4] Also check their website for additional series of interest: debates, letters, journals, bills and resolutions, and more.

LEGISLATIVE CLAIMS (Private Acts)

An easily accessible source is the *Digested Summary of Private Claims.*[5] Information in these alphabetically arranged name volumes is located by the surname of the claimant. Adjacent to the name is information indicating the nature of the claim, how it was brought to the House of Representatives, which committee handled it, the Congress and session, report number, dates, disposition, etc. the volumes cover many varied types of claims from military pensions, foreign affairs, commerce, and many others. Of particular interest to genealogical researchers are those claims for bounty land which were considered by the Public Lands committee.

An example will demonstrate the usefulness. Under the name of Frederick Copenrath, his heirs filed a claim for legalization of a transfer of bounty land warrant No. 7943. This came before the 30th Congress, 1st session, in the form of a petition. The report was No. 261, the subsequent number of the bill was 256. Armed with this

Copeland, William, and others, attorney for.	Compensation for services, &c., in revolutionary war.	1	3	Petition	378	....	....	....	......	Referred to Secretary War.
Copeland, William, and others, attorney for.	Compensation for services, &c., in revolutionary war.	3	2	Rep. of Secretary War.	278	....	....	....	......	Laid on table.
Copeland Zaccheus	Compensation for services as a revolutionary soldier.	23	1	Petition	440	Rev. Claims.				
Copeland, Zaccheus......	Compensation for services as a revolutionary soldier.	24	1	Petition	740	Claims	644	Adverse	......	Laid on table.
Copenrath, Frederic, heirs of.	Legalization of a transfer of bounty land warrant, No. 7943.	30	1	Petition	....	Public Lands.....	261	Report and bill.	256	Referred to Committee Whole House.
Copes, Thomas P........	Conditional pre-emption to certain inundated land in Missouri.	24	1	Petition	435	Public Lands.				
Copes, Thomas P........	Conditional pre-emption to certain inundated land in Missouri.	25	2	Petition	95	Public Lands.				
Copes, Thomas P........	Conditional pre-emption to certain inundated land in Missouri.	25	3	Petition	92	Public Lands	114	Adverse	......	Laid on table.
Copes, Thomas P........	(See Cornelius Campbell, and others.)									

Figure 7–3. From **Digested Summary of Private Claims.**

information the researcher can visit a library with a government documents section and access the report and the bill. Even better, make a photocopy of the page, highlight the item of interest, and contact:

The Center for Legislative Archives
700 Pennsylvania Ave., NW
Washington, DC 20408
<legislative.archives@nara.gov>

---

4   Visit their website at <http://memory.loc.gov/ammem/amlaw/lwsp.html>.

5   *Digested Summary and Alphabetical List of Private Claims which have been Presented to the House of Representatives from the First to the Thirty-first Congress, Exhibiting the Action of Congress on Each Claim, with References to the Journals, Reports, Bills, etc., Elucidating its Progress.* 3 volumes. 1853. Reprint. Baltimore, Md.: Genealogical Publishing Co., Inc., 1970, hereafter *Digested Summary of Private Claims.* A CD version of the *Digested Summary* which includes the first three volumes above, plus the 4th and 5th volume which include the 32nd to the 41st and the 42nd to the 46th Congress is available from Archive CD Books USA. Visit their website at <www.archivecdbooksusa.com>.

Request a quotation for the whole file from that office. The legislative consultants have access to the original records involving the claim, not just the published reports and bills.

Another example of what might be found is in the claim of Thomas Flowers, et al, for renewal of bounty land warrant. This came before the Public Land Claims committee. At the 20th Congress, 1st Session, a resolution was recorded in Journal page 175 in 1828; the Bill, No. 194, passed with an amendment. The actual file could add details for the Flowers descendants.

Occasionally the committee which handled private land claims (rather than public claims) also handled a bounty land related claim. The representative of Solomon Cooper, for example, petitioned for permission to locate 2,560 acres of revolutionary bounty land granted to the deceased, but from which he is barred by limitation. This came before the 25th Congress, 2nd session, Private Claims Committee, and is recorded in Journal Page 226. Accessing the original petition is likely to add additional details for interested family members.

SUNDRY OTHER AIDS

OTHER CONGRESSIONAL RECORDS: In addition to bounty land items among the private claims to the legislature are other congressional records. Check the *U.S. Statutes at Large,* and also session laws, debates, etc. Go to < http://memory.loc.gov/ammem/amlaw> to find those that have been digitized. Then check the index for each volume under such headings as "Bounty Land," "Land," "Revolutionary War," "War of 1812," etc. An unexpected document on a relative could be the reward.

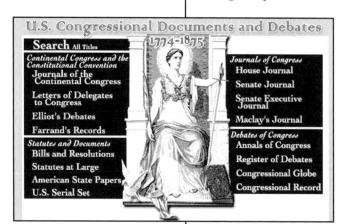

The Library of Congress website at <http://memory.loc.gov/ammem /amlaw>.

STATE LEGISLATURES: The state legislatures also became involved in the efforts to obtain the bounty land earned by the veterans. For example, a Resolution of the General Assembly of Indiana, February 13, 1840, states that Peter Houston, of the county of Monroe, Indiana, during the revolutionary war with Great Britain was a private in General Rutherford's regiment of North Carolina militia, and also under Colonial Bovard, during the battle of Romsaw's mill. Peter Houston never asked for compensation for his services, although in indigent circumstances. Now the General Assembly of Indiana was asked to use their influence to procure an act of Congress to grant to Peter a portion of the refuse lands lying east of Indianapolis State road, leading from Indianapolis in Bloomington, in the county of

Monroe, as reasonable compensation for his services. This was approved January 31, 1840.[6]

STATE ARCHIVES AND STATE LIBRARIES: A researcher, Ms. Petty of Carthage, Mississippi, attended two week-long courses coordinated by this author at the Institute of Genealogy and Historical Research at Samford University in Alabama. One was on land records, and the other on military records. These two courses included information on bounty land and as a result Ms. Petty has experienced great success in locating those records in her research. One discovery particularly surprised her and it is that event that she shares with us.

The target of the search was Mr. and Mrs. Joseph D. Eads, two early members of Ms. Petty's church which was formed in 1846. The purpose of the present-day quest was to locate records to help substantiate an application for a historical marker. What Ms. Petty discovered is that Mr. Eads, who was an attorney, kept ledgers and daybooks from his law practice and from a mercantile business. Those records eventually made their way to the Mississippi State Archives where Ms. Petty located them. She was astounded to find that many notes in connection with Mr. Eads' efforts to assist clients with their bounty land applications have been preserved. If an application was rejected, he listed the reason. When it was accepted, he recorded the warrant number. There were at least sixty of these entries for War of 1812, Indian Wars, and the Mexican Wars. The lesson learned—examine the manuscript catalogs of the various repositories that are visited!

NATIONAL UNION CATALOG OF MANUSCRIPT COLLECTIONS (NUCMC): A source that can be helpful for unusual finds is the National Union Catalog of Manuscript Collections. Use their search engine at <www.loc.gov/coll/nucmc/oclcsearch.html> and read about accessing the collection at <www.loc.gov/coll/nucmc>.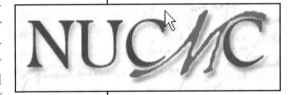

ADDITIONAL READING MATERIAL: There are many books and articles published regarding bounty land. Two that should be particularly mentioned for their overall comments and readibility are:

    E. Wade Hone, *Land & Property Research in the United States,* Salt Lake City, Utah: Ancestry, Incorporated, 1997.
    Sandra Hargreaves Luebking, "Land Records," in *The Source: A Guidebook to American Genealogy,* Loretto Dennis Szucs and Sandra Hargreaves Luebking, editors, Provo, Utah: Ancestry Publishing, 2006.

---

6   "Resolution of the General Assembly of Indiana, to obtain a donation of land to Peter Houston, for his services in the revolutionary war." 1st Session, 1840.

Reading the various articles and books suggested in the Bibliography is also encouraged. It will result in some interesting statistics and details such as the following chart:

BOUNTY LAND WARRANTS ISSUED TO JUNE 30, 1907		
WAR OF THE REVOLUTION, ACTS PRIOR TO 1800		
WAR OF THE REVOLUTION, ACTS PRIOR TO 1800	16,663	2,165,000
WAR OF 1812	29,186	4,845,920
ACT OF 1847	88,274	13.213,640
ACT OF 1850	189,145	13,168,480
ACT OF 1852	11,992	694,400
ACT OF 1855	263,100	34,151,500
		68,239,030

We might wonder, examining the above, how many of these patents were actually located by the patentee rather than an assignee or heir. Opponents of bounty land legislation would say far too few, and unfortunately, that appears to be so. We might also question whether the promise of land encouraged enlistments. In any event, the huge body of records the bounty land system generated is a boon to researchers eager to add details to their search.

Reading about bounty land and the laws that created them will enhance a researcher's documentation of their ancestry. It will provide tools needed to locate the valuable documents generated by this award for military service.

POINTS TO REMEMBER IN THIS CHAPTER

√ NARA's Archival Research Catalog (ARC) can be very useful in bounty search by providing details of each of the related collections.

√ Kvasnicka's *Trans-Mississippi West 1804–1914* only covers those states that are west of the river.

√ NARA's *Preliminary Inventory 22* is outdated but still useful for it includes states other than those covered by Kvasnicka.

√ NARA's Compiled Military Service Records (CMSR) do not directly relate to bounty land but can be useful in identifying those who served. Most who did serve (or their heirs) would at some point apply for bounty land.

8 WINDUP

THE INCREDIBLE TALE OF THE O'FLYNG FAMILY

The many laws generating and affecting bounty land could create some complex situations. As an example, let's view the circumstances surrounding the incredible tale of the O'Flyng family.

In preparation for the War of 1812, an act early in 1812 authorized the recruitment for five years of able-bodied men between the ages of eighteen and forty-five.[1] In 1814 a new act allowed recruitments of men between ages of eighteen and fifty.[2]

Additionally, commissioned officers were not eligible for bounty land in this war until 1850 and thus lost their claim to such lands when commissioned.

Enter now the O'Flyng family—Abigail the mother, Patrick the father, and sons Patrick, Temple E., and Edmund. This father and three sons all served the required time. But *all* were at first denied any benefits.

On February 26, 1816, it was communicated to the House of Representatives that Abigail O'Flyng was the wife of Patrick O'Flyng of the town of Batavia, New York.[3] During the "late war" (War of 1812) Patrick and three of his sons, Patrick, Temple E., and Edmund O'Flyng, enlisted and were honorably discharged: Edmund on account of his distinguished good conduct and bravery, was discharged and obtained a cadet's appointment to West Point; Patrick on account of his brave and meritorious conduct was promoted to a lieutenancy, and Temple to that of ensign.

The account continues that since the war Patrick (the son) died, without wife or child. Temple E. received a wound of which he died

---

1   2 *U.S. Stat.* 671-73, January 11, 1812.
2   3 *U.S. Stat.* 146-47, December 10, 1814.
3   *ASP,* IX Claims, 469, February 26, 1816.

the next day, leaving no wife or child. The petitioner Abigail stated that her husband, being old and infirm, was unable to attend to his business, but upon making application to the War Department for the bounty land of her husband and sons, she was denied because her husband Patrick, being above forty-five when enlisted, and her youngest son Edmund, being under eighteen at the time of his enlistment, the act of Congress did not authorize the Department to issue warrants because their age was higher and lower than had been required. Neither were her two other sons, Patrick and Temple, eligible in consequence of their promotion as commissioned officers, and that would have rendered Edmund ineligible too regardless of his age since Edmund had also been promoted.

Abigail, therefore, was left without means of support, even though three sons and her husband served in the War of 1812. Her husband was too old at enlistment for the benefit, one son was not only too young at enlistment for bounty land awards but had been promoted, and two sons who were meritoriously promoted as officers lost their benefits because officers were not at that time eligible for bounty land. This incredible set of circumstances did not however go unnoticed.

The Congressional Report went on to state "It cannot possibly be the policy of the Government to withhold the bounty land of a soldier because he has distinguished himself by his bravery and good conduct so as to merit and receive an appointment in the army." The committee "are of opinion that the persons interested are entitled to relief ..."

Fortunately Congress agreed. On April 16, 1816, the law was changed which corrected the iniquity based on age, and prevented the loss of land bounty benefits when promoted to a commissioned officer.[4]

A few days later on April 24th a private bill was passed by Congress for the relief of Patrick O'Flyng and Abigail O'Flyng and Edmund O'Flyng allowing a land warrant for 480 acres to Patrick (the father) and Abigail O'Flyng, and 160 acres to Edmund O'Flyng.[5] Additionally, Patrick and Abigail were allowed half pay for five years for each of their sons, Lieutenant Patrick O'Flyng, and Ensign Temple E. O'Flyng, who died while in service of the United States.[6]

Justice prevailed.

"JUSTICE PREVAILED"

4   3 *U.S. Stat.* 285–287, April 16, 1816.
5   *The Public Statues at Large of the United States of America, from the Organization of the Government in 1789, to March 3, 1845*, edited by Richard Peters, Esq. (Boston: Charles E. Little and James Brown, 1846). Vol. VI, "A List of the Private Acts of Congress." Online at: <http://memory.loc.gov/cgi-bin/ampage?collId=llsl&fileName=006/llsl006.db&recNum=4>.
6   6 *U.S. Stat.* 163, April 24, 1816.

APPENDIX A – The Laws

*Statutes of the Continental Congress and the
U.S. Congress Relating to Military Bounty Land*

In presenting the acts, in some instances only the portion relating to bounty land has been included, and other sections not pertinent to that subject omitted. If so, the notation "Rest omitted" is shown. Original marginal annotations are omitted; those marginal notes which do appear were prepared by the present author. Spelling and punctuation of the statutes has been retained. The following are presented chronologically and taken either from JCC (Journals of the Continental Congress, 1774-1789) and U.S. Stat. (the public statutes at large of the United States of America).

Journals of the Continental Congress.
Vol. V pp. 654–655.
Wed. August 14, 1776.

Resolved, Therefore, that these states will receive all such foreigners who shall leave the armies of his Britannic majesty in America, and shall chuse to become members of any of these states; that they shall be protected in the free exercise of their respective religions, and be invested with the rights, privileges and immunities of natives, as established by the laws of these states; and, moreover, that this Congress will provide, for every such person, 50 Acres of unappropriated lands in some of these states, to be held by him and his heirs in absolute property.

This statute encourages desertion from the British by offering 50 acres of unappropriated land.

Journals of the Continental Congress.
Vol. V 762–763.
Mon. September 16, 1776.

That eighty eight batallions be inlisted as soon as possible, to serve during the present war... That twenty dollars be given as a bounty to each non-commissioned officer and private soldier, who shall inlist to serve during the present war, unless sooner discharged by Congress.

That Congress make provision for granting lands, in the following proportions: to the officers and soldiers who shall so engage in the service, and continue therein to the close of the war, or until discharged by Congress, and to the representatives of such officers and soldiers as shall be slain by the enemy;

Such lands to be provided by the United States, and whatever expence shall be necessary to procure such land, the said expence shall be paid and borne by the states in the same proportion as the other expences of the war, viz.

To a colonel, 500 acres; to a lieutenant colonel, 450; to a major, 400; to a captain, 300; to a lieutenant, 200; to an ensign, 150; each non-commissioned officer and soldier, 100 ...[Rest omitted]

The first general statute providing for bounty land in various amounts for Revolutionary War enlistments. The highest officer in this initial resolution eligible for awards was a colonel. The non-commissioned officers and private soldiers received $20.00 in addition to land.

Journals of the Continental Congress.
Vol. V 781.
Wed. September 18, 1776

That the bounty and grants of land offered by Congress, by a resolution of the 16 instant, as an encouragement to the officers and soldiers to engage to serve in the army of the United States during the war, shall extend to all who are or shall be inlisted for that term; the bounty of ten dollars, which any of the soldiers have received from the continent on account of a former inlistment, to be reckoned in part payment of the twenty dollars offered by the said resolution:

Factors in a previous payment of $10.00 some may have already received.

Important provision making the bounty land unassignable.

Journals of the Continental Congress.
Vol. V 787–788.
Fri. September 20, 1776.
> [Omitted p. 787 and part of 1788]
> *Resolved,* That this Congress will not grant lands to any person or persons, claiming under the assignment of an officer or soldier.
> [Rest omitted]

Referred to the Board of Treasury.

Journals of the Continental Congress.
Vol. XIII 116.
Tues. January 26, 1779.
> A resolution of the general assembly of Virginia, dated December 18, 1778, for the more effectually enabling Congress to comply with the promise of a bounty in lands to the officers and soldiers of the army on continental establishment...*Ordered,* that this be referred to the Board of Treasury.

Journals of the Continental Congress.
Vol. XVI 10–11.
Mon. January 3, 1780.
> According to order, Congress took into consideration the report of the Medical Committee, *viz.* That each and every officer hereafter mentioned and described in this resolve, belonging to the medical department in the hospitals, or army, who is now in the service of the United States, and shall continue therein during the war, and not hold any office or profit under the United States, or any of them, shall after the conclusion of the war, be entitled to receive, annually, for the term of seven years, if they shall live so long, *viz;* the physicians general, surgeons general, the physician and surgeon general of the army, the deputy directors general, each, a sum equal to the half pay granted and extended to a colonel in the line of the army by a resolve of Congress, of the 15 of May, 1778; the senior surgeons and physicians, assistant deputy directors, and the apothecary general, each, a sum equal to the half pay of a lieutenant colonel, granted and extended by the resolve aforesaid; the junior or second surgeons of the hospitals and the regimental surgeons, each, a sum equal to the half pay of a major in the line, granted and extended as aforesaid; the mates of the regimental surgeons, the apothecary's mates, or assistants, each, a sum equal to the half pay granted and extended to a lieutenant in the line of the army, by the resolve aforesaid; the whole of the foregoing allowances are to be subject in every respect to the same rules, restrictions and limitations, upon which the half pay of the aforementioned officers of the line was granted and extended by the said resolve, of the 15 of May, 1778.

Adds benefits for officers belonging to the medical department.

> That each of the aforementioned and described officers in the medical department, or their legal representatives, respectively, shall be entitled to the like quantity of lands with the aforementioned and described officers of the line, in due proportion to the sums granted to them respectively by the preceding resolve, upon the same conditions, and subject to the same rules, restrictions and limitations, as the grants of lands to the aforementioned officers of the line, by a resolve of Congress of the 16 September, 1776.

Journals of the Continental Congress.
Vol. XVII 726–727.
Sat. August 12, 1780.
> ... That the provision for granting land, by the resolution of September 16th, 1776, be and is hereby extended to the general officers, in the following proportion to wit: a major general 1100 acres; a brigadier general 850 acres ...

Benefits for major general and brigadier general added.

Journals of the Continental Congress.
Vol. XVIII 847.
Fri. September 22, 1780.
> Congress resumed the consideration of the report of the committee on the medical department, and on the consideration of the following paragraph, viz.
> That the several officers whose pay is established as above, except the clerks and stewards, shall at the end of the war be entitled to a certain provision of land in the proportion following, viz.
> The director to have the same quantity as a brigadier general. Chief physicians and purveyors, the same as a colonel. Physicians and surgeons and apothecary the same as lieutenant colonel.

Regimental surgeons and assistants to the purveyor and apothecary, the same as a major. Hospital and regimental surgeons mates, the same as a captain.' "

A motion was made by Mr. [Frederick A.] Muhlenberg, seconded by Mr. [Theodorick] Bland, to amend the paragraph by inserting after the words, "intitled to" the words following, viz. "half pay in the same manner and under like restrictions as officers of the line"; and on the question to agree to the amendment, the yeas and nays being required by Mr. [John] Fell,

[Here appears a table of votes]

So it was resolved in the affirmative.

On the question to agree to the paragraph as amended, the yeas and nays being required by Mr. [Ezekiel] Cornell,

[table]

So it was resolved in the affirmative.

Further provisions regarding the medical department.

Journals of the Continental Congress.
Vol. XVIII 896–897.
Tues. October 3, 1780.

That the regiment commanded by Colonel Moses Hazen be continued on its present establishment, and that all non-commissioned officers and privates, being foreigners belonging to any of the reduced regiments and corps, be incorporated therewith, and all volunteers from foreign states, who are now in the service, or may hereafter join the American army, be annexed to the said regiment:

Whereas, by the foregoing arrangement, many deserving officers must become supernumerary, and it is proper that regard be had to them:

Resolved, That, from the time the reform of the army takes place, they be entitled to half pay for seven years, in specie, or other current money equivalent, and also grants of land at the close of war, agreeably to the resolution of the 16th September, 1776.

Benefits for the regiment commanded by Colonel Moses Hazen.

Supernumerary officers to receive half pay for life and also to receive land grants. [Supernumerary were those exceeding a fixed, prescribed number; extra. They exceeded the required or desired number of officers needed. They could become supernumerary for a variety of reasons.]

Journals of the Continental Congress.
Vol. XXVIII 379–382.
Fri. May 20, 1785.

[Omitted pp. 375-378]

And whereas Congress, by their resolutions of September 16 and 18 in the year 1776, and the 12th of August, 1780, stipulated grants of land to certain officers and soldiers of the late continental army, and by the resolution of the 22d September, 1780, stipulated grants of land to certain officers in the hospital department of the late continental army: for complying therefore with such engagements. Be it ordained, That the secretary at war, from the returns in his office, or such other sufficient evidence as the nature of the case may admit, determine who are the objects of the above resolutions and engagements, and the quantity of land to which such persons or their representatives are respectively entitled ... [here provides for certificates to be transmitted to the commissions of the loan offices of the different states which shall include the quantity of land he is entitled to, and the township, or fractional part of a township, and range out of which his portion is to be taken] ... Where any military claimants of bounty in lands shall not have belonged to the line of any particular state, similar certificates shall be sent to the board of treasury, who shall execute deeds to the parties for the same. ... [Omitted are other provisions for refugees from Canada, etc.] Saving and reserving always, to all officers and soldiers entitled to lands on the northwest side of the Ohio, by donation or bounty from the commonwealth of Virginia, and to all persons claiming under them, all rights to which they are so entitled, under the deed of cession executed by the delegates for the state of Virginia, on the first day of March, 1784, and the act of Congress accepting the same; and in the end, that the said rights may be fully and effectually secured, according to the true intent and meaning of the said deed of cession and act aforesaid. Be it Ordained, that no part of the land included between the rivers called the little Miami and Sciota, on the northwest side of the river Ohio, be sold, or in any manner alienated, until there shall first have been laid off and appropriated for the said Officers and Soldiers, and persons claiming under them, the lands they are entitled to, agreeably to the said deed of cession and act of Congress accepting the same.

Done by the United States in Congress assembled, the 20th day of May, in the year of our Lord 1785, and of our sovereignty and independence the ninth.

Provisions laying out some procedural matters regarding the Virginia Military District in Ohio. and providing that no part of the land set aside for Virginia's military district to be sold or alienated until land for the Officers and Soldiers was laid off.

Journals of the Continental Congress.
Vol. XXIII 666.

APPENDIX: The Acts

A tract to be set aside for satisfying military bounties only.

Fri. October 12, 1787.

Report...That a Tract of land to be bounded by [blank] be reserved and set a part for the purpose of satisfying the Military Bounties due to the late Army, and no locations other than for the said Bounties be permitted within the said Tract, until they shall be fully satisfied.

Journals of the Continental Congress.
Vol. XXXIII 695–696.
Mon. October 22, 1787.

That a million of Acres of land to be bounded east by the seventh range of townships, south by the land contracted for by Cutler and Sargent and to extend north as far as the ranges of townships and westward so far as to include the above quantity, also a tract to be bounded as follows beginning at the mouth of the river Ohio thence up the Mississippi to the river Au Vause thence up the same until it meets a west line from the mouth of the little Wabash thence easterly with the said West line to the Great Wabash, thence down the same to the Ohio and thence with the Ohio to the place of beginning, be reserved and set apart for the purpose of satisfying the military bounties due to the late Army and that no locations other than for the said bounties be permitted within the said tract until they shall be fully satisfied ...

Acreage set aside for the two tracts in Ohio and in Illinois. [Troubles with Indians forced the United States to later abandon these tracts for use by veterans.]

Journals of the Continental Congress.
Vol. XXXIV 307–309.
Wed. July 9, 1788.

Be it further ordained, That the Secretary of War issue warrants for bounties of land to the several Officers and soldiers of the late continental Army who may be entitled to such bounties, or to their respective assigns or legal representatives, certifying therein the rank or station of each Officer, and the line, regiment corps and company in which the Officer or soldier served.

Be it further ordained, That the Geographer by warrant under his hand and seal appoint one surveyor to each of the two tracts or districts of land set apart for satisfying the said bounties, by the Act of Congress of the 22ᵈ of October last; And that the persons entitled to lands by virtue of warrants issued as aforesaid, shall be at liberty to locate them on any part of the two tracts of land set apart as aforesaid, provided that each location and survey shall be bounded on one side by one of the external boundaries of one of the tracts aforesaid, or by some prior survey therein ... That if any Officer or soldier, or Assignee or grantee of either shall desire to have their bounty of land allotted in the townships or fractional parts thereof, lately drawn for the Army by the Secretary of War, out of the first four ranges of townships surveyed west of the Ohio, and shall cause such his desire in writing, together with his land warrant to be deposited in the Office of the Secretary At War before the first of July 1789, the said Secretary shall cause so much of the said Townships which, have been drawn for the Army, to be drawn for by lot as will satisfy the warrants so deposited ...

Makes warrants assignable. Eligibility for officers and soldiers of the Continental line (State line not mentioned).

Further provisions regarding the military lands in Ohio and Illinois but these two tracts were later abandoned.

1 *U.S. Statutes* **182–184.**
FIRST CONGRESS. Sess. II. 1790.

Chap. XL. *An Act to enable the Officers and Soldiers of the Virginia Line on continental Establishment, to obtain Titles to certain Lands lying northwest of the River Ohio, between the Little Miami and Sciota.*

SEC. 1. *Be it enacted by the Senate and House of Representatives of the United States of America in Congress assembled,* That the act of Congress of the seventeenth of July, one thousand seven hundred and eighty-eight, relative to certain locations and surveys made by, or on account of the Virginia troops on continental establishment upon lands between the Little Miami and Sciota rivers, northwest of the Ohio, be, and the same is hereby repealed.

And whereas the agents for such of the troops of the state of Virginia, who served on the continental establishment in the army of the United States, during the late war, have reported to the executive of the said state, that there is not a sufficiency of good land on the south-easterly side of the river Ohio, according to the act of cession from the said state to the United States, and within the limits assigned by the laws of the said state, to satisfy the said troops for the bounty lands due to them, in confirmity to the said laws: to the intent therefore that the difference between what has already been located for the said troops, on the south-easterly side of the side river, and the aggregate of what is due to the whole of the said troops, may be located on the north-westerly side of the said river, and between the Sciota and Little Miami rivers, as stipulated by the said state:

SEC. 2. *Be it further enacted,* That the secretary of the department of war shall make return to the executive of the state of Virginia of the names of such of the officers, non-commissioned of-

Repeals the establishment of the two tracts in Ohio and Illinois.

Provides the process by which those who served in Virginia's Continental line who were entitled to land in the Virginia Military District in Ohio can receive their patents.

ficers and privates of the line of the said state, who served in the army of the United States, on the continental establishment, during the late war, and who, in conformity to the laws of the said state, are entitled to bounty lands; and shall also in such return state the aggregate amount in acres due to the said line by the laws aforesaid.

SEC. 3. *And be it further enacted,* That it shall and may be lawful for the said agents to locate to and for the use of the said troops, between the rivers Sciota and Little Miami, such a number of acres of good land as shall, together with the number already between the said two rivers, and the number already located on the south-easterly side of the river Ohio, be equal to the aggregate amount, so to be returned as aforesaid by the secretary of the department of war.

[Sec. 4-7 omitted.]

Approved, August 10, 1790.

The Secretary of War shall return a list of names of officers, non-commissioned officers and privates of the Virginia Line who served in the army of the United States on Continental Establishment and who are entitled to bounty.

Agents to locate lands between the river Sciota and Little Miami for use of the troops.

1 *U.S. Statutes* 222.
FIRST CONGRESS. Sess. III. 1791.

Chap. XXVII. *An Act for granting lands to the Inhabitants and settlers at Vincennes and the Illinois country, in the territory northwest of the Ohio, and for confirming them in their possessions.*

[Sec. 1 through 5 omitted.]

SEC. 6: *And be it further enacted,* That the governor of the said territory be authorized to make a grant of land not exceeding one hundred acres, to each person who hath not obtained any donation of land from the United States, and who, on the first day of August one thousand seven hundred and ninety, was enrolled in the militia at Vincennes or in the Illinois country, and has done militia duty, the said land to be laid out at the expense of the grantees, and in such form and place as the governor shall direct. *Provided nevertheless,* That no claim founded upon purchase or otherwise, shall be admitted within a tract of land heretofore occupied by the Kaskaskia nation of Indians, and including their village, which is hereby appropriated to the use of the said Indians.

[Sec. 7 and 8 omitted.]

Approved, March 3, 1791.

Grants 100 acres to anyone who has not received any donation of land from the United States and who on 1 August 1790 was enrolled in the militia at Vincennes or in the Illinois country. Not to be located within the tract of the Kaskaskia nation of Indians.

1 *U.S. Statutes* 394.
THIRD CONGRESS. Sess. I. 1794.

Chap. LXII. *An Act to amend the act intituled "An act to enable the officers and soldiers of the Virginia line on Continental Establishment, to obtain titles to certain Lands lying northwest of the river Ohio, between the Little Miami and Sciota.*

Be it enacted by the Senate and House of Representatives of the United States of America in Congress assembled, That all and every officer and soldier of the Virginia line on continental establishment, his or their heirs or assigns, entitled to bounty lands on the northwest side of the river Ohio, between the Sciota and Little Miami rivers, by the laws of the state of Virginia, and included in the terms of cession of the said state to the United States, shall, on producing the warrant, or a certified copy thereof, and a certificate under the seal of the office where the said warrants are legally kept, that the same or a part thereof remains unsatisfied, and on producing the survey, agreeably to the laws of Virginia, for the tract or tracts to which he or they may be entitled, as aforesaid, to the Secretary of the Department of War, such officer and soldier, his or their heirs or assigns, shall be entitled to, and receive a patent for the same from the President of the United States, any thing in any former law to the contrary notwithstanding. *Provided,* that no letters patent shall be issued for a greater quantity of land than shall appear to remain due on such warrant, and that before the seal of the United States shall be affixed to such letters patent the Secretary of the department of War shall have endorsed thereon that the grantee therein named or the person under whom he claims was originally entitled to such bounty lands, and every such letters patent shall be countersigned by the Secretary of State and a minute of the date thereof, and the name of the grantee shall be entered in his office in a book to be specially provided for that purpose.

Approved, June 9, 1794.

Opens the Virginia Military District to Virginia's veterans but only those who served in the Continental Line.

1 *U.S. Statutes* 464–469.
FOURTH CONGRESS. Sess. I. 1796.

Chap. XXIX. *An Act providing for the Sale of the Lands of the United States, in the territory northwest of the river Ohio, and above the mouth of Kentucky river.*

Section 1. *Be it enacted by the Senate and House of Representatives of the United States of America in Congress assembled,* That a Surveyor General shall be appointed, whose duty it shall be to engage a sufficient number of skilful surveyors, as his deputies; whom he shall cause, without delay,

APPENDIX: The Acts

This May 18, 1796, act is known as the Land Act of 1796 and should not be confused with the military bounty act passed June 1, 1796, in 1 U.S. Stat. 490.

Changes numbering pattern of the 36 sections of the rectangular survey system.

to survey and mark the unascertained outlines of the lands lying northwest of the river Ohio, and above the mouth of the river Kentucky, in which the titles of the Indian tribes have been extinguished, and to divide the same in the manner herein after directed; he shall have authority to frame regulations and instructions for the government of his deputies; to administer the necessary oaths, upon their appointments; and to remove them for negligence or misconduct in office.

SEC. 2. *Be it further enacted,* That the part of the said lands, which has not been already conveyed by letters patent, or divided, in pursuance of an ordinance in Congress, passed on the twentieth of May, one thousand seven hundred and eight-five, or which has not been heretofore, and during the present session of Congress may not be appropriated for satisfying military land bounties, and for other purposes, shall be divided by north and south lines run according to the true meridian, and by others crossing them at right angles, so as to form townships of six miles square, unless where the line of the late Indian purchase, or of tracts of land heretofore surveyed or patented, or the course of navigable rivers may render it impracticable; and then this rule shall be departed from no further than such particular circumstances may require. The corners of the townships shall be marked with progressive numbers from the beginning; each distance of a mile between the said corners shall be also distinctly marked with marks different from those of the corners. One half of the said townships, taking them alternately, shall be subdivided into sections, containing, as nearly as may be, six hundred and forty acres each, by running through the same, each way, parallel lines, at the end of every two miles; and by marking a corner, on each of the said lines, at the end of every mile; the sections shall be numbered respectively, beginning with the number one, in the northeast section, and proceeding west and east alternately, through the township with progressive numbers, till the thirty-sixth be completed. And it shall be the duty of the deputy surveyors, respectively, to cause to be marked, on a tree near each corner made, as aforesaid, and within the section, the number of such section, and over it, the number of the township, within which such section may be; and the said deputies shall carefully note, in their respective field-books, the names of the corner trees marked, and the numbers so made: The fractional parts of townships shall be divided into sections, in manner aforesaid, and the fractions of sections shall be annexed to, and sold with, the adjacent entire sections. All lines shall be plainly marked upon trees, and measured with chains, containing two perches of sixteen feet and one half each, subdivided into twenty-five equal links, and the chain shall be adjusted to a standard to be kept for that purpose. Every surveyor shall note in his field-book the true situations of all mines, salt licks, salt springs and mill seats, which shall come to his knowledge; all water courses, over which the line he runs shall pass; and also the quality of the lands. These field-books shall be returned to the Surveyor General, who shall therefrom cause a description of the whole lands surveyed, to be made out and transmitted to the officers who may superintend the sales: he shall also cause a fair plat to be made of the townships, and fractional parts of townships, contained in the said lands, describing the subdivisions thereof, and the marks of the corners. This plat shall be recorded in books to be kept for that purpose; a copy thereof shall be kept open at the Surveyor General's office, for public information; and other copies sent to the places of the sale, and to the Secretary of the Treasury.

SEC. 3. *Be it further enacted,* That a salt spring lying upon a creek which empties into the Sciota river, on the east side, together with as many contiguous sections as shall be equal to one township, and every other salt spring which may be discovered, together with the section of one mile square which includes it, and also four sections at the centre of every township, containing each one mile square, shall be reserved, for the future disposal of the United States; but there shall be no reservations, except for salt springs, in fractional townships, where the fraction is less than three fourths of a township.

SEC. 4. *Be it further enacted,* That whenever seven ranges of townships shall have been surveyed below the Great Miami, or between the Sciota river and the Ohio company's purchase, or between the southern boundary of the Connecticut claims and the ranges already laid off beginning upon the Ohio river and extending westwardly, and the plats thereof made and transmitted, in conformity to the provisions of this act, the said sections of six hundred and forty acres (excluding those hereby reserved) shall be offered for sale, at public vendue, under the direction of the governor or secretary of the western territory, and the Surveyor General: such of them as lie below the Great Miami shall be sold at Cincinnati; those of them which lie between the Sciota and the Ohio company's purchase, at Pittsburg; and those between the Connecticut claim and the seven ranges, at Pittsburg. And the townships remaining undivided shall be offered for sale, in the same manner, at the seat of government of the United States, under the direction of the Secretary of the Treasury, in tracts of one quarter of a township lying at the corners thereof, excluding the four central sections, and the other reservations before mentioned; *Provided always,* that no part of the lands directed by this act to be offered for sale, shall be sold for less than two dollars per acre.

SEC. 5. *Be it further enacted,* That the Secretary of the Treasury, after receiving the aforesaid plats, shall forthwith give notice, in one newspaper in each of the United States, and of the territories northwest and south of the river Ohio, of the times of sale; which shall, in no case, be less than two months from the date of the notice; and the sales at different places shall not commence, within less than one month of each other: And when the governor of the western territory, or Secretary of the Treasury, shall find it necessary to adjourn, or suspend the sales under their direction, respectively, for more than three days, at any one time, notice shall be given in the public newspapers, of such suspension, and at what time the sales will re-commence.

Method of giving notice provided.

SEC. 6. *Be it further enacted,* That immediately after the passing of this act, the Secretary of the Treasury shall, in the manner herein before directed, advertise for sale, the lands remaining unsold in the seven ranges of townships, which were surveyed, in pursuance of an ordinance of Congress, passed the twentieth of May, one thousand seven hundred and eighty-five, including the lands drawn for the army, by the late Secretary of War, and also those heretofore sold, but not paid for; the townships which by the said ordinance, are directed to be sold entire, shall be offered for sale, at public vendue in Philadelphia, under the direction of the Secretary of the Treasury, in quarter townships, reserving the four centre sections, according to the directions of this act. The townships, which, by the said ordinance, are directed to be sold in sections, shall be offered for sale at public vendue, in Pittsburg, under the direction of the governor or secretary of the western territory, and such person as the President may specially appoint for that purpose, by sections of one mile square each, reserving the four centre sections, as aforesaid; and all fractional townships shall also be sold in sections, at Pittsburg, in the manner, and under the regulations provided by this act, for the sale of fractional townships: *Provided always,* That nothing in this act shall authorize the sale of those lots, which have been heretofore reserved in the townships already sold.

Public sales to be held in Pittsburg.

SEC. 7. *Be it further enacted,* That the highest bidder for any tract of land, sold by virtue of this act, shall deposit, at the time of sale, one twentieth part of the amount of the purchase money; to be forfeited, if a moiety of the sum bid, including the said twentieth part, is not paid within thirty days, to the treasurer of the United States, or to such person as shall be appointed by the President of the United States, to attend the places of sale for that purpose; and upon payment of a moiety of the purchase money, within thirty days, the purchaser shall have one year's credit for the residue; and shall receive from the Secretary of the Treasury, or the governor of the western territory, (as the case may be) a certificate describing the land sold, the sum paid on account, the balance remaining due, the time when such balance becomes payable; and that the whole land sold will be forfeited, if the balance is not then paid; but that if it shall be duly discharged, the purchaser, or his assignee, or other legal representative, shall be entitled to a patent for the said lands; And on payment of the said balance to the treasurer, within the specified time, and producing to the Secretary of State a receipt for the same, upon the aforesaid certificate, the President of the United States is hereby authorized to grant a patent for the lands to the said purchaser, his heirs or assigns: And all patents shall be countersigned by the Secretary of State, and recorded in his office. But if there should be a failure in any payment, the sale shall be void, all the money theretofore paid on account of the purchase shall be forfeited to the United States, and the lands thus sold shall be again disposed of, in the same manner as if a sale had never been made: *Provided nevertheless,* that should any purchaser make payment of the whole purchase money, at the time when the payment of the first moiety is directed to be made, he shall be entitled to a deduction of ten per centum on the part, for which a credit is hereby directed to be given; and his patent shall be immediately issued.

How payment is to be made.

SEC. 8. *Be it further enacted,* That the Secretary of the Treasury, and the governor of the territory north west of the river Ohio, shall respectively, cause books to be kept, in which shall be regularly entered, an account of the dates of all the sales made, the situation and numbers of the lots sold, the price at which each was struck off, the money deposited at the time of sale, and the dates of the certificates granted to the different purchasers. The governor, or secretary of the said territory shall, at every suspension or adjournment, for more than three days, of the sales under their direction, transmit to the Secretary of the Treasury a copy of the said books, certificated to have been duly examined, and compared with the original. And all tracts sold under this act, shall be noted upon the general plat, after the certificate has been granted to the purchaser.

Books to be kept.

SEC. 9. *And Be it further enacted,* That all navigable rivers, within the territory to be disposed of by virtue of this act, shall be deemed to be, and remain public highways: And that in all cases, where the opposite banks of any stream, not navigable, shall belong to different persons, the stream and the bed thereof shall become common to both.

SEC. 10. And *Be it further enacted,* That the surveyor general shall receive for his compensation, two thousand dollars per annum; and that the President of the United States may fix the compensa-

Compensation provided.

Provision for fees.

Oaths required.

Establishes the U.S. Military District.

Orders the survey of the land to be set aside for use of veterans.

Territory is northwest of the river Ohio and above the mouth of the Kentucky river.

Restricts sales of land in the U.S. Military District to a minimum of a quarter of a township.

tion of the assistant surveyors, chain carriers, and axe men: *Provided*, that the whole expense of surveying and marking the lines, shall not exceed three dollars per mile, for every mile that shall be actually run or surveyed.

SEC. 11. And *Be it further enacted,* That the following fees shall be paid for the services to be done under this act, to the treasurer of the United States, or to the receiver in the western territory, as the case may be; for each certificate for a tract containing a quarter of a township, twenty dollars; for a certificate for a tract containing six hundred and forty acres, six dollars; and for each patent for a quarter of a township, twenty dollars; for a section of six hundred and forty acres, six dollars: And the said fees shall be accounted for by the receivers, respectively.

SEC. 12. *And be it further enacted,* That the surveyor general, assistant surveyors, and chain carriers, shall, before they enter on the several duties to be performed under this act, severally take an oath or affirmation, faithfully to perform the same; and the person, to be appointed to receive the money on sales in the western territory, before he shall receive any money under this act, shall give bond with sufficient security, for the faithful discharge of his trust: That, for receiving, safe keeping, and conveying to the treasury the money he may receive, he shall be entitled to a compensation to be hereafter fixed.

Approved, May 18, 1796.

1 *U.S. Statutes* 490–491.
FOURTH CONGRESS. Sess. I. 1796.

Chap. XLVI. *An Act regulating the grants of land appropriated for Military services, and for the Society of the United Brethren, for propagating the Gospel among the Heathen.*

Section 1. *Be it enacted by the Senate and House of Representatives of the United States of America in Congress assembled,* That the Surveyor General be, and he is hereby required, to cause to be surveyed, the tract of land beginning at the northwest corner of the seven ranges of townships, and running thence fifty miles due south, along the western boundary of the said ranges; thence due west to the main branch of the Scioto river; thence up the main branch of the said river, to the place where the Indian boundary line crosses the same; thence along the said boundary line, to the Tuscaroras branch of the Muskingum river, at the crossing place above Fort Lawrence; thence up the said river to the point, where a line, run due west from the place of beginning, will intersect the said river; thence along the line so run to the place of beginning; and shall cause the said tracts to be divided into townships of five miles square, by running marking and numbering the exterior lines of the said townships, and marking corners in the said lines, at the distance of two and one half miles from each other, in the manner directed by the act, intituled "An act providing for the sales of the lands of the United States, in the territory northwest of the river Ohio, and above the mouth of Kentucky river;" and that the lands above described, except the salt springs therein, and the same quantities of land adjacent thereto, as are directed to be reserved with the salt springs, in the said recited act, and such tracts within the boundaries of the same, as have been heretofore appropriated by Congress, be, and they are hereby, set apart and reserved for the purposes herein after mentioned.

SEC. 2. And *Be it further enacted,* That the said land shall be granted only in tracts containing a quarter of the township to which they belong, lying at the corners thereof; and that the Secretary of the Treasury shall, for the space of nine months, after public notice in the several states and territories, register warrants for military services, to the amount of any one or more tracts, for any person or persons holding the same; and shall immediately after the expiration of the said time, proceed to determine, by lot, to be drawn in the presence of the secretaries of state and of war, the priority of location of the said registered warrants; and the person or persons holding the same, shall severally make their locations, after the lots shall be proclaimed, on a day to be previously fixed in the before mentioned notice; in failure of which, they shall be postponed in locating such warrants, to all other persons holding registered warrants: And the patents for all lands located under the authority of this act, shall be granted in the manner directed by the before mentioned act, without requiring any fee therefor.

SEC. 3. *And Be it further enacted,* That after the time limited for making the locations, as aforesaid, any person or persons holding warrants, of the before mentioned description, sufficient to cover any one or more tracts, as aforesaid, shall be at liberty to make their locations, on any tract or tracts not before located.

SEC. 4. *And Be it further enacted,* That all the lands set apart by the first section of this act, which shall remain unlocated on the first day of January, in the year one thousand eight hundred, shall be released from the said reservation, and shall be at the free disposition of the United States, in like manner as any other vacant territory of the United States. And all warrants or claims for lands on account of military services, which shall not, before the day aforesaid, be registered and located, shall be forever barred.

Bars claims after 1 January 1800, but this was later extended.

SEC. 5. *And Be it further enacted,* That the said surveyor general be, and he is hereby, required to cause to be surveyed three several tracts of land, containing four thousand acres each, at Shoenbrun, Gnadenhutten, and Salem; being the tracts formerly set apart, by an ordinance of Congress of the third of September, one thousand seven hundred and eight-eight, for the society of United Brethren for propagating the gospel among the heathen; and to issue a patent or patents for the said three tracts to the said society, in trust, for the uses and purposes in the said ordinance set forth.

These are non-military issues.

SEC. 6. *And be it further enacted.* That all navigable streams or rivers within the territory to be disposed of, by virtue of this act, shall be deemed to be and remain public highways. And that, in all cases, where the opposite banks of any stream not navigable shall belong to different persons, the stream and the bed thereof shall be common to both.

Approved, June 1, 1796.

1 *U.S. Statutes* 547.
FIFTH CONGRESS. Sess. II. 1798.

CHAP. XXVI. *An Act for the relief of the Refugees from the British provinces of Canada and Nova Scotia.*

Section 1. *Be it enacted by the Senate and House of Representatives of the United States of America in Congress assembled,* That to satisfy the claims of certain persons claiming lands under the resolutions of Congress, of the twenty third of April, one thousand Seven hundred and eighty-three, and the thirteenth of April, one thousand seven hundred and eighty five, as refugees from the British provinces of Canada and Nova Scotia, the Secretary for the Department of War be, and is hereby authorized and directed to give notice in one or more of the public papers, of each of the states of Vermont, Massachusetts, New York, New Hampshire, and Pennsylvania, to all persons having claims under the said resolutions, to transmit to the war office, within two years after the passing of this act, a just and true account of their claims to the bounty of Congress.

Pertains to the previous act of 23 April 1783 and 13 April 1785, regarding refugees from the British provinces of Canada and Nova Scotia.

SEC. 2. *And be it further enacted,* That no other persons shall be entitled to the benefit of the provisions of this act, than those of the following descriptions, or their widows and heirs, *viz:* First, those heads of families, and single persons, not members of any such families, who were residents in one of the provinces aforesaid, prior to the fourth day of July, one thousand seven hundred and seventy-six, and who abandoned their settlements, in consequence of having given aid to the United Colonies or States, in the revolutionary war against Great Britain, or with intention to give such aid, and continued in the United States, or in their service, during the said war, and did not return to reside in the dominions of the king of Great Britain, prior to the twenty-fifth of November, one thousand seven hundred and eighty three. Secondly, the widows and heirs of all such persons as were actual residents, as aforesaid, who abandoned their settlements as aforesaid, and died within the United States, or in their service, during the said war: And thirdly, all persons who were members of families at the time of their coming into the United States, and who, during the war, entered into their service.

Those entitled.

SEC. 3. *And be it further enacted,* That the proof of the several circumstances necessary to entitle the applicants to the benefits of this act, may be taken before a judge of the supreme or district court of the United States, or a judge of the supreme or superior court, or the first justice or first judge of the court of common pleas or county court of any state.

SEC. 4. *And be it further enacted,* That at the expiration of fifteen months from and after the passing of this act, and from time to time thereafter, it shall be the duty of the Secretary for the department of War, to lay such evidence of claims as he may have received, before the secretary and comptroller of the treasury, and with them, proceed to examine the testimony, and give their judgment what quantity of land ought to be allowed to the individual claimants, in proportion to the degree of their respective services, sacrifices and sufferings, in consequence of their attachment to the cause of the United States; allowing to those of the first class, a quantity not exceeding one thousand acres; and to the last class, a quantity not exceeding one hundred, making such intermediate classes as the resolutions aforesaid, and distributive justice, may, in their judgment, require; and make report thereof to Congress. And in case any such claimant shall have sustained such losses and sufferings, or performed such services for the United States, that he cannot justly be classed in any one general class, a separate report shall be made of his circumstances, together with the quantity of land that ought to be allowed him, having reference to the foregoing ratio: *Provided,* that in considering what compensation ought to be made by virtue of this act, all grants, except military grants, which may have been made by the United States, or individual states, shall be considered at the just value thereof, at the time the same were made, respectively, either in whole or in part, as the case, may be, a satisfaction to those who may have received the same: *Provided also,* that no claim under this law shall be assignable until after report made to Congress, as aforesaid, and until the said lands be granted to the persons intitled to the benefit of this act.

Not assignable until after report to Congress and until the land is granted to the persons entitled.

SEC. 5. *Be it further enacted,* That all claims, in virtue of said resolutions of Congress, which shall not be exhibited as aforesaid, within the time by this act limited, shall forever thereafter be barred.

APPROVED, April 7, 1798.

1 *U.S. Statutes* 724.
FIFTH CONGRESS. Sess. III. 1799.

Chap. XXIX. *An Act to amend the act intituled "An act regulating the grants of land appropriated for military services, and for the Society of the United Brethren, for propagating the Gospel among the Heathen."*

Section 1. *Be it enacted by the Senate and House of Representatives of the United States of America in Congress assembled,* That the fourth section of an act, intituled "An act regulating the grants of land appropriated for military services, and for the society of the United Brethren, for propagating the gospel among the Heathen," be, and the same is hereby repealed.

Section 4 of U.S. Stat. 490 repealed.

SEC. 2. *And Be it further enacted,* That all the lands set apart by the first section of the above mentioned act, which shall remain unlocated on the first day of January, in the year one thousand eight hundred and two, shall be released from the said reservation, and shall be at the free disposition of the United States, in like manner as any other vacant territory of the United States. And that all warrants or claims for lands on account of military services, which shall not, before the day aforesaid, be registered and located, shall be for ever barred.

Refers to land in U.S. Military District to be released after 1 January 1802, but this was later extended.

Approved, March 2, 1799.

2 *U.S. Statutes* 7.
SIXTH CONGRESS. Sess. 1. 1800.

Chap. VIII. *An Act giving further time to the holders of Military Warrants, to register, and locate the same.*

Be it enacted by the Senate and House of Representatives of the United States of America in Congress assembled, that the Secretary of the Treasury shall, for the space of fourteen days after the expiration of the nine months heretofore allowed for that purpose, by the act, intituled "An act regulating the grants of land, appropriated for military services, and for the society of the United Brethren for propagating the Gospel among the Heathen," register warrants for military services in the form and manner as is prescribed by the said recited act; and the priority of location of said warrants, and the warrants registered under the said recited act shall be determined by lot, immediately after the expiration of the said fourteen days, and a day for the location shall be fixed by the Secretary of the Treasury, in a public notice given in one of the gazettes of the city of Philadelphia.

Further time allowed to register and locate warrants.

Approved, February 11, 1800.

2 *U.S. Statutes* 14–16.
SIXTH CONGRESS. Sess. I. 1800.

Chap. XIII. *An Act in addition to an act entitled "An Act regulating the grants of land appropriated for Military services, and for the Society of the United Brethren for propagating the Gospel among the Heathen."*

[SEC. 1-4 omitted. Refers to boundaries of the quarter townships, deficiency certificates to be issued for the unsatisfied portion if the township taken up is less than 4000 acres, etc.]

SEC. 5. *And be it further enacted,* That after the priority of location shall have been determined, and after the proprietors or holders of warrants for military services shall have designated the tracts by them respectively elected; it shall be the duty of the Secretary of the Treasury to designate by lot, in the presence of the Secretary of War, fifty quarter townships, of the lands remaining unlocated, which quarter townships, together with the fractional parts of townships remaining unlocated, shall be reserved for satisfying warrants granted to individuals for their military services, in the manner hereafter provided.

Provides for fifty quarter townships and some fractional townships to be divided into 100-acre lots for the benefit of soldiers under certain provisions.

SEC. 6. *And Be it further enacted,* That the land in each of the quarter townships designated as aforesaid, and in such of the fractional parts of quarter townships, as may then remain unlocated, shall be divided by the Secretary of the Treasury, upon the respective plats thereof, as returned by the Surveyor General, into as many lots, of one hundred acres each, as shall be equal, as nearly as may be, to the quantity such quarter township or fraction is stated to contain; each of which lots shall be included, where practicable, between parallel lines, one hundred and sixty perches in length, and one hundred perches in width, and shall be designated by progressive numbers upon the plat, or survey of every such quarter township and fraction respectively.

SEC. 7. *And Be it further enacted,* That from and after the sixteenth day of March next, it shall be lawful for the holder of any warrant granted for military services, to locate, at any time before the first day of January, one thousand eight hundred and two, the number of hundred acres expressed in such warrant, or any lot or lots, from time to time, remaining unlocated within the tracts reserved as aforesaid, and upon surrendering such warrant for the treasury, the holder thereof shall be entitled to receive a patent in the manner, and upon the conditions heretofore prescribed by law; which patent shall in every case express the range, township, quarter township or fraction, and number of the lot located as aforesaid. But no location shall be allowed, nor shall any patent be issued for any lot or lots of one hundred acres, except in the name of the person originally entitled to such warrant, or the heir or heirs of the person so entitled; nor shall any land, so located and patented, to a person originally entitled to such warrant, be considered as in trust for any purchasr, or be subject to any contract made before the date of such patent, and the title to lands acquired, in consequence of patents issued as aforesaid, shall and may be alienated in pursuance of the laws, which have been, or shall be passed in the territory of the United States, northwest of the river Ohio, for regulating the transfer of real property, and not otherwise.

SEC. 8. *And be it further enacted,* That in all cases after the sixteenth of March next, where more than one application is made for the same tract, at the same time, under this act, or under the act to which this is in addition, the Secretary of the Treasury shall determine the priority of location by lot.

[SEC. 9-10 omitted. SEC. 9 provides that it shall be the duty of the Secretary of the Treasury to advertise the tracts that may be reserved for location, in lots of one hundred acres, in one newspaper in each of the states, and in the territory aforesaid, for and during the term of three months.]

Approved, March 1, 1800.

2 *U.S. Statutes* 155–156.
SEVENTH CONGRESS. Sess. I. 1802.

Chap. XXX *An Act in addition to an act, intituled "An act, in addition to an act regulating the grants of land appropriated for military services, and for the society of the United Brethren, for propagating the gospel among the Heathen."*

Be it enacted by the Senate and House of Representatives of the United States of America in Congress assembled, That from and after the passing of this act, and until the first day of January next, it shall be lawful for the holders or proprietors of warrants heretofore granted in consideration of military services, of register's certificates of fifty acres, or more, granted, or hereafter to be granted agreeable to the third section of an act intituled "An act in addition to an act, intituled An act regulating the grants of land appropriated for military services; and for the society of the United Brethren for propagating the gospel among the Heathen," approved the first day of March one thousand eight hundred, to register and locate the same, in the same manner, and under the same restrictions, as might have been done before the first day of January last: *Provided,* that persons holding register's certificates for a less quantity than one hundred acres, may locate the same on such parts of fractional townships, as shall, for that purpose, be divided by the Secretary of the Treasury into lots of fifty acres each.

SEC. 2. *And Be it further enacted,* That it shall be the duty of the Secretary of War to receive claims to lands for military services, and claims for duplicates of warrants issued from his office, or from the land-office of Virginia, or of plats and certificates of surveys founded on such warrants, suggested to have been lost or destroyed, until the first day of January next, and no longer; and immediately thereafter, to report the same to Congress, designating the numbers of claims of each description, with his opinion thereon.

Approved, April 26, 1802.

2 *U.S. Statutes* 236–237.
SEVENTH CONGRESS. Sess. II. 1803.

Chap. XXX. *An Act to revive and continue in force, an act in addition to an act intituled "An act in addition to an act regulating the grants of land appropriated for Military Services and for the Society of the United Brethren for propagating the Gospel among the Heathen," and for other purposes.*

Lessens the previous restrictions of quarter township of 4,000 acre lots. Provides that lots of 100 acres can be located if the warrantee is the original person entitled (thus usually the veteran) or the heirs of that person,.

Further provisions regarding smaller lots.

Be it enacted by the Senate and House of Represetatives of the United States of America in Congress assembled, That the first section of an act in addition to an act intituled "An act in addition to an act regulating the grants of land appropriated for military services, and for the society of the United Brethren for propagating the gosel among the heathen," approved the twenty-sixth of April, eighteen hundred and two, be, and the same is hereby revived and continued in force until the first day of April next.

SEC. 2. *And Be it further enacted,* That the Secretary of War be, and he hereby is authorized, from and after the first day of April next, to issue warrants for military bounty lands to the two hundred and fifty-four persons who have exhibited their claims, and produced satisfactory evidence to substantiate the same to the Secretary of War, in pursuance of the act of the twenty-sixth of April, eighteen hundred and two, intituled "An act in addition to an act, intituled An act in addition to an act regulating the grants of land appropriated for military services, and for the society of the United Brethren for propagating the gospel among the heathen."

Authorizes warrants to 254 persons.

SEC. 3. *And Be it further enacted,* That the holders or proprietors of the land warrants issued by virtue of the preceding section, shall and may locate their respective warrants only, on any unlocated parts of the fifty quarter townships and the fractional quarter townships which had been reserved for original holders, by virtue of the fifth section of an act intituled "An act in addition to An act intituled An act regulating the grants of land appropriated for military services, and for the society of the United Brethren for propagating the gospel among the heathen."

SEC. 4. And *Be it further enacted,* That the Secretary of War be, and he is hereby authorized to issue land warrants to Major General La Fayette, for eleven thousand five hundred twenty acres, which shall, at his option, be located, surveyed and patented, in conformity with the provisions of an act intituled "An act regulating the grants of land appropriated for military services, and for the society of the United Brethren for propagating the gospel among the heathen," or which may be received acre for acre, in payment for any of the lands of the United States north of the river Ohio, and above the mouth of the Kentucky river.

Grant to Major General LaFayette.

SEC. 5. *And be it further enacted,* That all the unappropriated lands within the military tract, shall be surveyed into half sections, in the manner directed by the act intituled "An act to amend the act intituled An act providing for the sale of the lands of the Unites States in the territory northwest of the Ohio, and above the mouth of Kentucky river;" and that so much of the said lands as lie west of the eleventh range within the said tract, shall be attached to, and made a part of the district of Chilicothe, and be offered for sale at that place, under the same regulations that other lands are within the said district.

SEC. 6. And *Be it further enacted,* That the lands within the said eleventh range, and east of it, within the said military tract, and all the lands north of the Ohio company's purchase, west of the seven first ranges, and east of the district of Chilicothe, shall be offered for sale at Zanesville, under the direction of a register of the land-office and receiver of public monies to be appointed for that purpose, who shall reside at that place, and shall perform the same duties and be allowed the same emoluments as are prescribed for and allowed to registers and receivers of the land-offices by law.

SEC. 7. *And Be it further enacted,* That all persons who have obtained certificates for the right of pre-emption to lands by virtue of two acts, the one intituled "An act giving a right of pre-emption to certain persons who have contracted with John Cleves Symmes, or his associates for lands lying between the Miami rivers in the territory of the United States northwest of the Ohio," and the other "An act to extend and continue the provisions of the said act, passed on the first day of May, eighteen hundred and two," and who have not made the first payment therefor, before the first day of January last, shall be allowed until the tenth day of April next to complete the same; and that all persons who have become purchasers of land by virtue of the aforesaid acts, be, and they are hereby allowed until the first day of January, eighteen hundred and five, to make the second instalment; until the first day of January, eighteen hundred and six, to make their third instalment; and until the first day of January, eighteen hundred and seven, to make their fourth and last instalment; any thing in the acts aforesaid, to the contrary notwithstanding.

Premption rights for certain persons who have contracted with John Cleves Symmes.

SEC. 8. *And Be it further enacted,* That where any warrants granted by the state of Virginia, for military services, have been surveyed on the northwest side of the river Ohio, between the Sciota and the little Miami rivers, and the said warrants, or the plats and certificates of survey made thereon, have been lost or destroyed, the persons entitled to the said land may obtain a patent therefor, by producing a certified duplicate of the warrant from the land-office of Virginia, or of the plat and certificate of survey from the office of the surveyor in which the same is recorded, and giving satisfactory proof to the Secretary of War, by his affidavit or otherwise, of the loss or destruction of said warrant, or plat and certificate of survey.

Replacing lost or destroyed warrants of the Virginia Military District.

Approved, March 3, 1803.

2 *U.S. Statutes* 274–275.
EIGHTH CONGRESS. Sess. I. 1804.

Chap. XXXIII. *An Act to ascertain the boundary of the lands reserved by the state of Virginia, northwest of the river Ohio, for the satisfaction of her officers and soldiers on continental establishment, and to limit the period for locating the said lands.*

Be it enacted by the Senate and House of Representatives of the United States of America in Congress assembled, That the line run under the direction of the surveyor-general of the United States, from the source of the Little Miami, towards the source of the Scioto, and which binds on the east, the surveys of the lands of the United States, shall, together with its course continued to the Scioto river, be considered and held as the westerly boundary line, north of the source of the Little Miami, of the territory reserved by the state of Virginia, between the Little Miami and Scioto rivers, for the use of the officers and soldiers of the continental line of that state: *Provided,* that the state of Virginia shall, within two years after the passing of this act, recognize such line as the boundary of the said territory.

Boundary designated for land reserved by the state of Virginia northwest of the river Ohio for the satisfaction of her officers and soldiers of the Continental Establishment

SEC. 2. *And Be it further enacted,* That all the officers and soldiers, or their legal representatives who are entitled to bounty lands within the above-mentioned reserved territory, shall complete their locations within three years after the passing of this act, and every such officer and soldier, or his legal representative, whose bounty land has or shall have been located within that part of the said territory, to which the Indian title has been extinguished, shall make return of his or their surveys to the secretary of the department of war, within five years after the passing of this act, and shall also exhibit and file with the said secretary, and within the same time, the original warrant or warrants under which he claims, or a certified copy thereof, under the seal of the office where the said warrants are legally kept; which warrant, or certified copy thereof, shall be sufficient evidence that the grantee therein named, or the person under whom such grantee claims, was originally entitled to such bounty land: and every person entitled to said lands and thus applying, shall thereupon be entitled to receive a patent in the manner prescribed by law.

Sets time limit.

SEC. 3, *And Be it further enacted,* That such part of the above mentioned reserved territory as shall not have been located, and those tracts of land, within that part of the said territory to which the Indian title has been extenguished, the surveys whereof shall not have been returned to the Secretary of War, within the time and times prescribed by this act, shall thenceforth be released from any claim or claims for such bounty lands, and shall be disposed of in conformity with the provisions of the act, intituled "An act in addition to, and modification of, the propositions contained in the act, intituled An act to enable the peple of the eastern division of the territory, northwest of the river Ohio, to form a constitution and state government, and for the admission of such state into the Union, on an equal footing with the original states; and for other purposes."

Approved, March 23, 1804.

2 *U.S. Statutes* 378.
NINTH CONGRESS. Sess. 1. 1806.

Chap. XXVI. *An Act to authorize the Secretary of War to issue land warrants; and for other purposes.*

Be it enacted by the Senate and House of Representatives of the United States of America in Congress assembled, That the Secretary of War be authorized to issue military land warrants, to such persons as have or shall, before the first day of March, one thousand eight hundred and eight, produce to him satisfactory evidence of the validity of their claims; which warrants, with those heretofore issued, and not yet satisfied, shall, and may be located in the name of the holders or proprietors thereof, at any time prior to the first day of October, one thousand eight hundred and eight, on any unlocated parts of the fifty quarter townships, and the fractional quarter townships, reserved by law, for original holders of military land warrants.

Authorizes the issuance of warrants.

SEC. 2. *And be it further enacted,* That it shall be the duty of the surveyor-general, under the direction of the Secretary of the Treasury, to cause to be surveyed so much of the fifty quarter townships, and the fractional quarter townships aforesaid, as have been, or hereafter may be located according to law, in conformity with the locations made on the plats of the said quarter townships: *Provided,* the whole expense of surveying the same shall not exceed three dollars for every mile actually surveyed.

Approved, April 15, 1806.

Extends time.

160 acres for every able-bodied man recruited or re-enlisted for five years unless sooner discharged. If killed or if he died in service, the heirs and representatives of non-commissioned officers and soldiers to receive the land.

Specifies recruitment of able-bodied men between ages of eighteen and forty-five for five years.

Allows 160 acres for non-commissioned officers or soldiers recruited as stated above (that is, ages eighteen to forty-five who served five years) or the heirs and representatives of those who die in service. (This age restriction was removed by the act of April 16, 1816, 3 U.S. Stat. 285–287.)

2 *U.S. Statutes* 424–426.
NINTH CONGRESS. Sess. II, 1807.

Chap. XXI. *An Act to extend the time for locating Virginia military [land] warrants, for returning surveys thereon to the office of the Secretary of the department of War, and appropriating lands for the use of schools, in the Virginia military reservation, in lieu of those heretofore appropriated.* [A footnote gives an excellent summation of the laws and intent of the Virginia military district.]

Be it enacted . . . That the officers and soldiers of the Virginia line on continental establishment, their heirs or assigns, entitled to bounty lands within the tract reserved by Virginia, between the little Miami and Scioto rivers, for satisfying the legal bounties to her officers and soldiers upon continental establishment, shall be allowed a further time of three years, from the twenty-third of March next to complete their locations, and a further time of five years from the said twenty-third of March next, to return their surveys and warrants . . .

[SEC. 2 & 3 omitted.]
Approved, March 2, 1807.

2 *U.S. Statutes* 669–670.
TWELFTH CONGRESS. Sess. I. 1811.

Chap. X. *An Act for completing the existing Military Establishment.*

Be it enacted by the Senate and House of Representatives ... That the military establishment, as now authorized by law, be immediately completed.

SEC. 2. *And be it further enacted,* That there be allowed and paid to each effective, able bodied man, recruited or re-enlisted for that service, for the term of five years, unless sooner discharged, the sum of sixteen dollars; but the payment of one half of the said bounty shall be deferred until he shall be mustered and have joined the corps in which he is to serve; and whenever any non-commissioned officer or soldier shall be discharged from the service, who shall have obtained from the commanding officer of his company, battalion or regiment a certificate that he had faithfully performed his duty whilst in service, he shall moreover be allowed and paid, in addition to the aforesaid bounty, three months' pay, and one hundred and sixty acres of land; and the heirs and representatives of those non-commissioned officers or soldiers, who may be killed in action, or die in the service of the United States, shall likewise be paid and allowed the said additional bounty of three months' pay, and one hundred and sixty acres of land, to be designated, surveyed and laid off at the public expense, in such manner and upon such terms and conditions, as may be provided by law.

Approved, December 24, 1811.

2 *U.S. Statutes* 671–673.
TWELFTH CONGRESS. Sess. I. 1812.

Chap. XIV. *An Act to raise an additional Military Force.*

Be it enacted by the Senate and House of Representatives ... That there be immediately raised, ten regiments of infantry, two regiments of artillery, and one regiment of light dragoons, to be enlisted for the term of five years, unless sooner discharged.

[SEC. 2 through 11 omitted. Section 11 provided commissioned officers employed in the recruiting service shall be entitled to receive $2.00 for every able bodied man between the ages of eighteen and forty-five years who he enlisted for for a term of five years. Those under twenty one need consent in writing of parent, guardian, or master.]

SEC. 12. *And be it further enacted,* That there shall be allowed and paid to each effective able bodied man, recruited as aforesaid to serve for the term of five years, a bounty of sixteen dollars; but the payment of eight dollars of the said bounty shall be deferred until he shall be mustered, and have joined some military corps of the United States for service. And whenever any non-commissioned officer, or soldier, shall be discharged from the service, who shall have obtained from the commanding officer of his company, battalion or regiment, a certificate, that he had faithfully performed his duty whilst in service, he shall moreover be allowed and paid, in addition to the said bounty, three months' pay, and one hundred and sixty acres of land, and the heirs and representatives of those non-commissioned officers or soldiers who may be killed in action, or die in the service of the United States, shall likewise be paid and allowed the said additional bounty of three months' pay and one hundred and sixty acres of land, to be designated, surveyed and laid off at the public expense, in such manner and upon such terms and conditions as may be provided by law.

[SEC. 13 through 24 omitted.]   Approved, January 11, 1812.

2 *U.S. Statutes* 676–677.
TWELFTH CONGRESS. Sess. I. 1812.

Chap. XXI. *An Act authorizing the President of the United States to accept and organize certain Volunteer Military Troops.* SEC. 1 through SEC. 5 omitted.]

SEC. 6. *And be it further enacted,* That the heirs and representatives of any non-commissioned officer or soldier, who may be killed in action, or die in the actual service of the United States, shall be entitled to receive one hundred and sixty acres of land; to be designated, surveyed and laid off at the public expense, in such manner, and upon such terms and conditions as may be provided by law.

[SEC. 7 through SEC. 8 omitted.]

Approved, February 6, 1812.

2 *U.S. Statutes* 728–730.
TWELFTH CONGRESS. Sess. I. 1812.

Chap. LXXVII. *An Act to provide for designating, surveying and granting the Military Bounty Lands.*

Be it enacted by the Senate and House of Representatives of the United States of America in Congress assembled, That the President of the United States be, and he is hereby authorized to cause to be surveyed a quantity of the public lands of the United States, fit for cultivation, not otherwise appropriated, and to which the Indian title is extinguished, not exceeding in the whole six millions of acres, two million to be surveyed in the territory of Michigan, two millions in the Illinois territory, north of the Illinois river, and two millions in the territory of Louisiana, between the river St. Francis and the river Arkansas; the said lands to be divided into townships, and subdivided into sections and quarter sections, (each quarter section to contain, as near as possible, one hundred and sixty acres,) in the manner prescribed by law for surveying and subdividing the other public lands of the United States; the same price to be allowed for surveying as is fixed for surveying the other public lands in the same territory. And the lands thus surveyed, with the exception of the salt springs and lead mines therein, and of the quantities of land adjacent thereto, as may be reserved for the use of the same by the President of the United States, and the section number sixteen in every township to be granted to the inhabitants of such township for the use of public schools, shall be set apart and reserved for the purpose of satisfying the bounties of one hundred and sixty acres, promised to the non-commissioned officers and soldiers of the United States, their heirs and legal representatives, by the act, entitled, "An act for completing the existing military establishment," approved the twenty-fourth day of December, one thousand eight hundred and eleven, and by the act, entitled, "An act to raise an additional military force," approved the eleventh day of January, one thousand eight hundred and twelve.

SEC. 2. *And Be it further enacted,* That the Secretary for the department of War, for the time being, shall, from time to time, issue warrants for the military land bounties to the persons entitled thereto by the two last mentioned acts, or either of them: *Provided always,* that such warrants shall be issued only in the names of the persons thus entitled, and be by them or their representatives applied for within five years after the said persons shall have become entitled thereto; and the said warrants shall not be assignable or transferable in any manner whatever.

SEC. 3. *And Be it further enacted,* That every person in whose favour such warrants shall have been issued, shall, on delivery of the same at the office of the Secretary of the Treasury or of such other officer as may at the time have, by law, the superintendence of the general land-office of the United States at the seat of government, be entitled to draw by lot in such manner as the officer, at the head of the land-office, under the direction of the President of the United States, may prescribe, one of the quarter sections surveyed by virtue of the first section of this act, in either of the said territories which the person in whose favour such warrant has issued may designate. And a patent shall thereupon be granted to such person, for such quarter section, without requiring any fee therefor.

SEC. 4. *And Be it further enacted,* That no claim for the military land bounties aforesaid shall be assignable or transferable in any manner whatever, until after a patent shall have been granted in the manner aforesaid. All sales, mortgages, contracts, or agreements, of any nature whatever, made prior thereto, for the purpose, or with the intent of alienating, pledging or mortgaging any such claim, are hereby declared and shall be held null and void; nor shall any tract of land, granted as aforesaid, be liable to be taken in execution or sold on account of any such sale, mortgage, contract or agreement, or on account of any debt contracted prior to the date of the patent, either by the person originally entitled to the land or by his heirs or legal representatives, or by virtue of any process, or suit at law, or judgment of court against a person entitled to receive his patent as aforesaid.

Approved, May 6, 1812.

NOTE: 2 U.S. Stat. 794-96 passed January 29, 1813. "An "Act in addition to the act entitled 'An act to raise an additional military force,' and for other purposes" in Section 5 states that all "officers, non-commissioned officers, musicians, and privates, authorized by this act, shall receive the like pay, forage, rations, clothing, and other emoluments (the land and bounty excepted) as the officers of the same grade and corps, non-commissioned officers, musicians, and privates, of the present military establishment." The exclusion referring to the land and bounty may be referring to the fact that officers were not under these early acts entitled to bounty land. This January 29, 1813 act also repealed parts of February 6, 1812 act though it seems to reserve the right for the heirs of the volunteers already enlisted to have bounty land.

Sets aside a military district in Michigan, Illinois, and Louisiana. To satisfy bounties of 160 acres promised to non-commissioned officers and soldiers in the acts of 24 December 1811 and 11 January 1812.

Must be applied for within five years, and are not assignable or transferable "in any manner whatever."

APPENDIX: The Acts

Extends time.

3 *U.S. Statutes* 3–4.
THIRTEENTH CONGRESS. Sess. I. 1813.

Chap. VII. *An Act further extending the time for issuing and locating military land warrants.*

Be it enacted ... That the Secretary of War be authorized to issue land warrants to such persons as have or shall, before the first day of March, one thousand eight hundred and sixteen, produce to him satisfactory evidence of the validity of their claims; which warrants, with those heretofore issued and not yet satisfied, shall and may be located in the name of the holders or proprietors thereof, prior to the first day of October, one thousand eight hundred and sixteen, on any unlocated parts of the fifty quarter townships, and the fractional quarter townships reserved by law for original holders of military land warrants. And patents shall be granted for the land located under this act, in the same manner as is directed by former acts for granting military lands.

Approved, July 5, 1813.

Recruiting officers authorized to enlist men between ages of eighteen and fifty; binding upon those under twenty one and of full age for new recruits under twenty-one given four days to reconsider.

3 *U.S. Statutes* 146–147.
THIRTEENTH CONGRESS. Sess. III. 1814.

Chap. X. *An Act making further provision for filling the ranks of the army of the United States.*

Be it enacted by the Senate and House of Representatives of the United States of America, in Congress assembled, That from and after the passing of this act, each and every commissioned officer who shall be employed in the recruiting service, shall be, and he hereby is authorized to enlist into the army of the United States, any free effective able-bodied man, between the ages of eighteen and fifty years; which enlistment shall be absolute and binding upon all persons under the age of twenty-one years, as well as upon persons of full age, such recruiting officer having complied with all the requisitions of the laws regulating the recruiting service.

SEC. 2. *And be it further enacted,* That it shall not be lawful for any recruiting officer to pay or deliver to a recruit under the age of twenty-one years, to be enlisted by virtue of this act, any bounty or clothing, or in any manner restrain him of his liberty, until after the expiration of four days, from the time of his enlistment; and it shall be lawful for the said recruit at any time during the said four days, to reconsider and withdraw his enlistment, and thereupon he shall forthwith be discharged and exonerated from the same.

SEC. 3. *And be it further enacted,* That so much of the fifth section of the act passed the twentieth day of January, one thousand eight hundred and thirteen, entitled "An act supplementary to the act, entitled 'An act for the more perfect organization of the army of the United States' " as requires the consent in writing of the parents, guardian, or master, to authorize the enlistment of persons under the age of twenty-one years, shall be, and the same is hereby repealed; *Provided however,* That in case of the enlistment of any person held to service as an apprentice, under the provisions of this act, whenever such persons at the time of his enlistment, shall be held by his indenture to serve for any term between two and three years, his master shall be entitled to receive one half of the money bounty; if held, in like manner, to serve between one and two years, the master shall be entitled to receive one-third of the money bounty as aforesaid; and if held, in like manner, to serve one year or less, the master shall be entitled to receive one-fourth of the money bounty as aforesaid.

The "double bounty warrant act" which doubled the bounty to 320 acres in order to encourage new enlistments.

Double bounty awards not to pass to collateral relatives.

SEC. 4. *And Be it further enacted,* That in lieu of the bounty of one hundred and sixty acres of land, now allowed by law, there shall be allowed to each non-commissioned officer and soldier, hereafter enlisted, when discharged from service, who shall have obtained from the commanding officer of his company, battalion, or regiment, a certificate that he had faithfully performed his duty whilst in service, three hundred and twenty acres of land, to be surveyed, laid off, and granted under the same regulations and in every respect in the manner now prescribed by law; and the widow and children, and if there by no widow nor child, the parents of every non-commissioned officer and soldier, enlisted according to law, who may be killed or die in the service of the United States, shall be entitled to receive the three hundred and twenty acres of land as aforesaid; but the same shall not pass to collateral relations, any law heretofore passed to the contrary notwithstanding.

[SEC. 5 omitted.]

Approved, December 10, 1814.

3 *U.S. Statutes* 212.
THIRTEENTH CONGRESS. Sess. III. 1815.

Chap. XLVIII. *An Act giving further time to complete the surveys and obtain the patents for lands located under Virginia resolution warrants.*

Be it enacted ... That the officers and soldiers of the Virginia line on continental establishment, or their legal representatives, to whom land warrants have issued by virtue of any resolution of the legislature of Virginia, as a bounty for services, which by the laws of Virginia, passed prior to the cession of the north-western territory to the United States, entitled such officers or soldiers to bounty lands, and whose location of such warrants shall have been made prior to the twenty-third of March, one thousand eight [hundred] and eleven, shall be allowed the further time of two years from the passing of this act to complete their surveys and obtain their patents . . . [and provides that the surveys and patents shall be as prescribed under act of 3 March 1807.]

Grants additional time to complete surveys on Virginia resolution warrants.

Approved, February 22, 1815.

3 *U.S. Statutes* 256–257.
FOURTEENTH CONGRESS. Sess. I. 1816.

Chap. XXV. *An Act granting bounties in land and extra pay to certain Canadian Volunteers.*

Be it enacted by the Senate and House of Representatives of the United States of America, on Congress assembled, That all such persons as had been citizens of the United States anterior to the late war, and were at its commencement inhabitants of the province of Canada, and who, during the said war, joined the armies of the United States, as volunteers, and were slain, died in service, or continued therein, till honourably discharged, shall be entitled to the following quantities of land respectively, viz: Each colonel nine hundred and sixty acres; each major to eight hundred acres; each captain six hundred and forty acres; each subaltern officer to four hundred and eighty acres; each non-commissioned officer, musician, or private, to three hundred and twenty acres; and the bounties aforesaid shall extend to the medical and other staff, who shall rank according to their pay. And it shall be lawful for the said persons to locate their claims in quarter sections, upon any of the unappropriated lands of the United States, within the Indiana Territory, which shall have been surveyed prior to such location, with the exception of salt springs, and lead mines therein, and of the quantities of land adjacent thereto, which may be reserved for the use of the same, by the President of the United States, and the section number sixteen, in every township to be granted to the inhabitants of such township, for the use of public schools; which locations shall be subject to such regulations, as to priority of choice, and the manner of location, as the President of the United States shall prescribe.

Involves certain Canadian Volunteers.

SEC. 2. *And Be it further enacted,* That the Secretary for the Department of War, for the time being, shall from time to time, under such rules and regulations as to evidence as the President of the United States shall prescribe, issue to every person coming within the description aforesaid, a warrant for such quantity of land as he may be entitled to by virtue of the aforesaid provision; and in case of the death of such person, then such warrant shall be issued to his widow, or if no widow, to his child or children.

[SEC. 3 omitted.]

Approved, March 5, 1816.

3 *U.S. Statutes* 285–287.
FOURTEENTH CONGRESS. Sess. I. 1816.

Chap. LV. *An Act making further provision for military services during the late war, and for other purposes.*

Be it enacted by the Senate and House of Representatives of the United States of America, in Congress assembled, That when any officer or private soldier of the militia, including rangers, sea fencibles and volunteers, or any non-commissioned officer, musician or private, enlisted for either of the terms of one year or eighteen months, or any commissioned officer of the regular army shall have died while in the service of the United States, during the late war, or in returning to his place of residence, after being mustered out of service, or who shall have died at any time thereafter, in consequence of wounds received whilst in the service, and shall have left a widow, or if no widow, a child or children, under sixteen years of age, such widow, or if no widow, such child or children, shall be entitled to receive half the monthly pay to which the deceased was entitled at the time of his death, for and during the term of five years; and in case of death or intermarriage of such widow before the expiration of said five years, the half pay for the remainder of the time shall go to the child or children of said decedent. *Provided always,* That the secretary of war shall adopt such forms of evidence in applications under this act, as the President of the United States may prescribe. *Provided also,* That the officers and private soldiers of the militia, as aforesaid, who have been disabled by wounds or otherwise, while in the service of the United States in the discharge of their duty, during the late war, shall be placed on the list of pensioners in the same manner as the officers and soldiers of the regular army, under such forms of evidence, as the President of the United States may prescribe. *Provided also,* That the

The "late war" referring to the War of 1812.

When any officer or private soldier of the militia, including rangers, sea fencibles and volunteers, or any non-commissioned officer, musician or private, enlisted for one year or eighteen months, or any commissioned officer of the regular army shall die in service and returning to his place of residence, or died of wounds, widow or children under sixteen to receive half of his pay for five years.

APPENDIX: The Acts

Provides for the militia, both officers and private soldiers.

Children under sixteen, through a guardian, may elect half pay for five years in lieu of bounty land.

All who enlisted to serve for five years or during the war and were above forty-five or under eighteen who were discharged, and representatives of soldiers who died while in service and all soldiers who served until they were promoted to rank of commissioned officers and would have been entitled to bounty land shall receive 160 acres or 320 acres according to term of enlistment.

(The above corrects a "wrong" done the servicemen by 2 U.S. Stat. 671-73 which restricted the bounty land to those ages eighteen to forty-five. It further corrected the inequity of non-commissioned officers losing their bounty land benefits when promoted.)

provisions of this act shall not extend to any person embraced in the provision of an act, entitled "An act to provide for the widows and orphans of militia slain, and for militia disabled in the service of the United States," passed the second day of August, one thousand eight hundred and thirteen.

SEC. 2. *And Be it further enacted,* That when any non-commissioned officer, musician or private soldier of the regular army of the United States shall have been killed in battle, or have died of wounds or disease, while in the service of the United States, during the late war, and have left a child or children under sixteen years of age, it shall be lawful for the guardian of such child or children, within one year from the passing of this act, to relinquish the bounty land, to which such non-commissioned officer, musician or private soldier, had he survived the war, would have been entitled; and, in lieu thereof, to receive half the monthly pay to which such deceased person was entitled, at the time of his death, for and during the term of five years, to be computed from and after the seventeenth day of February, one thousand eight hundred and fifteen, the payment thereof to be made when and where other military pensions are or shall be paid; and where a warrant for the military bounty land aforesaid shall have been issued to or for the use of the child or children of any such deceased non-commissioned officer, musician or private soldier, such child or children, or either of them, being under sixteen years of age, it shall be lawful for the guardian of such minor or minors, to surrender and deliver such warrant into the office for the department of war, within one year from the passing of this act; of which surrender and delivery, the secretary of that department shall give notice to the Secretary of the Treasury, who shall thereupon give the requisite orders for the payment of the half pay hereby provided for.

SEC. 3. *And Be it further enacted,* That all soldiers who have been enlisted to serve for five years, or during the war, and were above the age of forty-five, or under the age of eighteen years, who have faithfully served during the late war, and have been regularly discharged, and the representatives of such soldiers as shall have died whilst in the service of the United States, and all soldiers who have been enlisted, and have faithfully served during the late war, until they have been promoted to the rank of commissioned officers, who, if they had served during the war under their enlistment, and been regularly discharged, would have been entitled to a bounty in land, shall be entitled to one hundred and sixty or three hundred and twenty acres of land, according to the term of enlistment; the warrants and patents to issue in the same manner as in the case of soldiers enlisted of proper age, and discharged under similar circumstances.

SEC. 4. [Provides for Congress to appropriate additional lands for bounty.]

SEC. 5. [Provides that no transfer of land shall be valid until after the patent has been issued.]

Approved, April 16, 1816.

3 *U.S. Statutes* 317.
FOURTEENTH CONGRESS. Sess. I. 1816.

Chap. CXXVII. *An Act providing for cases of lost military land warrants, and discharges for faithful service.*

Be it enacted . . . , That when any soldier of the regular army having obtained a military land warrant shall have lost, or shall hereafter lose the same, or the said warrant shall have been or may be by accident destroyed, every such soldier shall, upon proof thereof, to the satisfaction of the Secretary of War, be entitled to a patent in like manner as if the said warrant was produced.

[SEC. 2. omitted. Involves lost discharges.]

Approved, April 27, 1816.

Provision for lost military warrants.

3 *U.S. Statutes* 332.
FOURTEENTH CONGRESS. Sess. I. 1816.

Chap. CLXIV. *An Act to authorize the survey of two millions of acres of the public lands, in lieu of that quantity heretofore authorized to be surveyed, in the territory of Michigan, as military bounty lands.*

Be it enacted by the Senate and House of Represtatives of the United States of America, in Congress assembled, That so much of the "Act to provide for designating, surveying, and granting the military bounty lands, approved the sixth day of May, one thousand eight hundred and twelve, as authorizes the President of the United States to cause to be surveyed two millions of acres of the lands of the United States, in the territory of Michigan, for the purpose of satisfying the bounties of land promised to the non-commissioned officers and soldiers of the United States, be, and the same is hereby repealed; and in lieu of the said two millions of acres of land, the President of the United States be, and he is hereby authorized to cause to be surveyed, of the lands of the United States fit for cultivation, not otherwise appropriated, and to which the Indian title is extinguished, one million

In lieu of land in Michigan 1,500,000 acres are to be surveyed in the Illinois territory and 500,000 in Missouri territory north of the river Missouri.

five hundred thousand acres in the Illinois territory, and five hundred thousand acres in the Missouri territory, north of the river Missouri; the said lands shall be divided into townships, and subdivided into sections and quarter sections, (each quarter section to contain, as near as possible, one hundred and sixty acres) in the manner prescribed by law for surveying and subdividing the other lands of the United States; and the lands thus surveyed, with the exception of the salt springs and lead mines therein, and of the quantities of land adjacent thereto as may be reserved for the use of the same by the President of the United States, and the section number sixteen in every township, to be granted to the inhabitants of such township for the use of public schools, shall, according to the provisions of the above-recited act, be set apart for the purpose of satisfing the bounties of land promised to the non-commissioned officers and soldiers of the late army of the United States, their heirs and legal representatives, by the act entitled "An act for completing the existing military establishment, approved the twenty-fourth day of December, one thousand eight hundred and eleven, and by the act, entitled "An act to raise an additional military force," approved the eleventh day of January, one thousand eight hundred and twelve.

SEC. 2. *And Be it further enacted,* That every person in whose favour any warrant for military land bounty is issued, shall be, and is hereby authorized, to draw by lot one of the quarter sections surveyed by virtue of this act, and shall obtain a patent therefor, in the same manner, in every respect, as is or shall be provided by law for patents to issue for other military land bounties, or as is provided by the act first above-recited for patents to issue for such lands.

Approved, April 29, 1816.

3 *U.S. Statutes* 408.
FIFTEENTH CONGRESS. Sess. I. 1818.

Chap. XVI. *An Act supplementary to the act, entitled "An act further extending the time for issuing and locating military land warrants, and for other purposes.*

Be it enacted . . . That the time limited by the act, . . . [passed 16 Apr. 1816, for issuing military warrants, be extended to 1 Mar. 1819].

Approved, March 9, 1818.

Extends time.

3 *U.S. Statutes* 411.
FIFTEENTH CONGRESS. Sess. I. 1818.

Chap. XXIII. *An Act extending the time for obtaining military land warrants in certain cases.*

Be it enacted . . . That the provisions of the second section of the act, entitled "An act to provide for designating, surveying, and granting, the military bounty lands," passed on the sixth day of May, one thousand eight hundred and twelve, which limits the time within which persons entitled to military bounty lands shall make their application for a land warrant to five years from and after such person shall have become entitled thereto, shall not be construed to apply to, affect, or bar, any application for a military land warrant, which may be made by the heirs and repersentatives of a deceased person, who was entitled thereto by services performed in the late war, or application by the heirs and representatives of any non-commissioned officer or soldier killed in action, or who died in the actual service of the United States, and entitled by existing laws to a bounty in lands; but the heirs and representatives of such persons shall be allowed to make their applications therefor at any time before the first day of May, one thousand eight hundred and twenty; any act to the contrary notwithstanding.

Approved, March 27, 1818.

Extends time.

3 *U.S. Statutes* 487.
FIFTEENTH CONGRESS. Sess. II. 1819.

Chap. XLI. *An Act allowing further time to complete the issuing and locating of military land warrants.*

Be it enacted... That the authority granted to the Secretary for the Department of War, by the second section of the act to provide for designating, surveying, and granting, the military bounty lands, . . . [approved 6 May 1812, and by fourth section of act approved December 10, 1814, shall be revived and continued for five years from 4 March next].

[SEC. 2 omitted.]   Approved, February 24, 1819.

Extends time.

3 *U.S. Statutes* 566–567.
SIXTEENTH CONGRESS. Sess. I. 1820.

Chap. LI. *An Act making further provision for the sale of the public lands.*

APPENDIX: The Acts

Land can be divided into as little as half-quarter sections (except for town lots.)

No credit to be allowed after July 1, 1820.

Price to be $1.25 per acre minimum with some exceptions.

Provides conditions for sale of reverted lands.

Be it enacted by the Senate and House of Representatives of the United States of America, in Congress assembled, That from and after the first day of July next, all the public lands of the United States, the sale of which is, of may be authorized by law, shall, when offered at public sale, to the highest bidder, be offered in half quarter sections; and when offered at private sate, may be purchased, at the option of the purchaser, either in entire sections, half sections, quarter sections, or half quarter sections; and in every case of the division of a quarter section, the line for the division thereof shall ran north and south, and the corners and contents of half quarter sections which may thereafter be sold, shall be ascertained in the manner, and on the principles directed and prescribed by the second section of an act entitled, "An act concerning the mode of surveying the public lands of the United States," passed on the eleventh day of February, eighteen hundred and five; and fractional sections, containing one hundred and sixty acres, or upwards, shall, in like manner, as nearly as practicable, be sub-divided into half quarter sections, under such rules and regulations as may be prescribed by the Secretary of the Treasury; but fractional sections, containing less than one hundred and sixty acres, shall not be divided, but shall be sold entire: *Provided,* That this section shall not be construed to alter any special provision made by law for the sale of land in town lots.

SEC. 2, *And be it further enacted,* That credit shall not be allowed for the purchase money on the sale of any of the public lands which shall be sold after the first day of July next, but every purchaser of land sold at public sale thereafter, shall, on the day of purchase, make complete payment therefor; and the purchaser at private sale shall produce, to the register of the land office, a receipt from the treasurer of the United States, or from the receiver of public moneys of the district, for the amount of the purchase money on any tract, before he shall enter the same at the land office; and if any person, being the highest bidder, at public sale, for a tract of land, shall fail to make payment therefor, on the day on which the same was purchased, the tract shall be again offered at public sale, on the next day of sale, and such person shall not be capable of becoming the purchaser of that or any other tract offered at such public sales.

SEC. 3. *And be it further enacted,* That from and after the first day of July next, the price at which the public lands shall be offered for sale, shall be one dollar and twenty-five cents an acre; and at every public sale, the highest bidder, who shall make payment as aforesaid, shall be the purchaser; but no land shall be sold, either at public or private sale, for a less price than one dollar and twenty-five cents an acre; and. all the public lands which shall have been offered at public sale before the first day of July next, and which shall then remain unsold, as well as the lands that shall thereafter be offered at public sale, according to law, and remain unsold at the close of such public sales, shall be subject to be sold at private sale, by entry at the land office, at one dollar and twenty-five cents an acre, to be paid at the time of making such entry as aforesaid; with the exception, however, of the lands which may have reverted to the United States, for failure in payment, and of the heretofore reserved sections for the future disposal of Congress, in the states of Ohio and Indiana, which shall be offered at public sale, as hereinafter directed.

SEC. 4. *And be it further enacted,* That no lands which have reverted, or which shall hereafter revert, and become forfeited to the United States for failure in any manner to make payment, shall, after the first day of July next, be subject to entry at private sale, nor until the same shall have been first offered to the highest bidder at public sale; and all such lands which shall have reverted before the said first day of July next, and which shall then belong to the United States, together with the sections, and parts of sections, heretofore reserved for the future disposal of Congress, which shall, at the time aforesaid, remain unsold, shall be offered at public sale to the highest bidder, who shall make payment therefore, in half quarter sections, at the land office for the respective districts, on such day or days as shall, by proclamation of the President of the United States, be designated for that purpose; and all lands which shall revert and become forfeited for failure of payment after the said first day of July next, shall be offered in like manner at public sale, at such time, or times, as the President shall by his proclamation designate for the purpose: *Provided,* That no such lands shall be sold at any public sales hereby authorized, for a less price than one dollar and twenty-five cents an acre, nor on any other terms than that of cash payment; and all the lands offered at such public sales, and which shall remain unsold at the close thereof, shall be subject to entry at private sale, in the same manner, and at the same price with the other lands sold at private sale, at the respective land offices.

SEC. 5. *And be it further enacted,* That the several public sales authorized by this act, shall respectively, be kept open for two weeks, and no longer; and the registers of the land office and the receivers of public money shall, each, respectively, be entitled to five dollars for each day's attendance thereon.

SEC. 6. *And be it further enacted,* That in every case hereafter, where two or more persons shall apply for the purchase, at private sale, of the same tract, at the same time, the register shall determine the preference, by forthwith offering the tract to the highest bidder.

Approved, April 24, 1820.

3 *U.S. Statutes* 612.
SIXTEENTH CONGRESS. Session II. 1821.

Chap. XI. *An Act to extend the time for locating Virginia military land warrants, and returning surveys thereon to the general land office.*

Be it enacted by the Senate and House of Representatives of the United States of America, in Congress assembled, That the officers and soldiers of the Virginia line on continental establishment, their heirs or assigns, entitled to bounty lands within the tract of country reserved by the State of Virginia, between the little Miami and Sciota rivers, shall be allowed a further time of two years, from the fourth day of January, one thousand eight hundred and twenty-one, to obtain warrants and complete their locations, and the further time of four years, from the fourth day of January, one thousand eight hundred and twenty-two, to return their surveys and warrants, or certified copies of warrants, to the general land office, to obtain patents.

Extends time to return surveys and warrants to the General Land Office for the Virginia Military District.

SEC. 2. *And be it further enacted,* That the provisions of the act, entitled "An act authorizing patents to issue for lands located and surveyed by virtue of certain Virginia resolution warrants," passed the third day of March, one thousand eight hundred and seven, shall be revived and in force, with all its restrictions, except that the respective times allowed for making locations, and returning surveys thereof, shall be limited to the terms prescribed by the first section of this act, for the location and return of surveys on other warrants, and that the surveys shall be returned to the general land office: *Provided,* That no locations as aforesaid, in virtue of this or the preceding section of this act, shall be made on tracts of land for which patents had previously been issued, or which had been previously surveyed; and any patent which may, nevertheless, be obtained for land located contrary to the provisions of this act, shall be considered null and void.

Extends Virginia resolution warrants.

Approved, February 9, 1821.

3 *U.S. Statutes* 612–614.
SIXTEENTH CONGRESS. Sess. II. 1821.

Chap. XII. *An Act for the relief of the purchasers of public lands prior to the first day of July, eighteen hundred and twenty.*

Be it anacted by the Senate and House of Representatives of the United States of America, in Congress assembled, That in all cases where lands have been purchased from the United States, prior to the first day of July, eighteen hundred and twenty, it shall be lawful for any such purchaser, or other person or persons, being the legal holder of any certificate or certificates of land, on or before the thirtieth day of September, eighteen hundred and twenty-one, to file, with the register of the land office, where any tract of land has been purchased, a relinquishment, in writing, of any section, half section, quarter section, half quarter section, or legal subdivision of any fractional section, of land so purchased, upon which the whole purchase money has not been paid, and all sums paid on account of the part relinquished, shall be applied to the discharge of any Instalments which may be, or shall hereafter become, due and payable upon such land, so purchased, as shall not have been relinquished, and shall be so applied and credited as to complete the payment on some one or more half-quarter sections where the payments by transfer are sufficient for that purpose: *Provided,* That all divisions and subdivisions, contemplated by this act, shall be made in conformity with the first section of an act making further provision for the sale of public lands, passed the twenty-fourth day of April, one thousand eight hundred and twenty: *And, provided, also,* That the right of relinquishment hereby given shall, in no case, authorize the party relinquishing to claim any repayment from the United States: *And provided, also,* That where any purchaser has purchased, at the same time, two or more quarter sections, he shall not be permitted to relinquish less than a quarter section.

Relief provided for purchasers of land purchased PRIOR to 1 July 1820. Relinquishment must be filed before 13 September 1821.

SEC. 2. *And be it further enacted,* That the interest which shall have accrued before the thirtieth day of September next, upon any debt to the United States, for public land, shall be, and the same is hereby, remitted and discharged.

Interest accrued before 13 September 1821 remitted and discharged.

SEC. 3. *And be it further enacted,* That the persons indebted to the United States, as aforesaid, shall be divided into three classes; the first class to include all such persons as shall have paid to the United States only one fourth part of the original price of the land by them respectively purchased or held; the second class to include ail such persons as shall have paid to the United States only one-half part of such original price; and the third class to include all such persons as shall have paid to the United States, three-fourth parts of such original price; and the debts of the persons included in the first class shall be paid in eight equal annual instalments; the debts of the persons included in the second class shall be paid in six equal annual instalments; and the debts of the persons included in the third class shall be paid in four equal annual instalments, the first of which instalments, in each of the classes aforesaid, shall be paid in manner following, to wit: of the third class, on the thirtieth day of September next; of the second class, on the thirty-first day of December next: and of the first class, on the thirty-first day of March, one thousand eight hundred and twenty-two; and the whole of the debt aforesaid, shall bear an equal annual interest at the rate of six per cent: *Provided always,* That the same shall be remitted upon each and every of the instalments aforesaid which shall be punctually paid when the same shall become payable as aforesaid.

SEC. 4. *And be it further enacted,* That in all cases where complete payment of the whole sum due, or which may become due, for any tract of land purchased from the United States, as aforesaid, shall be made on or before the thirtieth day of September, one thousand eight hundred and twenty-two, a deduction at the rate of thirty-seven and a half per centum, shall be allowed upon the sum remaining unpaid: *Provided,* That nothing herein contained shall authorize any discount upon payments made by a transfer of former payments under the provisions of the first section of this act.

A deduction is allowed when complete payment of whole sum due is made before September 30, 1822.

SEC. 5. *And be it further enacted,* That each and every individual or company that has laid off, on any lands by him or them purchased of the United States, any town, a part or the whole of the lots whereof have been sold, shall be entitled to the benefits of this act in relation to any half quarter, or quarter section of land, on which such town may be situated, and of all land by him or them owned, contiguous to, and adjoining said half quarter, quarter section, or section, on which said town is situated, upon condition only, that each and every person who has purchased of him, or them, a town lot, or part of a lot, or land in and adjoining the same, shall be entitled to a remission of all interest that has accrued, and to a discount of twenty per centum on the amount unpaid, and to discharge their debt by bonds, with security, in equal annual instalments of four years from the thirtieth day of December next. Nor shall the provisions of this act be construed to extend to any person or persons claiming title to land under the provisions of an act passed the third day of March, one thousand eight hundred and seventeen, entitled "An act to set apart and dispose of certain public lands for the encouragement of the cultivation of the vine and olive."

Certain discounts allowed.

SEC. 6. *And be it further enacted,* That, for failure to pay the several debts aforesaid, in manner aforesaid, and for the term of three months after the day appointed for the payment of the last instalment thereof, in each of the classes aforesaid, the land so purchased or held by the respective persons indebted to the United States as aforesaid, shall, ipso facto, become forfeited, and revert to the United States.

SEC. 7. *And be it further enacted,* That no person shall be deemed to be included within, or entitled to, the benefit of any of the provisions of this act, who shall not, on or before the thirtieth day of September next, sign, and file in the office of the register of the land office of the district where the land was purchased, or where the residue of the purchase money is payable, a declaration in writing, expressing his consent to the same; and shall pay to the register, for receiving, recording, and filing the same, fifty cents.

Written declaration is to be filed.

SEC, 8. *And be it further enacted,* That it shall be, and hereby is made, the duty of the several registers and receivers of the land offices of the United States, according to the forms and instructions which shall be given in that behalf by the Treasury Department, to assist in carrying this act in[to] execution, to keep full and faithful accounts and records of all proceedings under the same; and, within the term of three months after the said thirtieth day of September next, to transmit to the said department a correct report of the quantity of land relinquished to the United States; the quantity on which full payment shall have been made; and the quantity on which a further credit shall have been given, distinguishing the amount of the debt on which a farther credit shall have been allowed; and the registers and receivers, respectively, shall be entitled to receive fifty cents from the party relinquishing, for each half quarter section, quarter section, half section, section, or legal subdivision of a fractional section, so relinquished.

SEC, 9. *And be it further enacted,* That no lands purchased from the United States on or before the first day of July, eighteen hundred and twenty, which are not already forfeited, shall be considered as forfeited to the government, for failure in completing the payment thereon, until the said thirtieth day of September next; and all the lands which shall be relinquished to the United States, as aforesaid, shall be deemed and held to be forfeited, and, with all other lands which may become forfeited under this act, shall be sold according to the provisions of the act, entitled "An act making further provision for the sale of the public lands," passed the twenty-fourth day of April, eighteen hundred and twenty.

No lands are to be considered forfeited until September 13, 1821.

SEC.. 10. *And be it further enacted,* That no land which shall be surrendered under the provisions of this act, shall be offered for sale for the term of two years after the surrender thereof.

Approved, March 2, 1821.

No land surrendered under the provisions of this act to be offered for sale for two years from the surrender.

3 *U.S. Statutes* 617.
SIXTEENTH CONGRESS. Sess. II. 1821.

Chap. XV. *An Act extending the time for issuing and locating military land warrants to officers and soldiers of the revolutionary army.*

Be it enacted ... That the time limited, by the second section of the act approved on the twenty-fourth day of February, one thousand eight hundred and nineteen, for issuing military land warrants to the officers and soldiers of the revolutionary army, shall be extended to the fourth day of March, one thousand eight hundred and twenty-three; and the time for locating the unlocated warrants shall be extended to the first day of October thereafter.

Approved, March 2, 1821.

Extends time.

3 *U.S. Statutes* 641.
SIXTEENTH CONGRESS. Sess. II. 1821

Chap. XLIV. *An act to regulate the location of land warrants, and the issuing of patents, in certain cases.*

Be it enacted by the Senate and House of Representatives of the United States of America, in Congress assembled, That the holders, by assignment, of warrants issued under the acts of Congress, of the fifth of March, eighteen hundred and sixteen, the third of March eighteen hundred and seventeen, to Canadian volunteers, may be, and hereby are, authorized to locate the said warrants, and to receive patents therefor in their own names, as had been the practice before the twenty-sixth of December, eighteen hundred and nineteen: *Provided, however,* That in no case shall lands be so located, until, after having been exposed to public sale, shall remain unsold.

Approved, March 3, 1821.

Refers to the Canadian Volunteer acts.

3 *U.S. Statutes* 772–773.
SEVENTEENTH CONGRESS. Sess. II. 1823.

Chap. XXXIX. *An Act extending the time for locating Virginia military land warrants, and returning surveys thereon in the general land office.*

Be it enacted by the Senate and House of Representatives of the United States of America, in Congress assembled, That the officers and soldiers of the Virginia line, on the continental establishment, their heirs or assigns, entitled to bounty lands within the country reserved by the state of Virginia, between the little Miami and Scioto rivers, shall be allowed a further time of two years, from the fourth of January, one thousand eight hundred and twenty-three, to obtain warrants, and to complete their locations; and the further time of four years, from the fourth day of January, one thousand eight hundred and twenty-three, to return their surveys and warrants, or certified copies of warrants, to the general land office, to obtain patents.

Extends time on locating warrants in VMD.

SEC. 2. *And Be it further enacted,* That the provisions of the act, entitled "An act authorizing patents to issue for lands located and surveyed by virtue of certain Virginia resolution-warrants," passed the third day of March, one thousand eight hundred and seven, shall be revived, and in force, with all its restrictions, except that the respective times allowed for making locations, and returning surveys thereon, shall be limited to the terms prescribed by the first section of this act, for the location and return of surveys on other warrants; and that the surveys shall be returned to the general land office: *Provided,* That no locations, as aforesaid, in virtue of this or the preceding section of this act, shall be made on tracts of lands for which patents had previously been issued, or which had been previously surveyed; and any patent, which may nevertheless be obtained for land located contrary to the provisions of this act, shall be considered null and void.

Extends time on Virginia resolution warrants.

Sec. 3. *And be it further enacted,* That no holder of any warrant which has been, or may be, located, shall be permitted to withdraw or remove the same, and locate it on any other land, except in cases of eviction, in consequence of a legal judgment first obtained, or unless it can be found to interfere with a prior location and survey; nor shall any lands heretofore sold by the United States, within the boundaries of said reservation, be subject to location by the holder of any such unlocated warrant.   Approved, March 1, 1823.

4 *U.S. Statutes* 60.
EIGHTEENTH CONGRESS. Sess. I. 1824.

Extends time.

Chap. CLXXVII. *An Act to allow further time to complete the issuing and locating of military land warrants.*

Be it enacted by the Senate and House of Representatives of the United States of America, in Congress assembled, That the authority granted to the Secretary of the Department of War, by an act, approved the twenty-fourth day of February, one thousand eight hundred and nineteen, to issue warrants for the military land bounties, to persons entitled thereto, shall be revived and continued in force for the term of five years.

Approved, May 26, 1824.

4 *U.S. Statutes* 133.
EIGHTEENTH CONGRESS. Sess. II. 1825.

Chap. CXI. *An Act to extend the time of issuing and locating military land warrants to officers and soldiers of the revolutionary war.*

Be it enacted by the Senate and House of Representatives of the United States of America, in Congress assembled, That the time limited by the second section of the act approved the twenty-fourth day of February, one thousand eight hundred and nineteen, for issuing military land warrants to the officers and soldiers of the revolutionary army, shall be extended till the fourth of March, one thousand eight hundred and twenty-seven, and the time for locating the unlocated warrants shall be extended till the first day of October thereafter.

Extends time.

Approved, March 3, 1825.

4 *U.S. Statutes* 189–190.
NINETEENTH CONGRESS. Sess. I. 1826.

Chap. CXXXVIII. *An Act to extend the time for locating Virginia military land warrants, and returning surveys thereon to the general land office.*

Be it enacted by the Senate and House of Representatives of the United States of America, in Congress assembled, That the officers and soldiers of the Virginia line, on the continental establish-ment, their heirs or assigns, entitled to bounty lands within the tract of country reserved by the state of Virginia, between the Little Miami and Sciota rivers, shall be allowed until the first day of June, eighteen hundred and twenty-nine, to obtain warrants, and until the first day of June, eighteen hundred and thirty-two, to complete their locations, and until the first day of June, eighteen hundred and thirty-three, to return their surveys and warrants, or certified copies thereof, to the commissioner of the general land office, and to obtain patents: *Provided,* That no location shall be made by virtue of any warrant obtained after the first day of June, eighteen hundred and twenty-nine, and no patent shall issue in consequence of any location made after the first day of June, eighteen hundred and thirty-two; *And provided also,* That no patent shall be obtained, on any such warrant, unless there be produced, to the Secretary of War, satisfactory evidence that such warrant was granted for services which, by the laws of Virginia, passed prior to the cession of the north-western territory, would have entitled such officers, or soldier, his heirs or assigns, to bounty lands; and also a certificate of the register of the land office of Virginia, and no warrant has issued from the said land office for the same services.

Extends time.

Sec. 2. *And be it further enacted,* That no patent shall be issued, by virtue of the preceding section, for a greater quantity of land than the rank, or term of service, of the officer or soldier to whom or to whose heirs or assigns such warrant has been granted, would have entitled him to, un-der the aforesaid laws of Virginia; and whenever it appears, to the Secretary of War, that the survey made by virtue of any of the aforesaid warrants, is for a greater quantity of land than the officer or soldier is entitled to for his services, the Secretary of War shall certify, for each survey, the amount of such surplus quantity, and the officer or soldier, his heirs or assigns, shall have leave to withdraw his survey from the office of the Secretary of War, and re-survey his location, excluding such surplus quantity, in one body, from any part of his re-survey, and a patent shall issue upon such re-survey, as in other cases.

Provides for surplus to be paid.

Sec. 3. *And be it further enacted,* That no holder of any warrant which has been, or may be located, shall be permitted to withdraw or remove the same, and locate it on any other land, except in cases of eviction, in consequence of a legal judgment first obtained, from the whole or a part of the located land, or unless it be found to interfere with a prior location and survey; nor shall any lands heretofore sold by the United States, within the boundaries of said reservation be subject to location, by the holder of any such unlocated warrant; *Provided,* That no location shall, after the passage of this act, be made on lands for which patents had previously issued, or which had been previously surveyed, nor shall any location be made on lands lying west of Ludlow's line, and any patent which, nevertheless, may be obtained, contrary to the provisions of this section, shall be null and void.

Restrictions on withdrawals.

Approved, May 20, 1826.

4 *U.S. Statutes* 190–191.
NINETEENTH CONGRESS. Sess. I. 1826.

Chap. CXLVII. *An Act authorizing certain soldiers in the late war to surrender the bounty lands drawn by them, and to locate others in lieu thereof.*

Be it enacted by the Senate and House of Representatives of the United States of America, in Congress assembled, That it shall and may be lawful for any soldiers in the late war, or their heirs, to whom bounty lands have been patented, or may hereafter be patented, in the territory of Arkansas, and which land is unfit for cultivation, and who have removed, or shall hereafter remove, to the said territory, with a view to actual settlement on the lands by them drawn--in all such cases, where it shall be made to appear, in such manner as the commissioner of the general land office shall direct, to the satisfaction of the register and receiver of the proper district, that the land patented to them is unfit for cultivation, and on the surrender of the patent to them granted, accompanied with such a release of their interest as the commissioner of the general land office shall prescribe, such soldier, or his heirs, may locate and enter with the register of the land office, for the proper district, in the territory of Arkansas, according to the sectional and divisional lines, the like quantity on any of the unappropriated public lands in the military district in said territory; and upon such entry and location being made, it shall be the duty of the register to issue to the person so locating, a certificate specifying the quarter or half section of land so located and entered; and it shall be the duty of the commissioner of the general land office, if he is satisfied such certificate was fairly obtained, to issue a patent for the lands so located, whenever the certificate aforesaid shall be presented to him for that purpose. *Provided,* That before such certificate of location shall be granted, the applicant shall satisfy the register and receiver that his interest in the land originally patented to him, has not been divested, either by his own acts, or by the operation of law, for taxes, or otherwise. *And provided,* also, That such surrender and re-location shall be made on or before the first day of January, eighteen hundred and thirty. But, if said interest shall have been divested in either mode above mentioned, no title shall be acquired to the land subsequently patented.

Approved, May 22, 1826.

Provides that under certain conditions those who obtained their patent in Arkansas and found the land was unfit for cultivation could exchange the land before 1 January 1830 for lands deemed to be fit.

4 *U.S. Statutes* 219.
NINETEENTH CONGRESS. Sess. II. 1827.

Chap. XXXV. *An Act to extend the time of issuing and locating military land warrants to officers and soldiers of the revolutionary army.*

Be it enacted by the Senate and House of Representatives of the United States of America, in Congress assembled, That the time limited by the second section of the act, approved the twenty-fourth day of February, one thousand eight hundred and nineteen, for issuing military land warrants to the officers and soldiers of the revolutionary army, shall be extended till the fourth day of March, one thousand eight hundred and thirty; and the time for locating the unlocated warrants shall be extended till the first day of October thereafter.

Approved, March 2, 1827.

Extends time.

4 *U.S. Statutes* 333–334.
TWENTIETH CONGRESS. Sess. II. 1829.

Chap. XIV. *An Act to allow further time to complete the issuing and locating of military land warrants.*

Be it enacted by the Senate and House of Representatives of the United States of America, in Congress assembled, That the act entitled "An act to allow further time to complete the issuing and locating of military land warrants," approved the twenty-sixth day of May, one thousand eight hundred and twenty-four, and, also, the operations of the act, approved the twenty-fourth day of May, one thousand eight hundred and nineteen, which by the said act of one thousand eight hundred and twenty-four is revived, be, and the said acts are hereby, extended and continued in force for the term of five years from and after the twenty-sixth day of May next.

Approved, February 5, 1829.

Extends time.

4 *U.S. Statutes* 383.
TWENTY FIRST CONGRESS. Sess. I. 1830.

Chap. XXXVI. *An Act to continue in force "An act authorizing certain soldiers in the late war to surrender the bounty lands drawn by them, and to locate others in lieu thereof," and for other purposes.*

Be it enacted by the Senate and House of Representatives of the United States of America, in Congress assembled, That the act of the twenty-second of May, one thousand eight hundred and twenty-six, entitled "An act authorizing certain soldiers in the late war to surrender the bounty lands drawn by them, and to locate others in lieu thereof," be, and the same is hereby, continued in force for the term of five years. And the provisions of the above recited act shall be, and are hereby, extended to those having like claims in the states of Illinois and Missouri.

Approved, March 23, 1830.

4 *U.S. Statutes* 395–396.
TWENTY FIRST CONGRESS. Sess. I. 1830.

Chap. LXXIII. *An Act to amend an act, entitled "An act to extend the time for locating Virginia military land warrants, and returning surveys thereon in the general land office," approved the twentieth day of May, one thousand eight hundred and twenty-six.*

Be it enacted by the Senate and House of Representatives of the United States of America, in Congress assembled, That the officers and soldiers of the Virginia line, on the continental establishment, their heirs or assigns, entitled to bounty land within the tract of country reserved by the state of Virginia, between the Little Miami and Sciota rivers, shall be allowed until the first day of January, one thousand eight hundred and thirty-two, to obtain warrants, subject, however, to the conditions, restrictions, and limitations, relating to locations, surveys, and patents contained in the act of which this is an amendment.

Sec. 2. *And be it further enacted,* That no location shall be made by virtue of any warrant obtained after the said first day of January, one thousand eight hundred and thirty-two; and no patent shall issue in consequence of any warrant obtained after that time. And that the second proviso, inserted in the first section of the above recited act, except only that part thereof which requires "a certificate of the register of the land office of Virginia, that no warrant has issued from the said land office for the same services," be, and the same is hereby, repealed.

Approved, April 23, 1830.

4 *U.S. Statutes* 422–424.
TWENTY-FIRST CONGRESS. Sess. I. 1830.

Chap. CCXV. *An Act for the relief of certain officers and soldiers of the Virginia line and navy, and of the continental army, during the revolutionary war.*

Be it enacted by the Senate and House of Representatives of the United States of America, in Congress assembled, That the officers and soldiers, sailors and marines, who were in the service of Virginia on her own state establishment during the revolutionary war, and who were entitled to military land bounties, by the laws and resolutions of that state, their heirs, and assigns, shall be, and they are hereby, authorized to surrender, to the Secretary of the Treasury of the United States, such of their warrants for the said land bounties as shall remain unsatisfied, in whole or in part, and to receive certificates or scrip for the same, at any time before the first day of January, in the year one thousand eight hundred and thirty-five, which certificates or scrip shall be issued by the said Secretary, and signed by him, and countersigned by the commissioner of the general land office, in the following manner, that is to say: There shall be a separate certificate or scrip, for such sum as shall, at the time of issuing the same, be equal to the then minimum price of each quantity of eighty acres of land due by each warrant, and remaining unsatisfied at the time of such surrender, and a like certificate or scrip for such sum as, at the time, shall be equal to the minimum price of the quantity that shall so remain unsatisfied, of any such warrant after such subdivisions of the amount into quantities of eighty acres. And where any such warrant shall have been lost or mislaid, by time and accident, it shall and may be lawful for the party desiring to surrender the same, to surrender an official copy thereof, certified under the seal of the land office of Virginia, with the affidavit of the party endorsed upon, or accompanying the same, stating that such warrant has been lost or mislaid, and that the original hath not been sold or transferred, to the knowledge or belief of the party so surrendering, or his or her guardian.

SEC. 2. *And Be it further enacted,* That it shall be the duty of the commissioner of the general land office, to request the executive of Virginia to furnish him with a statement of all such warrants, within the purview of this act, as have already issued, showing the number and date of each warrant, and the quantity of acres granted by each, and also a monthly statement of the same description, showing the number, date and quantity, of such warrants as shall hereafter be granted. And no war-

Exchange act of unfit Arkansas land extended five years and also extended to like lands in Illinois and Missouri.

Extends time in the Virginia Military District and other provisions.

Officers and soldiers, sailors and marines who were in the service of Virginia on her own state establishment during the Revolutionary War and who were entitled to land bounties by that state are authorized to surrender their unsatisfied warrants and to receive certificates or scrip.

rant shall be taken to be within the provisions of this act, which shall hereafter be granted, unless the executive of Virginia shall cause a certificate to be endorsed thereon, signed by some proper officer, stating that the party to whom such warrant shall be so granted, his, her, or their ancestor or devisor, was entitled thereto by some law or resolution of the said state, in force at the time of the deed of cession, by the state of Virginia, to the United States.

SEC. 3. *And be it further enacted,* That before the Secretary of the Treasury shall issue the scrip required by the provisions of this bill, the applicants shall produce to him the certificate of the register of the land office in Kentucky, and the certificate of the surveyor of the military lands of the Virginia line, that the warrants (when the original is presented, or the copy, when the original has been lost or destroyed,) has not been located, surveyed, or patented, in Kentucky, attested by the seal of his office.

Virginia holders of military certificates to furnish proof the original was not located, surveyed or patented previously.

SEC. 4. *And Be it further enacted,* That the certificates or scrip to be issued by virtue of this act, shall be receivable in payment for any lands hereafter to be purchased, at private sale, after the same shall have been offered at public sale, and shall remain unsold at any of the land offices of the United States, established, or to be established, in the states of Ohio, Indiana, and Illinois. And all such certificates or scrip, as shall be issued by virtue of this act shall be assignable, by endorsement thereof, attested by two witnesses: *Provided,* That all certificates or scrip to be issued, in virtue of any warrant hereafter to be granted, shall be issued to the party originally entitled thereof, or his heir or heirs, devisee or devisees, as the case may be.

Certificates or scrip to be used for land offered at public sale or thereafter private sale in states of Ohio, Indiana, and Illinois where land is subject to private sale. Scrip to be assignable.

SEC. 5. *And Be it further enacted,* That the provisions of this act shall be deemed and taken to extend to all such officers, soldiers, sailors, marines, chaplains, musicians, surgeons, and surgeons' mates, in the land or sea service of the state of Virginia during the revolutionary war, and generally, to every person to whom the state had engaged to pay a land bounty for services in that war, or any description, by any law or resolution passed before, and in force at the date of the said deed of cession; except only such persons as are mentioned in, and provided for by the reservation contained in the said deed of cession in favour of the officers and soldiers of the said state on continental establishment: *Provided,* That no scrip issued under the provisions of this act, shall entitle the holder to enter or purchase any settled or occupied lands, without the written consent of such settlers or occupants, as may be actually residing on said lands at the time the same shall be entered or applied for: *And provided, also,* That the amount of land thus located, shall not exceed two hundred and sixty thousand acres.

Provisions to extend to officers, soldiers, sailors, marines, chaplains, musicians, surgeons, and surgeons mates, in the land or sea service of Virginia and generally to every person who served for Virginia except those on continental establishment provided for in Virginia's deed of cession.

No holder of scrip may not enter or purchase any settled or occupied land without written consent.

SEC. 6. *And Be it further enacted,* That the provisions of the first and fourth sections of this act, shall extend to and embrace owners of military land warrants, issued, by the United States, in satisfaction of claims for bounty land for services during the revolutionary war; and that the laws, heretofore enacted, providing for the issuing said warrants, are hereby revived and continued in force for two years.

Provisions of first and fourth sections shall extend to those holding warrants issued by the United States for Revolutionary War service.

SEC. 7. *And Be it further enacted,* That the provisions of this act shall also be deemed and taken to extend to all the unsatisfied warrants of the Virginia army on continental establishment: *Provided,* That the quantity thereof shall not exceed fifty thousand acres, in addition to the two hundred and sixty thousand acres heretofore authorized to be located by their state line.

Approved, May 30, 1830.

Provisions of this act also to extend to unsatisfield warrants of Virginia on continental establishment.

4 *U.S. Statutes* 560.
TWENTY-SECOND CONGRESS. Sess. I. 1832.

Chap. CLXIII. *An Act for the sale of the unlocated lots in the fifty quarter townships in the United States' military district, in the state of Ohio, reserved to satisfy warrants granted in individuals for their military services.*

Be it enacted . . . That the lots and fractional parts of lots lying in the fifty quarter townships, reserved by an act of Congress, passed the eleventh day of February, one thousand eight hundred, and entitled "An act giving further time to the holders of military warrants to register and locate the same," and which remain unlocated, shall, hereafter, be liable to be sold at private sale, in the respective land offices in which they lie, in the same manner, and for the same sum per acre, as other lands of the United States lying in said districts, and undisposed of.

Approved, July 3, 1832.

Provides for the sale of the remaining smaller lots in the U. S. Military District by private sale.

4 *U.S. Statutes* 578.
TWENTY-SECOND CONGRESS. Sess. I. 1832.

Extends time to file for scrip and appropriates additional land for scrip.

Chap. CCV. *An Act to extend the time of issuing military land warrants to officers and soldiers of the revolutionary war.*

Be it enacted by the Senate and House of Representatives of the United States of America, in Congress assembled, That the time allowed for issuing military land warrants to the officers and soldiers of the revolutionary army shall be extended to the first day of January, eighteen hundred and thirty-five.

SEC. 2. *And Be it further enacted,* That the further quantity of three hundred thousand acres of land be, and the same is hereby appropriated, in addition to the quantity heretofore appropriated by the act entitled "An act for the relief of certain officers and soldiers of the Virginia line and navy, and of the continental army during the revolutionary war," approved the thirtieth of May, eighteen hundred and thirty, which said appropriation shall be applied in the manner provided by the said act to the unsatisfied warrants which have been or maybe issued as therein directed to the officers and soldiers and others as described in the first, fifth, and seventh sections of said act.

SEC. 3. *And Be it further enacted,* That the last paragraph of the first section of the said act which authorizes the issuing of warrants upon an affidavit that the original as lost, and upon the production of an official copy thereof, shall be, and the same is hereby repealed.

Approved, July 13, 1832.

4 *U.S. Statutes* 665.
TWENTY-SECOND CONGRESS. Sess. II. 1833.

Chap. XCIV. *An Act granting an additional quantity of land for the location of revolutionary bounty land warrants.*

Be it enacted by the Senate and House of Representatives of the Untied States of America, in Congress assembled. That the further quantity of two hundred thousand acres of land be, and the same is here, appropriated, in addition to the quantity heretofore appropriated by the act, entitled, "An act for the relief of certain officers and soldiers of the Virginia line and navy, and of the continental army during the revolutionary war," approved the thirtieth May, one thousand eight hundred and thirty, and the act, entitled "An act to extend the time of issuing military land warrants to officers and soldiers of the revolutionary war," approved the thirteenth July, one thousand eight hundred and thirty-two; which said appropriations shall be applied in the manner provided by the said acts, to the unsatisfied warrants, whether original or duplicate, which have been or may be issued as therein directed, to the officers and soldiers, and others, as described in said acts: *Provided,* That the said certificates of scrip shall be receivable in payment of any of the public lands liable to sale at private entry.

Approved, March 2, 1833.

Appropriates more land and allows the warrant holder to locate the warrant anywhere in the public domain where public lands are available. Thus, by this act they are no longer restricted to Ohio, Illinois, and Indiana.

4 *U.S. Statutes* 749.
TWENTY-THIRD CONGRESS. Sess. II. 1835.

Chap. VI. *An Act to allow further time to complete the issuing and locating of military land warrants during the late war.*

Be it enacted by the Senate and House of Representatives of the United States of America, in Congress assembled, That the act entitled "An act to allow further time to complete the issuing and locating of military land warrants," approved the twenty-sixth day of May, one thousand eight hundred and twenty-four, and also the operations of the act approved the twenty-fourth day of February, one thousand eight hundred and nineteen, which, by said act of one thousand eight hundred and twenty-four, is revived, be, and the said acts are hereby, extended and continued in force for the term of five years from and after the twenty-sixth day of May last.

Approved, January 27, 1835.

Extends time.

4 *U.S. Statutes* 749.
TWENTY-THIRD CONGRESS. Sess. II. 1835.

Chap. VII. *An Act to extend the time of issuing military land warrants to the officers and soldiers of the revolutionary army.*

Be it enacted by the Senate and House of Representatives of the United States of America, in Congress assembled, That the time allowed for issuing military land warrants to the officers and soldiers of the revolutionary army shall be extended to the first day of January, eighteen hundred and forty.

Approved, January 27, 1835.

Extends time.

4 *U.S. Statutes* 760–771.
TWENTY-THIRD CONGRESS. Sess. II. 1835.

Chap. XXX. *An Act making appropriations for the civil and diplomatic expenses of government for the year one thouand eight hundred and thirty-five.*

Be it enacted by the Senate and House of Representatives of the United States of America, in Congress assembled, That the following sums be, and the same are hereby, appropriated, to be paid out of any unappropriated money in the treasury, viz:

[SEC. 1 omitted]

SEC. 2. *And Be it further enacted,* That six hundred and fifty thousand acres of land, in addition to the quantity heretofore appropriated by the act, entitled "An act for the relief of certain officers and soldiers of the Virginia line and navy, and of the continental army during the revolutionary war," approved the thirtieth day of May one thousand eight hundred and thirty, and the act entitled "An act to extend the time for issuing military land warrants to officers and soliders of the revolutionary war," approved the thirteenth day of July, one thousand eight hundred and thirty-two, and the act entitled "An act granting an additional quantity of land for the location of revolutionary bounty land warrants," approved the second day of March, one thousand eight hundred and thirty-three, be, and the same are hereby, appropriated, to be applied in the manner provided for in said acts, to the unsatisfied warrants whether original or duplicate, which have been or may be issued as therein directed to the officers, soldiers and others therein described; and the certificates of scrip, issued pursuant to said acts shall be receivable in payment for any of the public lands liable to sale at private entry: Provided, That no scrip shall be issued until the first day of September next, and warrants shall be received in the general land office until that day and immediately thereafter, if the amount filed exceed six hundred and fifty thousand acres, the commissioner of the general land office shall apportion the said six hundred and fifty thousand acres of land among the warrants which may be then on file, in full satisfaction thereof.

[SEC. 3 through SEC. 4 omitted.]

Approved, March 3, 1835.

Appropriates additional land for scrip.

5 *U.S. Statutes* 497.
TWENTY-SEVENTH CONGRESS. Sess. II. 1842.

Chap. LXIX. *An Act to provide for satisfying claims for bounty lands, for military services in the late war with Great Britain, and for other purposes.*

Be it enacted by the Senate and House of Representatives of the United States of America in Congress assembled, That in all cases of warrants for bounty lands for military services in the war of eighteen hundred and twelve with Great Britain, which remain unsatisfied at the date of this act, it shall be lawful for the person in whose name such warrant shall have issued, his heirs or legal representatives, to enter at the proper land office in any of the States or Territories in which the same may lie, the quantity of the public lands subject to private entry to which said person shall be entitled in virtue of such warrant in quarter sections: *Provide*d, Such warrants shall be located within five years from the date of this act.

SEC. 2. And *Be it further enacted,* That the terms prescribed for the issuing of warrants by the Secretary of the Department of War, under the act entitled, "An act to allow further time to complete the issuing and locating of military land warrants during the late war," and under the act entitled "An act to extend the time of issuing military land warrants to the officers and soldiers of the Revolutionary army," both of which acts were approved January twenty-seventh, eighteen hundred and thirty-five, be, and the same are hereby, respectively, renewed and contnued in force for the term of five years from and after the date of this act; and all cases which shall not, within the time aforesaid, be finally disposed of, shall be thereafter for ever barred from the benefits of all claim to bounty land for services performed within the spirit and meaning of said acts: *Provided,* That warrants issued under the provisions of this section may be located as is provided for warrants under the first section of this act: *And provided further,* That the certificate of location obtained under the provisions of this act, shall not be assignable, but the patent shall in all cases issue in the name of the person originally entitled to the bounty land, or to his heirs or legal representatives.

Approved, July 27, 1842.

Removes restriction on location. Now all warrants can be used in any state or territory in which public lands are available for private entry. Allows five years for warrants to be located.

9 U.S. Statutes 123–126.
TWENTY-NINTH CONGRESS. Sess. II. 1847.

Chap. VIII. *An Act to raise for a limited time an additional military Force, and for other Purposes.*

Be it enacted by the Senate and House of Representatives of the United States of America, in Congress assembled, That in addition to the present military establishment of the United States

APPENDIX: The Acts

The 1847 War with Mexico warrant act.

there shall be raised and organized, under the direction of the President, for and during the war with Mexico, one regiment of dragoons and nine regiments of infantry, each to be composed of the same number and rank of commissioned and non-commissioned officers, buglars, musicians, and privates, &c., as are provided for a regiment of dragoons and infantry, respectively, under existing laws, and who shall receive the same pay, rations, and allowances according to their respective grades, and be subject to the same regulations, and to the rules and articles of war: *Provided,* That it shall be lawful for the President of the United States alone to appoint such of the commissioned officers, authorized by this act, below the grade of field officers, as may not be appointed during the present session; *Provided,* That one or more of the regiments of infantry, authorized to be raised by this section, may, at the discretion of the President, be organized and equipped as voltigeurs, and as foot-riflemen, and be provided with a rocket and mountain howitzer battery.

SEC. 2. And *Be it further enacted,* That, during the continuance of the war with Mexico, the term of enlistment of the men to be recruited for the regiments authorized by this act, shall be during the war, unless sooner discharged.

[SEC. 3 through SEC. 8 omitted.]

Non-commissioned officer, musician, or private in the regular army or volunteer of not less than twelve months in the war with Mexico shall receive 160 acres. Warrants are not assignable though they could be inherited.

Warrant can be settled anywhere in the public domain subject to private entry except land where there is a preemption right or actual settlement and cultivation.

If the soldier died the warrant can be inherited by wife, child or children, in that order; but if none then to father; if no father to mother.

Claim to bounty is not subject to sales, mortgages or other instruments veteran made in writing prior to issuance of warrant.

Provides for the alternate option of scrip: $100 for those who served twelve months, and $25 for those who served for less.

SEC. 9. And *Be it further enacted,* That each non-commissioned officer, musician, or private, enlisted or to be enlisted in the regular army, or regularly mustered in any volunteer company for a period of not less than twelve months, who has served or may serve during the present war with Mexico, and who shall receive an honorable discharge, or who shall have been killed, or died of wounds received or sickness incurred in the course of such service, or who shall have been discharged before the expiration of his term of service in consequence of wounds received or sickness incurred in the course of such service, shall be entitled to receive a certificate or warrant from the war department for the quantity of one hundred and sixty acres, and which may be located by the warrantee, or his heirs at law at any land office of the United States, in one body, and in conformity to the legal subdivisions of the public lands, upon any of the public lands in such district then subject to private entry; and upon the return of such certificate or warrant, with evidence of the location thereof having been legally made, to the General Land Office, a patent shall be issued therefor. That in the event of the death of any such non-commissioned officer, musician, or private, during service, or after his discharge, and before the issuing of a certificate or warrant as aforesaid, the said certificate or warrant shall be issued in favor, and inure to the benefit, of his family or relatives, according to the following rules: first, to the widow and to his children; second, his father; third, his mother. And in the event of his children being minors, then the legally-constituted guardian of such minor children shall, in conjunction with such of the children, if any, as may be of full age, upon being duly authorized by the orphans' or other court having probate jurisdiction, have power to sell and dispose of such certificate or warrant for the benefit of those interested. And all sales, mortgages, powers, or other instruments of writing, going to affect the title or claim to any such bounty right, made or executed prior to the issue of such warrant or certificate, shall be null and void to all intents and purposes whatsoever, nor shall such claim to bounty right be in any wise affected by, or charged with, or subject to, the payment of any debt or claim incurred by the soldier prior to the issuing of such certificate or warrant; *Provided,* that no land warrant issued under the provisions of this act shall be laid upon any lands of the United States to which there shall be a preemption right, or upon which there shall be an actual settlement and cultivation; *Provided, further,* That every such non-commissioned officer, musician, and private, who may be entitled, under the provisions of this act, to receive a certificate or warrant for one hundred and sixty acres of land, shall be allowed the option to receive such certificate or warrant, or a treasury scrip for one hundred dollars; and such scrip, whenever it is preferred, shall be issued by the Secretary of the Treasury to such person or persons as would be authorized to receive such certificates or warrants for lands; said scrip to bear an interest of six per cent per annum, payable semi-annually, redeemable at the pleasure of the government. And that each private, non-commissioned officer, and musician, who shall have been received into the service of the United States, since the commencement of the war with Mexico, for less than twelve months, and shall have served for such term or until honorably discharged, shall be entitled to receive a warrant for forty acres of land, which may be subject to private entry, or twenty-five dollars in scrip, if preferred; and in the event of the death of such volunteer during his term of service, or after an honorable discharge, but before the passage of this act, then the warrant for such land or scrip, shall issue to the wife, child, or children, if there be any, and, if none, then to the father, and, if there be no father, then to the mother of such deceased volunteer: *Provided,* That nothing contained in this section shall be construed to give bounty land to such volunteers as were accepted into service, and discharged without being marched to the seat of war.

[SEC. 10 omitted.]

Approved, February 11, 1847.

140

9 U.S. Statutes 232-233.
THIRTIETH CONGRESS. Sess. I. 1848.

Chap. XLIX. *An Act explanatory of the Act entitled "An Act to raise, for a limited Time, an additional Military Force, and for other Purposes," approved eleventh February, eighteen hundred and forty-seven.*

[Sec. 1 omitted.]

Sec. 2. *And be it further enacted,* That the benefits of the said act of eleventh February, eighteen hundred and forty-seven, shall not be construed as forfeited by the privates and non-commissioned officers who have been, or may be, promoted to the grade of commissioned officer during their service in Mexico, and who shall have subsequently fulfilled the condition of their engagements: *Provided,* Such promotion shall have been made subsequent to the original organization of the company, corps, or regiment to which such privates and non-commissioned officers may have belonged.

Approved, May 27, 1848.

9 *U.S. Statutes* 240.
THIRTIETH CONGRESS. Sess. I. 1848.

Chap. LXXIV. *An Act giving further Time for satisfying Claims for Bounty Lands, and for other Purposes.*

Be it enacted by the Senate and House of Representatives of the United States of America in Congress assembled, That the act of the second session of the twenty-ninth [twenty-seventh] Congress, chapter sixty-nine, entitled "An Act to provide for satisfying claims for bounty lands for military services in the late war with Great Britain, and for other purposes," approved July twenty-seven, eighteen hundred and forty-two, and also the two acts approved January twenty-seventh, eighteen hundred and thirty-five, therein and thereby revived, shall be, and the same are hereby, revived, and continued in force for five years, to be computed from and after the passage of this act.

Approved, June 26, 1848.

The act of July 27, 1842 and the acts of January 27, 1835 continued for five years from passage of this act.

9 *U.S. Statutes* 520–521.
THIRTY-FIRST CONGRESS. Sess. I. 1850.

[The full text]

Chap. LXXXV. *An Act granting Bounty Land to certain Officers and Soldiers who have been engaged in the Military Service of the United States.*

Be it enacted by the Senate and House of Representatives of the United States of America in Congress assembled, That each of the surviving, or the widow or minor children of deceased commissioned and non-commissioned officers, musicians, or privates, whether of regulars, volunteers, rangers, or militia, who performed military service in any regiment, company, or detachment, in the service of the United States, in the war with Great Britain, declared by the United States on the eighteenth day of June, eighteen hundred and twelve, or in any of the Indian wars since seventeen hundred and ninety, and each of the commissioned officers who was engaged in the military service of the United States in the late war with Mexico, shall be entitled to lands, as follows: Those who engaged to serve twelve months or during the war, and actually served nine months, shall received one hundred and sixty acres, and those who engaged to serve six months, and actually served four months, shall receive eighty acres, and those who engaged to serve for any or an indefinite period, and actually served one month, shall receive forty acres; *Provided,* That wherever any officer or soldier was honorably discharged in consequence of disability in the service, before the expiration of his period of service, he shall receive the amount to which he would have been entitled if he had served the full period for which he had engaged to serve; *Provided,* The person so having been in service shall not receive said land, or any part thereof, if it shall appear, by the muster rolls of his regiment or corps, that he deserted, or was dishonorably discharged from service, or if he has received, or is entitled to, any military land bounty under the act of Congress heretofore passed.

SEC. 2. *And Be it further enacted,* That the period during which any officer or soldier may have remained in captivity with the enemy shall be estimated and added to the period of his actual service, and the person so detained in captivity shall receive land under the provisions of this act in the same manner that he would be entitled in case he had entered the service for the whole term made up by the addition of the time of his captivity, and had served during such time.

SEC. 3. *And Be it further enacted,* That each commissioned and non-commissioned officer, musician, or private, for whom provision is made by the first section hereof, shall receive a certificate

Includes surviving veterans, or widow or minor children of deceased commissioned and non-commissioned officers, musicians, privates (whether regulars, volunteers, rangers, or militia) who performed military services in the War of 1812 or in any of the Indian wars since 1790 and the commissioned officers who were engaged in War with Mexico. If enlisted for twelve months and served nine shall receive 160 acres; if engaged to serve six months and served four to receive 80 acres; and if engaged to serve for any or an indefinite period and served one month to receive 40 acres.

APPENDIX: The Acts

Credit for period of captivity.

Widow is to receive 160 acres if her husband was killed in battle and provided she is unmarried at the time of application, but it is not to go to her heirs if she is deceased. No land warrant issued under this act is to be laid on land where there is a pre-emption right, or actual settlement and cultivation, without the consent of the seller.

Excludes any person who is a member of the then-present Congress from benefits.

An important act making the warrants assignable.

If land subject to entry is at a greater amount than $1.25 per acre, the locator to pay the U.S. the difference.

or warrant from the Department of the Interior for the quantity of land to which he may be entitled, and which may be located by the warrantee or his heirs at law, at any land office of the United States, in one body and in conformity to the legal subdivisions of the pubic lands, upon any of the public lands in such district then subject to private entry; and upon the return of such certificate or warrant, with evidence of the location thereof having been legally made to the general land office, a patent shall be issued therefor. In the event of the death of any commissioned or non-commissioned officer, musician, or private, prior or subsequent to the passage of this act, who shall have served as aforesaid, and who shall not have received bounty land for said services, a like certificate or warrant shall be issued in favor, and enure to the benefit of his widow, who shall receive one hundred and sixty acres of land in case her husband was killed in battle, but not to her heirs, *Provided,* She is unmarried at the date of her application. *Provided further,* That no land warrant issued under the provisions of this act shall be laid upon any land of the United States to which there shall be a pre-emption right, or upon which there shall be an actual settlement and cultivation, except with the consent of such settler, to be satisfactorily proven to the proper land officer.

SEC. 4. *And Be it further enacted,* That all sales, mortgages, letters of attorney, or other instruments of writing, going to affect the title or claim to any warrant or certificate issued, or to be issued, or any land granted, or to be granted, under the provisions of this act, made or executed prior to the issue, shall be null and void to all intents and purposes whatsoever; nor shall such certificate or warrant, or the land obtained thereby, be in any wise affected by, or charged with, or subject to, the payment of any debt or claim incurred by such officer or soldier, prior to the issuing of the patent: *Provided,* That the benefits of this act shall not accrue to any person who is a member of the present Congress. *Provided further,* That it shall be the duty of the commissioner of the general land office, under such regulations as may be prescribed by the Secretary of the Interior, to cause to be located, free of expense, any warrant which the holder may transmit to the general land office for that purpose in such State and land district as the said holder or warrantee may designate, and upon good farming land, so far as the same can be ascertained from the maps, plats, and field notes of the surveyor, or from any other information in the possession of the local office, and, upon the location being made as aforesaid, the Secretary shall cause a patent to be transmitted to such warrantee: *And provided further,* That no patent issued under this act shall be delivered upon any power of attorney or agreement dated before the passage of this act, and that all such powers of attorney or agreements be considered and treated as null and void.

Approved, September 28, 1850.

10 *U.S. Statutes* 3–4.
THIRTY-SECOND CONGRESS. Sess. I. 1852.
[The full text]

Chap. XIX. *An Act to make Land Warrants assignable, and for other Purposes.*

Be it enacted by the Senate and House of Representatives of the United States of America in Congress assembled, That all warrants for military bounty lands which have been or may hereafter be issued under any law of the United States, and all valid locations of the same which have been or may hereafter be made, are hereby declared to be assignable, by deed or instrument of writing made and executed after the taking effect of this act according to such form and pursuant to such regulations as may be prescribed by the Commissioner of the General Land-Office, so as to vest the assignee with all the rights of the original owner of the warrant or location: *Provided,* That any person entitled to preemption right to any land shall be entitled to use any such land warrant in payment for the same at the rate of one dollar and twenty-five cents per acre, for the quantity of land therein specified: *Provided,* That the warrants which have been, or may hereafter be issued in pursuance of said laws or of this act may be located according to the legal subdivisions of the public lands in one body upon any lands of the United States, subject to private entry at the time of such location, at the minimum price. *Provided, further,* That when said warrant shall be located on lands which are subject to entry at a greater minimum than one dollar and twenty-five cents per acre, the locator of said warrants shall pay to the United States in cash the difference between the value of such warrants at one dollar and twenty-five cents per acre and the tract of land located on.

SEC. 2. And *Be it further enacted,* That the registers and receivers of the land-offices shall hereafter be severally authorized to charge and receive for their services in locating all military bounty land warrants issued since the eleventh day of February, eighteen hundred and forty-seven, the same compensation or percentage to which they are entitled by law for sale of the public lands for cash, at the rate of one dollar and twenty-five cents per acre, the said compensation to be hereafter paid by the assignees or holders of such warrants.

SEC. 3. *And Be it further enacted,* That registers and receivers, whether in or out of office at the passage of this act, or their legal representatives in case of death, shall be entitled to receive from the treasury of the United States, for services heretofore performed in locating military bounty land warrants, the same rate of compensation provided in the preceding section for services hereafter to be performed, after deducting the amount already received by such officers under the act entitled "An act to require the holders of military land warrants to compensate the land-officers of the United States for services in relation to the location of those warrants," approved May seventeenth, eighteen hundred and forty-eight: *Provided,* That no register or receiver shall receive any compensation out of the treasury for past services, who has charged and received illegal fees for the location of such warrants; *And provided further,* That no register or receiver shall receive for his services during any year a greater compensation than the maximum now allowed by law.

SEC. 4. *And Be it further enacted,* That in all cases where the militia or volunteers, or State troops of any State or Territory were called into military service, and whose services have been paid by the United States subsequent to the eighteenth June, eighteen hundred and twelve, the officers and soldiers of such militia, volunteers or troops shall be entitled to all the benefits of the act entitled, "An act granting bounty land to certain officers and soldiers who have been engaged in the military service of the United States," approved September twenty-eighth, eighteen hundred and fifty, and shall receive lands for their services according to the provisions of said act, upon proof of length of service as therein required, and that the last proviso of the ninth section of the act of the eleventh of February, eighteen hundred and forty-seven, be, and the same is hereby repealed: *Provided,* That nothing herein contained shall authorize bounty land to those who have heretofore received or become entitled to the same.

SEC. 5. *And Be it further enacted,* That where any company, battalion or regiment, in an organized form, marched more than twenty miles to the place where they were mustered into the service of the United States, or were discharged more than twenty miles from the place where such company, battalion or regiment was organized; in all such cases, in computing the length of service of the officers and soldiers of any such company, battalion or regiment, with a view to determine the quantity of land any officer or soldier is entitled to under said act,approved twenty-eighth September eighteen hundred and fifty. There shall be allowed one day for every twenty miles from the place where the company, battalion or regiment was organized, to the place where the same was mustered into the service of the United States; and also one day for every twenty miles from the place where such company, battalion or regiment was discharged, to the place where it was organized, and from whence it marched to enter the service.

If mustered in or discharged more than twenty miles from the place where the company, battalion or regiment was organized, one day for every twenty miles shall be added in computing time in service.

Approved, March 22, 1852.

10 *U.S. Statutes* 143.
THIRTY-SECOND CONGRESS. Sess. I. 1852.

Chap. CXIV. *An Act making further Provisions for the Satisfaction of Virginia Land Warrants.*

Be it enacted by the Senate and House of Representatives of the United States of America in Congress assembled. That all unsatisfied outstanding military land-warrants or parts of warrants issued or allowed prior to the first day of March, eighteen hundred and fifty-two, by the proper authorities of the Commonwealth of Virginia, for military services performed by the officers and soldiers, seamen or marines, of the Virginia State and continental lines in the Army or Navy of the Revolution, may be surrendered to the Secretary of the Interior, who, upon being satisfied, by a revision of the proofs or by additional testimony, that any warrant thus surrendered was fairly and justly issued in pursuance of the laws of said Commonwealth, for military services so rendered, shall issue land scrip in favor of the present proprietors of any warrant thus surrendered, for the whole or any portion thereof yet unsatisfied, at the rate of one dollar and twenty-five cents for each acre mentioned in the warrant thus surrendered and which remains unsatisfied, which scrip shall be receivable in payment for any lands owned by the United States subject to sale at private entry; and said scrip shall, moreover, be assignable by indorsement attested by two witnesses. In issuing such scrip, the said Secretary is authorized, when there are more persons than one interested in the same warrant to issue to each person scrip for his or her portion of the warrant; and where infants or feme coverts may be entitled to any scrip, the guardian of the infant and the husband of the feme covert may receive and sell or locate the same. *Provided,* that no less than a legal subdivison shall be entered and paid for by the scrip issued in virtue of this act.

This scrip to be full and final adjustment of all bounty land claims to the officers and soldiers, seamen, and marines of the state of Virginia for the war of the Revolution provided that Virginia shall by act of the legislature relinquish all claim to lands in the Virginia Military District.

SEC. 2. *And be [it] further enacted,* That this act shall be taken as a full and final adjustment of all bounty-land claims to the officers and soldiers, seamen and marines of the State of Virginia, for services in the war of the Revolution *Provided,* That the State of Virginia shall by a proper act of legislature thereof relinquish all claim to the lands in the Virginia military land district in the State of Ohio.

SEC. 3. [Omitted] Approved, August 31, 1852.

10 *U.S. Statutes* 150–151.
THIRTY-SECOND CONGRESS. Sess. II. 1853

Chap. VIII. *An Act authorizing certain soldiers of the late war with Great Britain to surrender the Bounty Lands drawn by them, and to locate others in lieu thereof.*

Be it enacted by the Senate and House of Representatives of the United States of America in Congress assembled, That it shall be and may be lawful for any soldier in the late war with Great Britain, to whom bounty land has been allotted and patented in any State of this Union, by virtue of the laws of the United States passed prior to the year 1850, which was and is unfit for cultivation, to surrender said patent, and to receive in lieu thereof the same quantity of any of the public land subject to private entry at the minimum price as he may select: *Provided,* That before receiving such new land, it shall be proven to the satisfaction of the Commissioner of the General Land Office, that the land so allotted and patented to said soldier is unfit for cultivation, and that said soldier has never disposed of his interest in said land by any sale of his own, and that the same has not been taken or disposed of for his debts due to any individual, and that he shall release all his interest in the same to the United States in such way as said Commissioner shall prescribe, —and such surrender and location shall be made within five years from the passage of this act.

Approved, January 7, 1853.

Allows anyone who obtained bounty land unfit for cultivation prior to 1850 to exchange it for the lowest rate anywhere on the public domain provided that he proves he has not used or transferred his interest in the land. He must do it within five years of the passage of this act.

10 *U.S. Statutes* 267.
THIRTY-THIRD CONGRESS. Sess. I. 1854.

Chap. X. *An Act giving further Time for Satisfying Claims for Bounty Lands and for other purposes.*

Be it enacted ... That the act entitled "An act to provide for satisfying claims for bounty lands for military services in the late war with Great Britain, and for other purposes," approved July twenty-seventh, eighteen hundred and forty-two, and also the two acts approved January twenty-seventh eighteen hundred and thirty-five, therein and thereby revived, shall be and the same are hereby revived and continued in force for five years, to be computed from the twenty-sixth day of June, one thousand eight hundred and fifty-three.

Approved, February 8, 1854.

Extends time for 1842 act and two acts of 1835.

10 *U.S. Statutes* 701.
THIRTY-THIRD CONGRESS. Sess. II. 1855.

Chap. CCVI. *An Act allowing the further time of two Years to those holdings Lands by Entries in the Virginia Military District in Ohio, which were made prior to the first [of] January, eighteen hundred and fifty-two, to have the same surveyed and patented.*

Be it enacted by the Senate and House of Representatives of the United States of America in Congress assembled,That the officers and soldiers of the Virginia line on continental establishment, their heirs or assigns, entitled to bounty lands, which have, prior to the first day of January, Anno Domini eighteen hundred and fifty-two, been entered within the tract reserved by Virginia, between the Little Miami and Sciota Rivers, for satisfying the legal bounties to her officers and soldiers upon continental establishment, shall be allowed the further time of two years from and after the passage of this act to make and return their surveys and warrants, or certified copies of warrants, to the General Land-Office.

SEC. 2. *And Be it further enacted,* That the act entitled "An act allowing the further time of two years to those holding lands by entries in the Virginia milituary district in Ohio, which were made prior to first January, eighteen hundred and fifty-two, to have the same surveyed and patented," approved December nineteenth, eighteen hundred and fifty-four, be, and the same is hereby, repealed.

Approved, March 3, 1855.

Further time of two years for officers and soldiers of the Virginia line on continental establishment to return their surveys and warrants to the GLO.

10 *U.S. Statutes* 701–702.
THIRTY-THIRD CONGRESS. Sess. II. 1855.

Chap. CCVII. *An Act in Addition to certain Acts granting Bounty Land to certain Officers and Soldiers who have engaged in the Military Service of the United States.*

Be it enacted by the Senate and House of Representatives of the United States of America in Congress assembled, That each of the surviving commissioned and non-commissioned officers, musicians, and privates, whether of regulars, volunteers, rangers, or militia, who were regularly mustered into the service of the United States, and every officer, commissioned and non- commissioned, seaman, ordinary seaman, flotilla-man, marine, clerk, and landsman in the navy, in any of the wars in which this country has been engaged since seventeen hundred and ninety, and each of the survivors of the militia, or volunteers, or State troops of any State or Territory, called into military service, and regularly mustered therein, and whose services have been paid by the United States, shall be entitled to receive a certificate or warrant from the Department of the Interior for one hundred and sixty acres of land; and where any of those who have so been mustered into service and paid shall have received a certificate or warrant, he shall be entitled to a certificate or warrant for such quantity of land as will make, in the whole, with what he may have heretofore received, one hundred and sixty acres to each such person having served as aforesaid: *Provided,* The person so having been in service shall not receive said land warrant if it shall appear by the muster-rolls of his regiment or corps that he deserted, or was dishonorably discharged from service: *Provided further,* That the benefits of this section shall be held to extend to wagon-masters and teamsters who may have been employed, under direction of competent authority in time of war in the transportation of military stores and supplies.

SEC. 2. *And Be it further enacted,* That in case of the death of any person who, if living, would be entitled to a certificate or warrant as aforesaid under this act, leaving a widow, or, if no widow, a minor child or children, such widow, or, if no widow, such minor child or children, shall be entitled to receive a certificate or warrant for the same quantity of land that such deceased person would be entitled to receive under the provisions of this act, if now living: *Provided,* That a subsequent marriage shall not impair the right of any such widow to such warrant if she be a widow at the time of making her application: *And provided, further,* That those shall be considered minors who are so at the time this act shall take effect.

SEC. 3. *And Be it further enacted,* That in no case shall any such certificate or warrant be issued for any service less than fourteen days, except where the person shall actually have been engaged in battle, and unless the party claiming such certificate or warrant shall establish his or her right thereto by record evidence of said service.

SEC. 4. *And Be it further enacted,* That said certificates or warrants may be assigned, transferred, and located by the warrantees, their assignees, or their heirs-at-law, according to the provisions of existing laws regulating the assignment, transfer, and location of bounty-land warrants.

SEC. 5. And *Be it further enacted,* That no warrant issued under the provisions of this act shall be located on any public lands, except such as shall at the time be subject to sale at either the minimum or lower graduated prices.

SEC. 6. *And Be it further enacted,* That the registers and receivers of the several land-offices shall be severally authorized to charge, and receive for their services, in locating all warrants under the provisions of this act, the same compensation or percentage ot which they are entitled by law, for sales of the public lands, for cash, at the rate of one dollar and twenty-five cents per acres; the said compensation to be paid by the assignee or holders of such warrants.

SEC. 7. *And be it further enacted,* That the provisions of this act, and all the bounty-land laws heretofore passed by Congress, shall be extended to Indians, in the same manner, and to the same extent, as if the said Indians had been white men.

SEC. 8. *And Be it further enacted,* That the officers and soldiers of the revolutionary war, or their widows or minor children, shall be entitled to the benefits of this act.

SEC. 9. *And Be it further enacted,* That the benefits of this act shall be applied to and embrace those who served as volunteers at the invasion of Plattsburg, in September, eighteen hundred and fourteen; also at the battle of King's Mountain, in the revolutionary war, and the battle of Nickojock, against the confederated savages of the South.

SEC. 10. *And be it further enacted,* That the provisions of this act shall apply to the chaplains who served with the army, in the several wars of this country.

SEC. 11. *And be it further enacted,* That the provisions of this act be applied to those who served as volunteers at the attack on Lewistown, in Delaware, by the British fleet, in the war of eighteen hundred and twelve-fifteen.

Approved, March 3, 1855.

11 *U.S. Statutes* **8–9.**
THIRTY-FOURTH CONGRESS. Sess. I. 1856.

Eligible service includes commissioned officers, non-commissioned officers, musicians, privates whether regulars, volunteers, rangers, or militia, also commissioned and non-commissioned seaman, ordinary seaman, flotilla-man, marine, clerk, and landsman in the navy in wars since 1790. Also eligible are survivors of militia, or volunteers, or State troops of any State of Territory regularly mustered in and paid by the United States. They are entitled to 160 acres. The act also extends benefits to wagon masters and teamsters who were employed under the direction of competent authorities during the war.

Widow and minor children are eligible. Remarriage of the widow does not prevent her eligibility if she is not married at the time of application.

Those with under fourteen days service are not eligible unless engaged in battle.

Warrants may be assigned.

Provisions are extended to Indians. Various others also named and included, including revolutionary war, Plattsburg, King's Mountain, Nickojock, and those who served against "confederated savages of the South."

Provisions for Revolutionary War veterans and heirs.

Provisions added for chaplains.

Provisions for volunteers in attack on Lewistown.

If any officer or soldier or widow or minor child received less than 160 acres, they may get the difference to total that amount.

Eighth section of March 3, 1855 act to be construed as including officers, marines, seamen, and other persons in naval service in Revolutionary War, and their widows and minor children.

Benefits extended to Major David Bailey's battalion of Illinois for service in the Black Hawk war.

Chap. XXVI. *An Act to amend the Act in addition to certain Acts granting Bounty Land to certain Officers and Soldiers who have been engaged in the Military Service of the United States, approved March third, eighteen hundred and fifty-five.*

SEC. 2. Be it enacted ... That in all cases where a certificate or warrant for bounty land for any less quantity than one hundred and sixty acres, shall have been issued to any officer or soldier, or to the widow or minor child or children of any officer or soldier, under existing laws, the evidence upon which such certificate or warrant was issued shall be received to establish the service of such officer or soldier in the application of himself, or of his widow or minor child or children, for a certificate or warrant for so much land as may be required to make up the full sum of one hundred and sixty acres, on proof of the identity of such officer or soldier, or in the case of his death, of the marriage and identity of his widow, or in case of her death, of the identity of his minor child or children: *Provided, nevertheless,* That if, upon a review of such evidence, the Commissioner of Pensions shall not be satisfied that the former certificate or warrant was properly granted, he may require additional evidence, as well of the term as of the fact of service.

[SEC. 3 OMITTED, allows for the use of parol evidence to be used as evidence of service when no other evidence exists.]

SEC. 4. *And be it further enacted,* That the eighth section of the act above mentioned, approved the third day of March, in the year eighteen hundred and fifty-five, shall be construed as embracing officers, marines, seamen, and other persons engaged in the naval service of the United States during the revolutionary war, and the widows and minor children of such officers, marines, seamen, and other persons engaged as aforesaid.

SEC. 5. *And be it further enacted,* That the provisions of the said act shall extend to all persons who have served as volunteers with the armed forces of the United States, subject to military orders, for the space of fourteen days, in any of the wars specified in the first section of the said act, whether such persons were or were not mustered into the service of the United States.

SEC. 6. *And be it further enacted,* That the widows and minor children of all such persons as are specified in the last preceding section of this act, and are now dead, shall be entitled to the same privileges as the widows and minor children of the beneficiaries named in the act to which this is an amendment.

SEC. 7. And be it further enacted, That when any company, battalion, or regiment, in an organized form, marched more than twenty miles to the place where they were mustered into the service of the United States, or were discharged more than twenty miles from the place where such company, battalion, or regiment was organized, in all such cases, in computing the length of service of the officers and soldiers of any such company, battalion, or regiment, there shall be allowed one day for every twenty miles from the place where the company, battalion, or regiment was organized to the place where the same was mustered into the service of the United States, and also one day for every twenty miles from the place where such company, battalion, or regiment was discharged, to the place where it was organized, and from whence it marched to enter the service: *Provided,* That such march was in obedience to the command or direction of the President of the United States, or some general officer of the United States, commanding an army or department, or the chief executive officer of the State or Territory by which such company, battalion, or regiment was called into service.

Approved, May 14, 1856.

11 *U.S. Statutes* 249–250.
THIRTY-FOURTH CONGRESS. Sess. III. 1857.

Chap. CXV. *An Act to extend the Provisions of the Act entitled "An Act in Addition to certain Acts granting Bounty Land to certain Officers and Soldiers who have been engaged in the Military Services of the United States," to the Officers and Soldiers of Major David Bailey's Battalion of Cook County (Illinois) Volunteers.*

Be it enacted ... That all those officers and soldiers of Major David Bailey's battalion of Cook county (Illinois) volunteers stationed at Fort Dearborn, in the Black Hawk war of eighteen hundred and thirty-two, who have never received warrants for bounty land for services in said war, shall be entitled to receive a certificate or warrant from the Department of the Interior for one hundred and sixty acres of land, upon making proof either by record evidence or such parol evidence as the commissioner of pensions may require of having served in said war for the term of at least fourteen days; the provisions of this act to extend to the widows and minor childrenn of said officers and soldiers who have died or may die before receiving such warrant or certificate.

Approved, March 3, 1857.

13 *U.S. Statutes* 378–379.
THIRTY-EIGHTH CONGRESS. Sess. I. 1864.

CHAP. CCXXVI. An Act providing for satisying claims for Bounty Lands, and for other Purposes.

Be it enacted ... That the act entitled "An act to provide for satisfying claims for bounty lands for military services in the late war with Great Britain, and for other purposes," approved July twenty-seventh, in the year one thousand eight hundred and forty-two, and the two acts approved January twenty-seventh, in the year one thousand eight hundred and thirty-five, therein and thereby revived, and also the two acts to the same intent and purpose, respectively approved the twenty-sixth day of June, in the year eighteen hundred and forty-eight, and the eighth day of February, in the year eighteen hundred and fifty-four, be, and the same are hereby, renewed and continued in force and effect, without restriction or limitation as to the time of location of said warrants issued in virtue thereof.

SEC. 2. *And be it further enacted,* That all warrants for bounty lands heretofore issued in virtue of any of the several acts hereinbefore named, may be located at any time subsequent to the passage of this act, in conformity with the general laws in force at the time of such location; and that all entries and locations heretofore made with such warrants shall be as valid and effectual as if the several acts aforesaid had not expired at the time of such entry and location, any law to the contrary notwithstanding.

SEC. 3. *And be it further enacted,* That all acts and parts of acts inconsistent with the provisions of this act, be, and the same are hereby, repealed.

Approved, July 2, 1864.

Extends time for claims under acts of July 27, 1842, the two acts of January 27, 1835, the 26 June 1848, and 8 February 1854, without limitation as to time of location of those warrants.

BIBLIOGRAPHY

Adkinson, Kandie. "The Kentucky Land Grant System." *Saddlebag Notes*. Technical Leaflet, The Circuit Rider, Historical Confederation of Kentucky. 13 no. 3 (May/June 1990).

American State Papers: Documents, Legislative and Executive, of the Congress of the United States. Public Lands, eight volumes. Claims, one volume. Washington, D.C.: Gales and Seaton, 1832+.

Bacon, Lee D. "Early Navy Personnel Records at the National Archives 1776–1860," *Prologue: Quarterly of the National Archives and Records Administration*. 27 no. 1 (Spring 1995).

Balloting Book and Other Documents Relating to Military Bounty Land in the State of New York, The. 1825. Reprint, with added index, Ovid, N.Y.: W. E. Morrison & Co., 1983.

Beahan, Gary W. *Missouri's Public Domain: United States Land Sales, 1818–1922*. Jefferson City: State of Missouri Office of Secretary of State Records Management and Archives Service, Archives Information Bulletin II no. 3 (July 1980).

Bockstruck, Lloyd deWitt and Sandra Hargreaves Luebking, " Military Records," in Loretto Dennis Szucs and Sandra Hargreaves Luebking, *The Source: A Guidebook of American Genealogy*. 3d ed. Salt Lake City: Ancestry, a division of MyFamily.com, 2006. ch. 11: 513.

Bockstruck, Lloyd deWitt. *Bounty and Donation Land Grants in British Colonial America*. Baltimore: Genealogical Publishing Company, 2007.

_____. *Revolutionary War Bounty Land Grants: Awarded by State Governments*. Baltimore: Genealogical Publishing Company, 1996.

_____. "Revolutionary War Bounty Lands Awarded for Clearing the Road over the Cumberland Mountain into Kentucky County, Virginia, in 1779." *Magazine of Virginia Genealogy* 45 (May 2007): 129–130. See also 10 *Hening* 443–44 for the act upon which this article was based.

Brookes-Smith, Joan E. *Master Index Virginia Surveys and Grants 1774–1791 [in Ky.]*. Frankfort, Ky.: Kentucky Historical Society, 1976.

Brown, Margie G. *Genealogical Abstracts, Revolutionary War Veterans, Scrip Act 1852, Astracted from Bureau of Land Management Record Group 49 National Archives Branch, Suitland*. 1990. Reprint. Lovettsville, Va.: Willow Bend Books, 1997.

Brumbaugh, Gaius Marcus, M.D. *Revolutionary War Records. Virginia Army and Navy Forces with Bounty Land Warrants for Virginia—Military District of Ohio; and Virginia Military Scrip; from Federal and States Archives*. volume 1. 1936. Reprint. Baltimore: Genealogical Publishing Company, 1967.

Burgess, Louis A. *Virginia Soldiers of 1776, Compiled from Documents on File in the Virginia Land Office Together with Material found in the Archives Department of the Virginia State Library, and other Reliable Sources*. 3 volumes. 1927–1929. Reprint. Baltimore, Md.: Clearfield Company, Inc., 1994.

Butler, Stuart L. "Genealogical Records of the War of 1812," *Prologue: Quarterly of the National Archives and Records Administration*. 23 no. 4 (Winter 1991).

Carstensen, Vernon, ed. *The Public Lands: Studies in the History of the Public Domain*. Madison: University of Wisconsin Press, 1963.

Christensen, Katheren (Mrs. Paul). *[Index to] Arkansas Military Bounty Grants, War of 1812*. [Hot Springs]: Arkansas Ancestors, 1971.

Clark, Murtie June. *American Militia in the Frontier Wars, 1790–1796*. Baltimore: Genealogical Publishing Company, 1990.

_____. *Colonial Soldiers of the South, 1732–1774*. Baltimore: Genealogical Publishing Company, 1983.

_____. *Index to U.S. Invalid Pension Records 1801–1815*. Baltimore: Genealogical Publishing Company, 1991.

Davis, Robert S. Jr. *Georgia Citizens and Soldiers of the American Revolution*. Easley, S.C.: Southern Historical Press, 1999.

Digested Summary and Alphabetical List of Private Claims which have been Presented to the House of Representatives from the First to the Thirty-first Congress, Exhibiting the Action of Congress on Each Claim, with References to the

Bibliography

Journals, Reports, Bills, etc., Elucidating its Progress. 3 volumes. 1853. Reprint. Baltimore, Md.: Genealogical Publishing Company, Inc., 1970.

Dixon, Ruth Priest. "Genealogical Fallout from the War of 1812," *Prologue: Quarterly of the National Archives and Records Administration.* 24 no. 1 (Spring 1992).

Donaldson, Thomas. *The Public Domain Its History.* Revised edition. Washington, D.C.: Government Printing Office, 1884.

Dunaway, Maxine. *Missouri Military Land Warrants, War of 1812.* Springfield, Mo.: Maxine Dunaway, 1985.

Eales, Anne Bruner and Robert M. Kvasnicka. *Guide to Genealogical Research in the National Archives.* 3d edition. Washington, D.C.: National Archives and Records Service. 2000. In particular, consult Section B, Military Records, Chapters 4, 5, 6, 7, 8 and 9.

Eckenrode, Hamilton J. *Virginia Soldiers of the American Revolution.* 1912–1913. Reprint. Richmond: Virginia State Library and Archives, 1989.

Egle, William Henry. *Virginia Claims to Lands in Western Pennsylvania with an Account of the Donation Lands of Pennsylvania.* Baltimore: Reprint, from *Pennsylvania Archives,* Third Series, Volume III, Harrisburg, 1896. Baltimore: Clearfield Co., 2001.

Ford, Amelia Clewly. *Colonial Precedents of our National Land System as it Existed in 1800.* Madison, Wisc.: no pub.,1919, 108.

Freund, Rudolph. "Military Bounty Lands and the Origins of the Public Domain" in Vernon Carstensen, *The Public Lands: Studies in the History of the Public Domain.* Madison: The University of Wisconsin Press, 1963, 15–34.

_____. "Military Bounty Land and the Origins of the Public Domain," *Agricultural History.* 20 (1946): 8–18.

Gates, Paul W. *History of Public Land Law Development, with Chapter by Robert W. Swenson.* Washington, D.C.: Public Land Law Review Commission, 1968.

Gentry, Daphne S. *Virginia Land Office Inventory. 3d edition, revised and enlarged by John S. Salmon.* Richmond: Virginia State Library and Archives, 1981.

Gwathmey, John H. *Historical Register of Virginians in the Revolution, Soldiers, Sailors, Marines, 1775–1783.* 1938. Reprint. Baltimore: Genealogical Publishing Company, 1973.

Hatcher, Patricia Law. *Locating Your Roots: Discover Your Ancestors Using Land Records.* Cincinnati, Ohio: Betterway Books, 2003.

Hawkins, Kenneth. *Research in the Land Entry Files of the General Land Office Record Group 49.* Revised edition. Washington, D.C.: National Archives and Records Administration, 1998.

Hening, William Waller. *The Statutes at Large being a Collection of all the Laws of Virginia from the First Session of the Legislature, in the year 1619.* 13 volumes. New York: R & W. & G. Bartlow, 1823.

Heitman, Francis B. *Historical Register and Dictionary of Officers of the United States Army, from its organization, September 19, 1789, to March 2, 1903.* 1903. Reprint. Baltimore: Genealogical Publishing Company, 1994.

Hemperley, Marian. *Military Certificates of Georgia 1776–1800 on File in the Surveyor General Department.* Atlanta, Georgia: State Printing Office, 1983.

Hibbard, Benjamin Horace. *A History of the Public Land Policies.* 1924. Reprint. The University of Wisconsin Press, 1965.

Hite, Alex M. "Georgia Bounty Land Grant," *Georgia Historical Quarterly* 38 (December 1954): 337–48.

Hone, E. Wade. *Land & Property Research in the United States.* Salt Lake City, Utah: Ancestry, Incorporated, 1997.

Hopkins, William Lindsay. *Virginia Revolutionary War Land Grant Claims 1783–1850 (Rejected).* Richmond, Va.: priv. pr. [P.O. Box 7254, Richmond, Va. 23221.]

Hutchinson, William Thomas. "Military Bounty Lands of the American Revolution in Ohio." University of Chicago, June 1927. Unpublished Ph.D. Dissertation.

Jillson, Willard Rouse. *The Kentucky Land Grants: A Systematic Index to All of the Land Grants Recorded in the State Land Office in Frankfort, Kentucky, 1782–1924.* Filson Club Publication No. 33. 1925. Reprint. Baltimore: Genealogical Publishing Company, 1972.

_____. *Old Kentucky Entries and Deeds: A Complete Index to All of the Earliest Land Entries, Military Warrants, Deeds and Wills of the Commonwealth of Kentucky.* Filson Club Publication, No. 34. Louisville: Filson Club, 1926.

Journals of the Continental Congress, 1774–1789, ed. Multi-volumes. Worthington C. Ford et al. Washington, D.C., 1904–37.

Knepper, George W., Dr. *The Official Ohio Lands Book*. Columbus, Ohio: The Auditor of State, 2002.

Kvasnicka, Robert M. *The Trans-Mississippi West 1804–1912. A Guide to Records of the Department of the Interior for the Territorial Period. Section 3: Records of the General Land Office. Part IV*. Two volumes. [Washington, D.C.]: National Archives and Records Administration, 2007. The second volume: *The Guide Supplement Containing State Lists and Other Appendixes*.

Laws, Treaties and Other Documents, Having Operation and Respect to the Public Domain. Collection per act of Congress Apr. 27, 1810. Washington City: Joseph Gales Jun., [1810].

Lichtenberg, Caroline. "Beginnings of the United States Military Bounty Policy, 1637–1812." Unpublished Master's Thesis, University of Wisconsin, 145.

Lindregren, A. M. "The History of the Land Bonus of the War of 1812." M.A. Thesis, University of Wisconsin, 1922.

Luebking, Sandra Hargreaves. "Land Records." In *The Source.: A Guidebook to American Genealogy*, Loretto Dennis Szucs and Sandra Hargreaves Luebking, editors. Provo, Utah: Ancestry Publishing, 2006.

Lutz, Paul V. "A State's Concern for the Soldiers Welfare: How North Carolina Provided for her Troops During the Revolution," *North Carolina Historical Review* 42 (July 1965): 315–18.

_____. "Land Grants for Service in the Revolution," *New York Historical Society Quarterly* 48 (1964): 221–235.

Maxwell, Richard S. "The Public Land Records of the Federal Government, 1800–1950, and Their Statistical Significance." Paper presented at the Conference on the National Archives and Statistical Research, May 1968, 11.

Military Land Warrants in Missouri, 1819. Denver, Colo.: Stagecoach Library for Genealogical Research, 1988.

Military Service Records: A Select Catalog of National Archives Microfilm Publications. Washington, D.C.: National Archives and Service Administration, 1985. See: <www.archives.gov/publications/genealogy/microfilm-catalogs.html>.

Morrow, Mary Frances. "Indian Bounty Land Applications," *Prologue* 25 (Fall 1993) no. 3, available at <www.archives.gov/publications/prologue>.

National Archives Microfilm Resources for Research: A Comprehensive Catalog. Washington, D.C.: National Archives and Records Service, 2000.

National Genealogical Society, *Index of Revolutionary War Pension Applications in the National Archives*, NGS special publication no. 40. Washington, D.C.: National Genealogical Society, 1976. (Known as "Hoyt's Index"; named for one of its original compilers.)

Oberly, James W. "Military Bounty Land Warrants of the Mexican War." *Prologue* 14 (1982) 25–34.

_____. *Sixty Million Acres, American Veterans and the Public Lands before the Civil War*. Kent, Ohio: Kent State University, 1990.

O'Callaghan, Jerry. "The War Veteran and the Public Lands." *Agricultural History* 28 (1954): 163–168.

O'Kelley, Nicole and Mary Bondurant Warren. *Georgia Revolutionary Bounty Land Records 1783–1785*. Athens, Ga.: Heritage Papers, 1992.

Paullin, Charles Oscar and John Kirtland Wright. *Atlas of the Historical Geography of the United States*. Carnegie Institution of Washington Publication, 1932, 401.

Pay Rolls [Va.] of Militia Entitled to Land Bounty Under the Act of Congress of Sept. 28, 1850, copied from rolls in the Auditor's Office at Richmond. Richmond: William F. Ritchie, Public Printer, 1851.

Peters, William Edwards. *Ohio Lands and Their Subdivison*. 2d edition. Athens, Ohio: The Messenger Printery Company, 1918.

Pioneer Collections: Collections and Researches made by the Pioneer Society of the State of Michigan. 2d edition. Lansing: Wynkoop Hallenbeck Crawford Company, State Printer, 1908, X:61–62.

Revolutionary Soldiers' Receipts for Georgia Bounty Grants. Atlanta, Ga.: Foote and Davies Company, 1928.

Robbins, Roy M. *Our Landed Heritage The Public Domain, 1776–1970*. 2nd edition revised 1976. Lincoln & London: University of Nebraska, 1942, 3–91.

Rohrbough, Malcolm J. *The Land Office Business: The Settlement and Administration of American Public Lands, 1789–1837*. N.Y.: Oxford University Press, 1968.

Rose, Christine. *Military Pension Acts 1776–1858*. San Jose, Calif.: CR Publications, 2001.

Salmon, John. "Revolutionary War Records in the Archives & Records Division of the Virginia State Library," *Genealogy* 70 (July 1982): 2–10

Bibliography

Shepherd, Samuel. *The Statutes at Large of Virginia–October Session 1792 to December Session 1806 in Three Volumes* (New Series) being a continuation of Hening. 1835. Reprint. Richmond, 1970.

Smith, Clifford Neal. *Federal Land Series: A Calendar of Archival Materials on the Land Patents Issued by the United States Government, with Subject, Tract, and Name Indexes.* Volume 1: 1788–1810. Chicago: American Library Association, 1972.

_____. *Federal Land Series: A Calendar of Archival Materials on the Land Patents Issued by the United States Government, with Subject, Tract, and Name Indexes.* Volume 2: 1799–1835. Federal Bounty-Land Warrants of the American Revolution. Chicago: American Library Association, 1973.

_____. *Federal Land Series: A Calendar of Archival Materials on the Land Patents Issued by the United States Government, with Subject, Tract, and Name Indexes.* Volume 3. Chicago: American Library Association, 1980.

_____. *Federal Land Series: A Calendar of Archival Materials on the Land Patents Issued by the United States Government, with Subject, Tract, and Name Indexes.* Volume 4: 1810–1814. Grants in the Virginia Military District of Ohio. Chicago: American Library Association. Part 1, 1982. Part 2, 1986.

Treat, Payson Jackson, Ph.D. *The National Land System 1785–1820.* 1910. Reprint. New York: Russell & Russell, 1967.

Vivian, Jean H. "Military Land Bounties During the Revolutionary and Confederation Periods," Maryland Historical Magazine 61 (1966): 231–56.

Volkel, Lowell M. *War of 1812 Bounty Lands in Illinois.* Introduction by James D. Walker. Thomson, Ill.: Heritage House, 1977. Originally published House Doc. 262, 26th Congress, 1st Session 1840.

Weisiger, Minor T. *Using Virginia Revolutionary War Records.* Richmond: Library of Virginia, 1999. This is a comprehensive overview of both published and archival materials.

White, Virgil D. *Genealogical Abstracts of Revolutionary War Pension Files.* 4 volumes. Waynesburg, Tenn.: National Historical Publishing Co., 1990.

_____. *Index to Indian Wars Pension Files 1892–1926.* 2 volumes. Waynesboro, Tennessee: The National Historical Publishing Company, 1987.

_____. *Index to Mexican War Pension Files.* Waynesboro, Tenn.: The National Historical Publishing Company, 1989.

_____. *Index to Old Wars Pension Files 1815–1926.* Waynesboro, Tenn.: the National Historical Publishing Company, 1993.

_____. *Index to War of 1812 Pension files.* 2 volumes. Waynesboro, Tenn.: The National Historical Publishing Company, 1991.

Wilson, Samuel Mackay. *Virginia Land Bounty Warrants.* Baltimore: Southern Book Co., 1953.

Yoshpe, Harry P. and Philip P. Brower. *Preliminary Inventory of the Land-Entry Papers of the General Land Office. Preliminary Inventory No. 22.* 1949. New edition, San Jose, Calif.: Rose Family Association, 1996.

INDEX

Note that "fn" = footnote; "m" after the page number indicates it is in the margin of that page.

Index

154